The Autobi...

B. H. RO~~BERTS~~

D0118207

Dear Bampa

Merry Christmas 1995, I
thought you might be interested
in B.H., since he was such a
colorful character.

Stephen & Elaine

The Autobiography of

B. H. ROBERTS

Edited by
Gary James Bergera

Foreword by
Sterling M. McMurrin

SIGNATURE BOOKS
SALT LAKE CITY
1990

Cover design: Randall Smith Associates, Han Vu

∞Printed on acid free paper.

94   93   92   91   90   6   5   4   3   2   1

LIBRARY OF CONGRESS CATALOGING-IN-PUBLICATION DATA

Roberts, B. H. (Brigham Henry), 1857–1933.
    The autobiography of B. H. Roberts / edited by Gary James Bergera;
    foreword by Sterling M. McMurrin.
        p.   cm.
    Includes bibliographical references and index.
    ISBN 1-56085-005-1
    1. Roberts, B. H. (Brigham Henry), 1857–1933. 2. Mormons–United
States–Biography.
I. Bergera, Gary James. II. Title.
BX8695.R58A3 1990
289.3'092–dc20
[B]   90–39781
                                                                        CIP

CONTENTS

B. H. Roberts: Historian and Theologian

Sterling M. McMurrin

Although the fundamentals of Mormon thought were quite firmly established in the first generation of the Church of Jesus Christ of Latter-day Saints, it was the second generation which pulled the philosophical and theological strands together. Among the intellectual leaders of this generation Brigham H. Roberts (1857-1933) was preeminent in both abilities and influence. It was in this period that the outlines of a systematic theology were shaped and developed as well the perspectives which placed the church as an institution within the framework of history and provided the Mormon people with the instruments for rationalizing and defending their beliefs and practices. Though perhaps less radical and less creative than the first, the second generation was more reflective, more reasonable, and intellectually more responsible. The church had already become defensive, where before it had exhibited a quite admirable independence in both thought and action, and argument and scholastic justification had displaced the facile prophetic pronouncements of the first years. Something very important to Mormonism had been lost with the death of the prophet Joseph Smith and the passing of those who had known him and were close to him and had been creators with him of the new church and its faith. But just as inevitably something was gained by their successors in the necessity for explaining and justifying the doctrine and exploring and exploiting its numerous entailments for both thought and action. Above all a new intellectual vitality was gained by the "defense of the faith and the saints."

Since his death in 1933, Roberts has been a neglected figure in the Mormon church. Where once he was easily the most interesting and exciting and stimulating person in its leadership, its most prolific writer, its chief theologian and historian, and its most capable defender, today his name is scarcely known to large segments of the membership of the church. He has been eclipsed by a deluge of writers of varying but lesser talent, many of whom lack even the grace to acknowledge their indebtedness to him. Therefore, a resurgence of interest in Roberts and his work and the reissue of some of his writings are fortunate, for in him the Mormon people have a spokesman of uncommon stature and ability. His name should be kept very much alive by those who value the traditions of the church, who have any attachment to its robust and romantic past, or who have genuine appreciation for the ideas and institutions that have been the substance and strength of Mormonism.

Roberts belonged to the era of great Mormon oratory, and for a third of a century he was the church's great orator in the days when the tabernacle in Salt Lake City sounded and resounded with the voices of impassioned advocates and defenders, the days before the microphone and camera robbed the Mormon conferences of much of their character and vitality and inspiration, the days when the church both valued and invited argument and debate.

There was then a kind of intellectual openness about the church, which encouraged thought and discussion. Its faith and confidence were firm, and it was ready and anxious to take on all comers. The church could justifiably boast a roster of admirable talent, but Roberts was its chief exhibit and its most competent advocate.

The high value which the church in those days placed on intellectual strength and achievement yielded a good return, for it gathered into its leadership a quite impressive group whose thought and writings made a permanent impress upon its character. Among these Roberts was the recognized leader. Often in rebellion and conflict, he nevertheless commanded both the confidence and admiration of his colleagues and of the rank and file of the church. His native intellectual powers, his wide and intelligent reading, his forensic skills, the forcefulness of his pen, his enthusiastic and even impetuous speech, and the sheer impact of his uncommon personality made him the intellectual leader of the Mormon people in the era of Mormonism's finest intellectual attainment. Since his death the church has suffered a steady intellectual decline among its leaders in matters pertaining to theology, a decline accompanied by a growth of irrationalism and anti-intellectualism. Perhaps a resurgence of interest in Roberts's work will point toward a better future.

It seems to me that Roberts's central importance for Mormon thought derives largely from the reliability of his instincts in assessing the crucial elements in the Mormon intellectual foundation, both philosophical and theological, and in his capacity to exploit these elements within a historical framework of large perspectives and vision. He was not a creator of doctrine like Joseph Smith or even Brigham Young, nor did he import doctrine into Mormonism as did Sydney Rigdon. And he was somewhat less original in his thought than Orson Pratt. Certainly he lacked Pratt's disposition for speculative metaphysics as well as his analytic and logical talent. There is nothing in Roberts's writings, for instance, comparable in character to Pratt's finest philosophical piece, "The Absurdities of Immaterialism." But Roberts had a better historical sense than any of these and a far better knowledge of history, and he was in a better position to achieve perspective on the place of Mormonism as a religious and social movement. If less analytical and innovative than Pratt, Roberts had a better feel for relevance and a firmer grasp of the large implications of Mormon doctrine, and he had, I believe, more common sense in his treatment of religious issues. Roberts was less legalistic and literalistic than his contemporary James E. Talmage, and if his talents in treating doctrinal issues were less refined than those of Talmage, he had a more expansive intellect and a far greater sensitivity to philosophic issues.

Roberts lived during a crucial period for Mormonism. The original prophetic and sectarian impulse was waning, the major feats of pioneering were accomplished, and the struggles with the federal government and their aftermath were taking a severe toll of human energy and threatening the economic and institutional life of the church. More than anything else, the church needed defenses that would justify its existence, establish its moral and intellectual respectability, and guarantee its own integrity. But there were additional challenges which engrossed Roberts: the coming of statehood for Utah and the creation of a political life for the Mormon people and the secular threat to religion that was carried largely by the new humanism and by Darwinism and the sciences generally. Roberts seemed born to these tasks, and he entered into them with quite remarkable energy and dedication and with the self-assurance and determination of those whose commitment and faith are firm.

Roberts's prose style is rhetorical and dramatic. He was at all times the orator. He lacked the precision of Talmage's diction and the poetic qualities of Orson F. Whitney. But he was without pedantry, and both his oral and written words drew strength from his directness and enthusiasm. Roberts wrote as he spoke, and his written pages often read not with finely composed and polished sentences but as if they were edited reports of extemporaneous statements–direct, often repetitive, somewhat personal as if writer and reader were in conversation, sometimes careless in construction but always to the point and effective.

Roberts's writing like his public address was argumentative and polemical. He enjoyed nothing more than argument. Indeed he liked nothing better than a good fight. If no one was available to engage in debate, he would produce a battle by monologue. He was at his best in the heat of controversy, and it is not surprising that his most commendable theological piece, *The Mormon Doctrine of Deity*, certainly the most competent theological statement to come from a Mormon leader, was in its most important part a literary debate, an argument with a Roman Catholic scholar set within the larger dispute on Mormon doctrine that aroused widespread public interest near the turn of the century.

In his private as well as public life, Roberts was a controversial figure. His autobiography is a fascinating, moving story of a lonely child in England left to shift for himself by irresponsible guardians after his mother had migrated to Utah; of his walking barefoot from the Platte River to Salt Lake City; of a rough and tumble youth; of his admirable struggle for education;

of his fight with the church to get into politics; of his role in the struggle for statehood; of his dramatic losing battle with the United States Congress, which refused him his seat in the House of Representatives because of his polygamy. The full story of his life will tell of his double struggle against the inroads of secularism in the church and against the anti-scientific bias of some of his ecclesiastical colleagues; of his battle as historian to publish an uncensored history of the church; of his fights over doctrine and evolution; of his missionary controversies with Christian sects; of his fight to get into action in the First World War, when he was commissioned a chaplain above the age limit because of his demonstrated physical strength and abilities; of his determination to make Mormonism intellectually acceptable; of his endless battle with its critics; of his struggle to maintain the prestige and influence of his quorum, the First Council of the Seventy; and of his internal struggles with his own faith, the struggles of a man who wanted to believe and yet be honest.

When Roberts died a packed tabernacle paid him homage, and he was buried with military rites in the cemetery of the little village of Centerville, where much of his life was lived. His grave is marked by a monument erected by missionaries who had served under him in the eastern United States. Those who can remember his death can remember what, for Mormons, was the end of an era.

Roberts's strength as a historian, it seems to me, was especially in his intense historical consciousness, his quite spacious perspectives on history, his capacity for historical research and talent for narrative, his sense of personal involvement with his subject, his passion for it, and his deep-lying desire to be honest and open with his readers. His histories are not without bias and prejudice. They are clearly pro-Mormon—sometimes with a vengeance. They are written to justify the Mormon church, but they are written with honesty and sincerity. They have the mark of a desire for objectivity even when it is not achieved. "The historian's line of delineation between things," Roberts wrote in his autobiography, "must follow justly, firmly, and without hesitation, or he will fail in his absolute duty to the truth of things." Often in his writings the church comes out second best where a man of lesser character under similar circumstances would have found it easy to bring it out on top. "History to be of any worth," he wrote, "must not only tell of your successes, but also of your failures or semi-failures in your work."

There have been and are a number of highly competent historians of Mormonism. Indeed some of the very best are now at their work. Of these, however, most are students of specialized facets of Mormon history. The time is near when a general history of high order should make its appearance, as the materials are available and they have been well worked over. But as yet nothing like a definitive history has been published. There are excellent works of historical fiction and equally good biographical, sociological, economic, political, and local studies, and some good general commentaries, but no full-fledged history – none, that is, except Roberts's *A Comprehensive History of the Church of Jesus Christ of Latter-Day Saints*, a large and expansive work. This work, whatever Roberts's deficiencies as a historian and whatever his prejudices, is still the best account of the first hundred years of the church.

It is well known that most work on the Mormons produced until recently has been strongly biased pro or con with prejudices which violently distort the facts. No historian, of course, can be expected to achieve anything like a full objectivity. In history this is a concept quite without meaning, for historians must pick and choose their materials from an enormous and unwieldy mass of events, and if they are to be anything more than chroniclers, they must run the risk of causal explanation and interpretation which must sooner or later get them into trouble. Anyone who reads written history must have the grace to take all such matters into consideration.

But until recently Mormon history was written under the stress of exaggerated propaganda and controversy, propaganda that was excessive and controversy that as often as not was more passionate than reasonable, generating more heat than light. Today we can find numerous professional historians who have a calm competence on various phases of Mormon history. Some of these turn out historical essays of the highest quality. I mention this because I think it is essential to see that Roberts was not the end of history writing on the subject of Mormonism. He lacked many of the talents and opportunities represented in today's better and more-specialized historians, and no one should read his *Comprehensive History* and suppose that this is the end of the matter. Indeed it is only the beginning, and this is my point. For the historically minded and history-based Mormons, Roberts composed a strong and carefully researched comprehensive historical statement, laid out many of the fundamental issues and basic problems, and did so with courage and honesty. He had a large capacity for work, a fine sensitivity for the controversial, and a talent for research, comprehension, and synthesis. And while he wrote as he argued and debated, he achieved a measure of understanding admirable in a man who was personally living through the impassioned events which he described and who wrote as both a high official of the church and as its official historian. But the very ground which he covered must be worked again and again if the church is to have the written history which it deserves.

Though historians must adopt a position from which they select their material if they are to avoid confusion and frustration, I personally regret that Roberts was so strongly inclined toward what I would call the "political" theme in his history. This is a confession of my own bias, of course, and I suppose he would have been untrue to his own political nature if he had done otherwise. But it is still disappointing to find so much of political and institutional conflict and controversy and so little of what might be called cultural history in his work. Yet he was himself a man of action, and quite certainly he told the narrative where the action was.

I feel, moreover, that Roberts did not fully and properly examine and exploit the origins of Mormonism; and partly because of this, the generality of Mormon people today, who depend so heavily upon his work for their historical interpretations, do not understand and appreciate the multiple forces that went into the making of their religion and the historical movement of their church. The picture is altogether too simple and is too much affected by the strong desire to vindicate and justify the church.

But enough of criticism. If readers seek evidence of special virtue in Roberts as a historian, his determination to lay things out as he saw them, however distasteful they might be to some of his ecclesiastical colleagues and many of his readers, let them read his commentary on the destruction of the press of the *Nauvoo Expositor*, the account of and notes on the so-called "Canadian Copyright Incident," both in the *Comprehensive History*, or the fascinating "case of Pelatiah Brown," included in his editing of the documentary materials of the *History of the Church, Period I*. Or let them note the omission by Roberts of blocks of myth and legend which many accepted as history in his day.

Finally it should at least be noted that Roberts's perspectives on history and his competence to treat some of the large problems in Christian history were due in part to his intelligent and broad reading. There was much that he neglected in intellectual history, through no fault of his own, for his formal education was at best very elementary. He seems to have known too little of Greek and Roman philosophy and their bearing upon Christianity or of medieval philosophy and theology. And he neglected some of the great minds among his own contemporaries in favor of second- and third-raters. But he was acquainted with Emerson and Fiske and profited much from such writers as Andrew White, Kitto, Draper, and Gibbon. His works are well furnished with telling references to such greats as Mosheim, Milner, Edersheim, Milman, and Eusebius. When still a youth employed as a blacksmith, Roberts read extensively from all of these and from Renan, Blackstone, Macaulay, and an assortment of major philosophers, ancient and modern – no mean accomplishment for one who first learned the alphabet at the age of eleven. His work indicates too a broad acquaintance with the Bible and with Bible commentaries, though he seems to have been little affected by the historical and literary scriptural criticism which had such a large impact during his lifetime. Partly because of this neglect by Roberts and his contemporary fashioners of Mormon ways of thinking, the Mormon people even today are in general the victims of traditional patterns of biblical thought, which often tie them to an outworn and intellectually frustrating scriptural fundamentalism.

Roberts's treatments of Christian history were polemical and propagandistic. He dealt altogether too casually with the large cultural forces that produced Christianity and its institutions, and while his factual materials are in the main reliable, much that he wrote on this subject is difficult to defend. He failed to grasp the character of early hellenistic Christianity, to see its very beginnings in Paul as a departure from the Palestinian religion, and failed therefore, as did most Christian historians, to fairly judge the subsequent course of Christian thought and institutions. Nevertheless, he wrote intelligently, and though he depended excessively on secondary sources, the church historians, he described the main historical foundations upon which Mormons have rested their case, the apostasy of the Christian church as the necessity for a restoration. I refer here especially to his *Outlines of Ecclesiastical History*, his *The Falling Away*, and to his introduction for the *History of the Church, Period I*.

At the turn of the century, the Mormons had special problems of their own which kept them well occupied, but their intellectual leaders did not escape the main controversy of the time, religion versus evolution. The organic evolution controversy reached the United States rather late, and it reached the Mormons a little later, but Roberts was in the thick of it, determined to make the case for orthodoxy by discrediting Darwinism. His main, and early, essay on the subject, "Man's Relationship to Deity," does him little credit, but it is an important part of the story of his work. It is interesting that his argument was not anti-scientific in spirit, an attitude that would have betrayed his confidence in the virtues of reason. The errors of Darwinism, he insisted, were not due to the scientists. They were the fault rather of the churches, whose nonsense regarding the creation and age of the earth had driven the scientists far from the truth in their efforts to find a ground upon which they could make sense. Roberts's efforts to reconcile the findings of science with a liberalized biblical literalism were typical of the times and do not deserve serious attention today, but it should be said in his defense that in later years he appears to have developed a much greater sophistication in such matters. He was interested in the science-religion controversy and he read quite widely in the field, but he was better prepared to see the dispute in past centuries than to contribute importantly to it in the present.

Roberts's main strength as a theologian for Mormonism was not at all in his capacity for theological dialectic or refinement or in any originality for this discipline. It was rather in his instinct for the philosophical relevance of the Mormon theological ideas—this combined with his sense of history. This combination in temperament, talent, and interest brought both breadth and depth to his thought, giving his work a profundity that was uncommon among Mormon writers. Certainly one of the best exhibits of these qualities is his 1907 discourse, *Joseph Smith, the Prophet-Teacher*.

More than any other Mormon writer Roberts sensed the radical heresy in Mormon theology, its complete departure from the traditional Christian doctrines of God and man, its denial of the divine absoluteness, and its rejection of the negativism of the orthodox dogma of the human predicament, the doctrine of original sin. Roberts was not a creator of doctrine in these matters, but he had a clear vision of what was entailed by the basic ideas already laid down by his predecessors. He did more than any other person to set forth the full character of Mormonism that followed inevitably from the theological ideas of Joseph Smith, from the doctrine, for instance, of the uncreated intelligence or ego and the denial of the orthodox dogma on the creation of the world. Roberts was not repulsed by the unorthodox implications of the finistic conception of God. He delighted in them, for they made room for a positive doctrine of man. Yet he kept the discussion of the nature of God on a more defensible level than did some who confused the old absolutism with the new doctrine. It was a bold and audacious religion, which combined elements of traditional fundamentalism with the modern liberal doctrine of humanity and the optimism of the nineteenth century, and it required a bold and rebellious and spacious mind to grasp its full implication.

Today religious liberalism is largely spent, and the facts of life too often fail to support its claims. And there is little justification remaining for genuine optimism. Even in Mormonism the old Christian orthodoxy in new clothes is gaining ground. We are a tired and disillusioned generation which has suffered a new loss of nerve, and too often we prefer our religion in negative rather than positive terms. We prefer the comforts of resignation to the dangers and uncertainties of crusade and adventure. But however sanguine its claims and extravagant its vision, there is something noble and heroic about the authentic Mormon orthodoxy which Roberts and his generation believed and defended and which is still the religion of uncorrupted Mormonism. For it joins faith in God with faith in man, and unless this can be done effectively not only in theology but as well in the minds and experience of men, religion in any viable and acceptable form may not prevail.

EDITOR'S INTRODUCTION

Eight or nine months before his death in September 1933 at the age of seventy-six, Brigham H. Roberts began the bittersweet task of composing his autobiography. Known variously as "biographical notes" and "Life Story," Roberts's memoirs span the breadth of his life from the late 1850s as a neglected child in Dickensian England to post-World War I Utah as a respected, outspoken official of the Church of Jesus Christ of Latter-day Saints.

Roberts's episodic autobiography emphasizes his adventures in pioneer Utah, his missions for the LDS church, his career in partisan politics (including his opposition to women's suffrage and to prohibition), his bid for the United States House of Representatives (from which he was barred for polygamy), and his activities as one of seven presidents of the First Quorum of Seventy of the LDS church.

Only briefly does Roberts broach his marriages and family life; the historical and theological writings for which he had become well known such as his *Comprehensive History of the Church*; or the last fifteen or so years of his life. He does not mention his appointment as a chaplain in France during World War I; his controversial study of the origin of the Book of Mormon; his unpublished theological magnum opus, "The Truth, The Way, The Life"; his treatises on *Joseph Smith: Prophet, Teacher, The Mormon Doctrine of Deity, Defense of the Faith and the Saints,* or *Succession in the Presidency*; or his numerous disagreements with ecclesiastical colleagues over politics and church doctrine. As Roberts approached more contemporary events perhaps he was unwilling to be as revealing as he had been in recounting earlier experiences; perhaps the job of dictating his life story was simply too much of a strain for a man already suffering the debilitating effects of diabetes, depression, and old age.

Of his autobiographical notes, Roberts once disingenuously commented, "I do not think much of them. The conviction grows upon me that they ought not to be published. First, because my life is not of sufficient importance for a biography; second that it could not be fully told without arraigning others, and if told it must be fully and of course truthfully told; if that were done all Israel [the LDS church] could be greatly shocked. The only thing that would induce me to publish it would be to prevent someone else half and weakly doing it." Of course, had Roberts lived longer there is little doubt that he would have seen to the completion of his "notes." More than most, Roberts appreciated the lasting historical, social, literary, and political value of publication.

Although not completely reliable in every detail, nor as definitive and as thorough as might be hoped for, Roberts's autobiography reveals a man of considerable complexity and contradiction. For example, Roberts insists that he loved his mother deeply, yet it is apparent that he was devastated as a child when she abandoned him and his sister to abusive strangers while she emigrated with two of her other children to America. Her subsequent less-than-enthusiastic greeting at their reunion in Salt Lake City only underscored her apparent ambivalence. Roberts's later relationships with women, especially his three wives and fifteen children, were probably colored by the conflicting emotions he felt toward his mother.

In addition, although Roberts points out that Mormon leaders hoped to double their political clout by granting women's suffrage, he nonetheless was much slower than his contemporaries to be converted to equal rights for women. It is difficult to imagine that the same person who would later argue against prohibition–saying that nothing is "so dear to me as the liberty of the individual"–would not be similarly supportive of women's suffrage. But such are the contradictions and inconsistencies that spot Roberts's life.

At least two versions of B. H. Roberts's autobiography exist. The first he dictated to his secretary Elsa Cook, beginning either in December 1932 or January 1933 and continuing for three or four months, and is some 473 double-spaced typewritten pages long. The second is a copy of the original subsequently made by his daughter, Georgia Roberts Livingston, and is 237 single-spaced typewritten pages long. Both versions are currently housed in the B. H. Roberts Papers at the Marriott Library, University of Utah, although the library's copy of the original manuscript is incomplete. Both previously unpublished versions have been used in preparing the present edition for publication.

In its original form, the autobiography was written almost entirely in third person, presumably at Roberts's instruction and probably in an attempt to avoid self-aggrandizement. Only occasionally did Roberts lapse into first person. This awkward, artificial device unnecessarily distances author from reader and results in convoluted sentence constructions and ambiguous pronominal antecedents. Therefore, in editing the autobiography, all third-person pronouns referring to Roberts have been changed to first person. Also, spelling and grammar have been silently corrected, paragraph breaks inserted, transitions occasionally inserted, and missing text supplied. Finally, two lengthy and distracting excerpts from the Salt Lake City *Argus* and the autobiography of Orson F. Whitney have been deleted, as have two redundant paragraphs from Roberts's sermonizing against prohibition. This material would have otherwise appeared in chapter 21. Aside from this, Roberts's life story remains unchanged.

Despite its relatively minor drawbacks, "The Autobiography of B. H. Roberts" is a moving, insightful, sometimes painfully honest account that more than deserves publication. Ironically, Roberts's important published writings, which made him famous to Mormons throughout the world, will probably not survive as his most enduring legacy. A more promising candidate is his life story: a forthright account of events and acquaintances contributing to the unique faith and intellectual independence of one of Mormonism's most memorable leaders.

The
Autobiography

CHAPTER 1

The Promise

It was June the 6th, 1866, in Old Castle Gardens on the upper bay of New York, the landing place where nearly all European emigrants filed into the United States. A lad midway between nine and ten years of age, I could be seen seated on a bench on the south side of Castle Gardens. I was waiting the time when the large company of Mormon emigrants, which filled the gardens, would embark for the zig-zag route across the United States, through Canada, for the distant valley of Salt Lake, Utah.

I was a boy of no prepossessing appearance. In the first place I was clad in just a pair of barn-door trousers and jacket (made from the old trousers of an English policeman), a pair of iron-rimmed wooden clogs, and on my head was what was supposed to be a jaunty Scotch cap, faced with bright plaid around the rim and ending in two black streamers behind—a headgear which I heartily despised. My eyes were restless, keen, blue and deep set, my nose decidedly ill-shaped and upturned, and my face was freckled, my lips full, but not tender nor sweet. My head appeared to be crunched down into my shoulders, amounting almost to a deformity. My teeth were ugly, misshapen, with a wide gap between the two frontal ones through which I had learned to send forth a shrill whistle on occasion. My body was rather heavy, such as is described for lads as "chunky." My hair was of light mouse-colored hue, ill kept, slightly wavy and unruly of management—no amount of training seemed to affect it. On the whole I was stolid, and sober-faced. There was no joy in boyhood in my appearance, no disposition to mill round with the seven hundred other emigrants thronging the Old Castle Gardens. I seemed to be without companions and doubtless would have been repulsed by me if they manifested friendliness. I was a boy evidently who was accustomed to being alone—apart from the throng. I was not restless, but rather solemn and gloomy.

I seemed, however, to be watching somewhat and trying to keep within vision a young girl about nineteen years of age. She was rather shabbily attired, and the dress she wore was not only threadbare but torn in places. Her head was uncovered and the hair, glossy black, was pasted close to her head. She had my ill-shaped nose—it evidently was a family defect. Her brow was high and broad, and there was nothing to relieve the plainness of the face except the deep-set, hazel eyes, intensely bright, and the friendly smile which at times graced the generous mouth and full lips. She was

sociable and evidently having both a sad and a cheerful time in prospective
partings with the friends that thronged about her. Her social disposition was
in marked contrast with my surly disposition of an ill-favored lad of the
bench.

We were brother and sister on the way with this great throng of nearly
a thousand emigrants bound for Utah. By my side were several packages,
some in canvas wrappings or small canvas bags. These proved to be pieces
of fat-side bacon, made greenish by the intense pickling of the pork to make
it suitable for food on the long voyage by the sailing vessel which had just
ended. I also had some loaves of bread, some packages of hard tack. This
food was common to sea voyages, which took for sailing vessels over six
weeks in crossing from Liverpool to New York in those days (1866). It had
been a terrific voyage we had made in the ship *John Bright* of the Union
Line. The ship still lay some distance out in upper New York harbor.

A short distance west of Ireland, the *John Bright* had encountered three
days of severe storm with high seas and had to sail with hatches down and
sails reefed. The three-decked serviceable ship was seaworthy but tub-like
in movements, and during the three days of fierce storm little progress had
been made on the western journey—in fact it was said among the passengers
to have been driven backward. In six weeks and two days, however, the *John
Bright* had made New York harbor, and had disgorged its nearly one
thousand emigrants on the shores of the New World.

It was a motley crowd of Mormon emigrants that were chiefly from the
working classes of English people, of various grades: trades people, shop-
keepers, household servants, followers of odd jobs, such could be had from
any source of industry. Yet Charles Dickens, three years before on the 6th of
June 1863, said of a similar company of about the same number, in his
capacity of "Uncommercial Traveler," that they were in their degree "the
pick and flower of England." This company so described by Dickens was
made up of emigrants of English and Welch Latter-day Saints. It was equally
true of the Saints from the Scandinavian and other European countries, and
through all the years that the immigration or "gathering to Zion" continued.
This gathering was of the common people, purely, of the same class that
"heard Jesus gladly" (Mark 12:37), that God must love, because he had
"made so many of them." It is true of all the Mormon immigration to Utah,
for they were practically of one class from first to last—the common people.
And yet Mr. Dickens said of this group he visited in London harbor on the
emigration ship *Amazon*, the company numbering eight hundred:

"Now, I have seen emigrant ships before this day in June. And these
people are so strikingly different from all other people in like circumstances whom I have ever seen, that I wonder aloud, 'What would a stranger
suppose these emigrants to be!'

"The vigilant bright face of the weather-browned captain of the *Amazon*
is at my shoulder, and he says, 'What indeed! The most of these came

aboard yesterday evening. They came from various parts of England in small parties that had never seen one another before. Yet they had not been a couple of hours on board when they established their own police, made their own regulations, and set their own watches at all the hatchways. Before nine o'clock the ship was as orderly and as quiet as a man-of-war . . . . A stranger would be puzzled to guess the right name for the people . . . '

" 'Mr. Uncommercial,' says the captain, . . . 'if you hadn't known, could you ever have supposed?'

" 'How could I! I should have said they were in their degree, *the pick and flower of England.*'

" 'So should I,' says the captain.

" . . . I, Uncommercial Traveler for the firm of Human Interest, Brothers, had come aboard this emigrant ship to see what eight hundred Latter-day Saints were like, and I found them (to the rout and overthrow of all my expectations) like what I now describe with scrupulous exactness. . . .

"*Uncommercial.* 'These are a very fine set of people you have brought together here' [he said to the Mormon agent].

"*Mormon Agent.* 'Yes, sir, they are a very fine set of people.'

"*Uncommercial* (looking about). 'Indeed, I think it would be difficult to find eight hundred people together anywhere else, and find so much beauty and so much strength and capacity for work among them.'

"*Mormon Agent* (not looking about, but looking steadily at Uncommercial). 'I think so. We sent out about a thousand more yesterday from Liverpool. . . .'

"Among all the fine, handsome children, I observed but two with marks upon their necks that were probably scrofulous. Out of the whole number of emigrants, but one old woman was temporarily set aside by the doctor, on suspicion of fever; but even she afterwards obtained a clean bill of health. . . .

"I afterwards learned that a dispatch was sent home by the captain before he struck out into the wide Atlantic, highly extolling the behavior of those emigrants, and the perfect order and propriety of all their social arrangements. What is in store for the poor people on the shore of the Great Salt Lake, what happy delusions they are laboring under now, on what miserable blindness their eyes may be open then, I do not pretend to say. But I went on board their ship to bear testimony against them if they deserved it, as I fully believed they would; to my great astonishment they did not deserve it, and my predispositions and tendencies must not affect me as an honest witness. I went over the *Amazon*'s side, feeling it impossible to deny that, so far, some remarkable influence had produced a remarkable result, which better known influences have often missed" (*A Comprehensive History of the Church of Jesus Christ of Latter-day Saints, Century, I,* 5:92-93).

Such Dickens vouched the Mormon emigrants of the *Amazon* to be, three years before; such the emigrants of the *John Bright* were, three years later, so far as I can be sure of my boyish recollection when analyzed by observation and manhood experiences.

The passengers of the *John Bright* were awaiting the time when they would be transferred to river boats or barges for the beginning of the trans-continental journey; and as they were waiting, there suddenly rang out wild, unearthly screams, one following another, that spoke of great agony of heart. I slipped from the bench, looked in the direction whence the screams came, and saw a tall, angular woman, with sunken cheeks and streaming hair, her clothes half torn from her body, rushing through the crowd, seeking for her children. Afterwards I learned that the poor woman had broken down into violent insanity. It was a case of which there were many in that day among these gathering Latter-day Saints, that had divided families in order to make this journey of gathering to Zion. This Scotch family of which the crazed woman was the mother had been so divided, the parents bringing several children with them but leaving the other children in the care of fellow religionists. The poor mother had brooded over this incident in her experience until at last nature could hold out no longer and there came the unbalanced mind with its uncontrollable frenzy of insanity. She was vainly screaming for her offspring from whom she was separated. The husband was in close pursuit of her, trying to overtake and calm her. Presently he halted her flight and gathered her in his arms near the bench where I sat, where she continued heart-rended sobbing.

This incident with its explanation awakened in my mind a shadowy experience in my own family. About four years before a like separation had taken place in the family of which I was a member. Only my father was not in the picture. Somehow or other he was out of it. But I remembered the separation from my own mother, who had brought with her upon the voyage to the New World a babe in arms, about two years old, and a girl six or seven years of age and had left me, scarce four years old, with strangers. The girl of our picture, my sister Mary, had been left with distant relatives to be cared for until our mother from the far distant west could make the means and send for her and me. This at last had been effected, and we were as far as Castle Gardens, on our way to the longed-for reunion. But this separation had not occasioned the mental undoing of our stern-faced mother, who had faced her problem. All, however, are not equal to such a strain, and this poor woman of Scotch-like appearance was one who broke down. Her case was a sad one as we shall see in the progress of the trans-continental journey, for she will make one or two other intrusions into our story before I and my better-favored sister arrive at our destination.

The gospel of the New Dispensation had not been altogether a happy circumstance to the Roberts family. The proclamation of restored gospel through Joseph Smith, the Mormon prophet, had been a message of divine importance to our mother, Ann Everington Roberts, but to Benjamin Roberts, her husband, it was a matter that tested his credulity. Though he had accepted it, it was a perfunctory thing to him and of doubtful credibility. But his young wife had accepted it wholly and with such spiritual commendatory testimony that it became her life. It had been said of her that she was a "natural-born Israelite" and that since the New Dispensation message had within it the proclamation for the "gathering of Israel" wherever found in the world, the completeness of her faith was heralded as an evidence of Israelitish origin. In any event, her conversion was complete and nothing doubting. She had accepted baptism by immersion as a complete symbol of acceptance of the Christ and his latter-day gospel and as the door of entrance into the new fold of the Christ, under the sanctions of the special dispensation, which had come to the world. She had secretly accepted this entrance into the New Dispensation Church, against the wishes of her husband. She was secretly baptized into the fold in the North Sea and confirmed by the laying on of hands both in confirmation of membership into the church and for reception of the Holy Ghost, an inner light, to become the soul-voice of the church member.

This would be her spiritual guide. Later the husband followed the wife into the church fellowship, only half timorously accepting it however, as already indicated.

It was a strong pair, this man and wife, but the wife loved her faith more than she did her husband, and his reluctance at accepting this "call" to gather with the church and also certain unconquered intemperate habits and wild craving for independence began to suggest the possibility of a family rupture. The thought was some time suggested that Benjamin–"Ben" to the wife–would have to be sacrificed to her full realization of faith. The intemperate habits referred to on the part of the husband led to occasional and sometimes protracted separations. As the question of "gathering to Zion"–even at the sacrifice of Ben–became more and more insistent, at the close of one of these separations when money was sent by the husband to bring his wife and us to him, the question to his wife became: shall the money be used to make the local journey and reunite her family or shall it meet the principal part of the migration to Zion. Being near the headquarters of the European and British Mission at that time, Mrs. Roberts referred the question to the church authorities and received encouragement to separate her family. She and two of her children would undertake the long journey and trust to the Providence of God to bring her two remaining children, my sister and I, to the same destination with the reunion at last of mother and children in Zion–even at the risk of a fixed separation from her husband and their father. It was a tremendous undertaking. I can recall some of the occasions of grief which the contemplated action produced in the family life.

Of my father I can remember but little, but some incidents were pleasant and favorable to my father's character and genial good nature. I remember some fragment of the songs he sang. One has as a refrain:

> I've a darling little wife,
> She's the comfort of my life,
> And her, I always will adore –
> I am sitting by the fire;
> With my children by my side,
> And what can a poor man ask for more.

"Old Dog Tray" is vividly remembered:

> Old Dog Tray is ever faithful,
> Grief cannot drive him away,
> He is gentle, he is kind,
> You'll never, never find,
> A better friend than Old Dog Tray.

And also a snatch of "Old Horse" – he must have lived to an old age after a hard life of work, for the fragment remembered must have been just a refrain:

> Whip him, strip him, and turn him out –
> Poor old horse, Poor old horse!

I remember family misunderstandings, my father coming home and no supper prepared – perhaps no food in the house – my father standing at the pantry door and twirling the plates across the room to the table. They would settle with a whirling motion and a clatter to the respective places of the members of the household – a wonderful performance, so I thought childishly! I remember a sickness, a great weakness following. During that time – it must have been on a Sunday morning, it was summer time, the window was open and a large pigeon flew into the sitting room – my father caught the bird. Its neck was wrung, the feathers plucked off, the bird dressed and soon in the pot to be made into soup for me, who was sick at the time. These are the items that memory holds of my father. There are other items that I cherish, some traditions in the family that relate to what my father had done.

One account told of my father's rescuing an apprentice lad from the brutality of two fellow workmen in a blacksmith shop at which he worked. The apprentice lad was constantly scolded and kicked and cuffed about by this pair of workmen to the suffering of the boy and against the protests of Ben Roberts. One day, when they had been unusually cruel, Ben knocked one of them down by a blow of his strong right fist. The other workmen – by the way, they were both Irish – attacked him, and Ben had to give them both a sound beating before they would promise to let the apprentice chap alone for the future.

Another story was told by my mother. She and Ben were going through a side street in Liverpool, crowded with fighting men. Something of a riot was on. Every man's hand was against every other man apparently, and no one seemed to know his opponent. My mother clung firmly to her husband's arm, and he was trying to lead her from the tumult. Suddenly they were confronted by a half-drunken chap, who said to Ben: "I believe you are an Irishman." "Perhaps I am," said Ben. "Then down you go," said the burley rioter and struck but missed. Ben, without letting go of his wife, struck and knocked out his assailant and quietly walked on without further ado of interference.

With reference to the breaking up of the family home, I retain a vivid recollection of my mother weeping as she went about her household duties. On this occasion, left alone with her except for the babe, my mother as she stepped from dining table to pantry door was weeping. With childish sympathy I plucked her gown and in my broad Lancashire dialect said: "Mother, What oop? And why art' crying?" My mother knelt on the floor beside me and with her arms about my shoulders told me of the intended journey to America–Zion–and how I would have to be left behind with Brother and Sister Tovey. My sister Mary would be left with some distant relatives by the name of Pie, and it was only now a day or two when this separation would take place.

As she held on to me telling the story, sobs and tears became more profuse, and at last folding me in her arms, she sought of me brokenly to promise that when I grew up to be a man I would come to her in "Zion." Freeing myself from the embrace, I stood erect in the middle of the floor and with childish solemnity promised her that "I would come."

CHAPTER 2.

The Prophecy

The four-year period of life with the Toveys following the separation from my mother bound to Zion and the separation from my older sister, Mary, was far from being a happy childhood. The Toveys were scarcely ideal people for honesty and right living, although church members of the New Dispensation. Certain shadowy references to the past of their lives indicated to me that something was irregular. For one thing, there arose a doubt as to the real name of the pair–who by the way were childless–and disclosed the fact that Tovey was not the real name nor the only name they used. It developed that sometimes they were known by, and sometimes they themselves used, the name of Gaily. There was in the offing of their experience a brother of the old lady who was connected with some criminal transaction and had been in prison. Furthermore, notwithstanding their church membership, they were both addicted to periodical heavy drinking, and as I afterwards remembered, most of their evenings were spent in country taverns and city saloons, ending frequently in absolute drunkenness. To these taverns and saloons, they dragged me with them, who curled up under the tables where the drinking went on and slept. Out of the drear loneliness, I longed for the time to go to the wretched home which was all they ever seemed able to maintain.

As the years passed I became something of a bone of contention with them. Their frequent quarrels ended in temporary separation when each sought to establish claims for possession of me. With the passing years, as I became more useful in the household and in the occupation of John Tovey, the desire of each to have control of me increased.

As manifestation of this contested control over me, the following incident was sharply placed in my mind. A dispute about me arose in a public market place of some city not now remembered. As the controversy sharpened, I was disgusted and took to my heels, whereupon both of the worthy pair pursued me. Losing in the race, the old lady took up a shout of "Stop thief," and this set the pack in the market place on the run to catch me. Having witnessed such scenes before, I knew how my opportunity for escape was diminishing. Presently a policeman outrunning the crowd grabbed me and held me until the pair of my pursuers came up. Then explanations were due, and it was quickly disclosed that I was no thief, since I had nothing upon me, nor had I taken anything in my flight. An

awkward explanation had to be made to the officer, who severely repri-
manded the old lady for making a false cry of "stop thief" merely to hold
me to her bondage. The explanations were at last straightened out and a
severe reproof given by the policeman and the trio thus strangely united
went on our way.

John Tovey (for such I shall continue to call him notwithstanding his
frequent lapses into the use of John Gaily) was a stone sawyer by trade. In
this vocation I could be quite useful in sifting the sand and carrying it to the
sloping board above the slashes cut into the sandstone by the moving
backward and forward of a heavy steel blade set in a frame something like a
bucksaw, but much larger and heavier. This blade pushed across the
sandstone, and the sand on the sloping board above the slash was washed
into the crevices by the dripping of water from the spigot of the keg. This
movement cut the stone into the desired slab. It was my business through
the day to keep the board supplied with sand and the water in the keg. Both
water and sand were carried upon the head. This continuing through a
number of years, my head was pressed between my shoulders until it
amounted almost to a deformity. It was not until the occupation ceased and
the arrival of a robust boyhood at about twelve or thirteen years of age was
attained that my shoulders assumed normal conditions. Thus through these
years of early boyhood, there was almost a hunchback appearance given to
me.

While pursuing this unfortunate vocation, I held in memory a very
pleasant incident. The great building from which the stone had been cut
was finished, and the company directing the building gave a banquet to the
workmen on the yards about the building. It was the first feast I had ever
attended and "My," I was wont to say, "what a grand affair it was." A great
hall was brilliantly lighted by gas, long tables extending the length of the
hall with great roasts of beef alternating down the lengths of the tables with
roasted young pigs, baked apples in their mouths. There was an abundance
of vegetables and fruits and table adornments for accompaniment and at the
head of each table an elegantly dressed gentleman who spoke kindly to the
workmen and invited them to partake heartily of the feast prepared. There
was an abundance of all this, with plenty of ale supplied.

As I took my part in the feasting, I remembered the little old woman at
the bare wretched home, Mrs. Tovey. Some of the thick slices of bread and
some of the famous English roast beef were crowded into the pockets of my
jacket for her, which later in the night with some ale brought from the
neighboring pub made her a hearty meal. I enjoyed this as much as I had
my own gorging feast, and I remember the happiness that came from this
rude service to one whom I knew was not infrequently hungry. It will be
seen from this description of occupation how I could be useful to the
sawyer John Tovey.

Also I had recollections of polishing marble slabs for mantel pieces and hearthstones, table tops, and other interior uses. Marble blocks were sawed up into possibly from an inch to two inches in thickness according to the purpose for which they were to be used. The first treatment of the stones was by long rubbing with sandstone until the surface was made reasonably smooth. Then a substance called snake-stone, of a finer grain, was employed. This rubbing generally was performed by children and brought on the polish of the fine marble, so it was ready for uses in ornamentation of inside buildings.

Strangely enough John Tovey was a remarkable preacher of the Mormon doctrine, and his way of life seemed not to interfere especially with the effectiveness of his testimony and preaching. The custom of the church in England about this time was to hold morning services, where they partook of the "sacrament." After this those who were sufficiently gifted were appointed to go to street corners and to public squares and sometimes cut in the fields to hold preaching service, and at this kind of work, John Tovey was especially noted. It was perhaps this association with the church that led my mother at the pair's solicitation to take charge of me and confirmed to her the righteousness of their lives and suitableness of their character. It is quite certain that without such confirmation Ann Roberts would never have committed me to be placed in their charge. In the outdoor preaching service, I usually accompanied John Tovey. I had something of a boyish voice that seemed to be attractive in singing some of the early church hymns of the Mormon cult, and with me to sing for him, John Tovey and I made a full missionary team.

John Tovey could neither read nor write, but his wife could do both, and she read to him the passages of the scripture over and over again that would sustain the Mormon point of view, and these John Tovey committed to memory and marked their location in the Bible. When controversies arose from his preaching, he would turn to these special texts in the Bible and, running his finger along the lines, would pretend to be reading them and would offer his Bible in confirmation to those who disputed him. My thought at such times was that this was not quite honest, because I knew John Tovey could not read but was pretending he could.

Sometimes violence attended upon these occasions, especially on the Old Clock Square at Wolverampton, England. This square was sort of an open forum for the people. It was so called because of the old town clock erected upon the fluted columns surrounded by a few yards of iron railings, inside of which were two cannons placed there as momentoes from Sebastopol and the Crimean war. Pyramids of solid shot were stacked by the wheels, and here many meetings were held. The custom was to bring a chair from the home. At the commencement of the meeting, I was placed upon the chair and would sing some of the early church hymns, after which Mr. Tovey would mount the chair and preach. Sometimes in the surgings of the crowd, Tovey would get pushed off the chair, and several times the old man would have to take to his heels to get away from his violent opposers. I then shouldered the chair and marched off home, being, of course, too insignificant to attract attention of the crowd. Those occurrences, however, were early lessons in much mob violence witnessed by me in later years.

During this time the Tovey home was located in an obscure street called "Old Horsefair Street" in Wolverampton. It received its name because through this street passed the great Norman Horse parades on their way to the place of exhibition, the horses decorated with bright colored ribbons woven into their manes and their bob tails.

For a time this pair of nondescript Mormons, the Toveys, opened and ran a cake and pie shop, their wares being sold to rag-muffin children of the neighborhood. Here occurred a very violent quarrel and an assault upon the person of old Mrs. Tovey, and here came up reference to the criminal brother of the woman. I remember seeing her struck down by the use of a chair. The blood spurted fiercely from the wide wound across the temple and face. She must have been knocked unconscious, for I remember her lying in a shapeless heap and blood flowing from her head and spreading out upon the floor. Tovey was evidently alarmed and seized a half bag of flour, evidently about to make the pastry for the little shop. He shook it out to cover up the blood, but it only soaked through it and made it seem more gruesome and larger and more terrible than it really was. Then there was a hasty departure; grabbing me by the hand, Tovey fled from the scene. As I remember it, the separation of the pair that time was a long one, and for some time the old man's anxiety was very great as to whether the old woman had died or not.

About this time when attending meetings and coming in contact with the Saints, I heard remarks in their conversations that an effort was being made for me to go to America to join my mother. It afterwards developed that President Brigham Young had sent word to the mission and branch authorities to find me and have me join one of the emigration companies gathering to Zion that year, but the efforts failed. Another year had to pass before the proper connections could be made, and I could be rescued from these conditions.

That last year with the Toveys was increasingly difficult. I remember one effort that was made by the old lady to separate me from Tovey by apprenticing me to a trade. At that time boys were put out to apprenticeship for trade in boyhood and were expected to remain until they were of age twenty-one. Mrs. Tovey took me to an institution in the city that managed these things, and my name was entered upon the books in application for an apprenticeship in this district. I was to be brought the next day to be taken in charge by the institution. The poverty of the pair at this time was very great. The shop had broken down and was given up, and frequently hunger and gauntness were visited upon the three of us. I remember that the home was a tumbled-down house. We lived in an upper room. There was neither bed nor bedding, and my sleeping place was in one corner of the room. It was a mere huddle under various pieces of day clothing under which I generally shivered through the night. On this night following the registering for an apprenticeship, after sleeping some time, I awoke and was strangely awake, eyes staring out into the darkness which was only relieved by the dim lights from the streets coming in through the windows and patterning the windows on the opposite walls. Restless I tossed from side to side. Then presently a calmness, and a voice was heard saying: "If you are apprenticed to the shoemaker's trade tomorrow, you will never see your mother in America." Then stillness and the recurring question in my disturbed mind: What should be done?

How much time elapsed during these questions I did not know, but presently I found the resolution formed in my mind that I would run away. Gathering up such clothing as I had, I stole downstairs and out into the steps of the house that led down to the brick pavement of the sidewalk. Putting on my clogs which I had carried in my hand, I stole down the side street into the wider ones and thence on into the main streets. On and on I walked without objective. Off to my left I saw the flare of furnaces that I knew to be in the edge of the city by a canal, and to them I guided my footsteps. I did not know the nature of the manufactures and the use of the furnaces, only that red hot slag was occasionally dumped on the accumulating slag heaps. Getting as close as possible, I sat in the glowing welcome warmth of the red hot slag and remained there until daybreak. Then there were wanderings, the direction and nature of which cannot be remembered, but weeks passed. I lived as a gamin in a town some distance away to which I had gone, and then at last I was discovered by the pair hunting for me. I went back to their adventures seeking for a new home. The danger, however, of apprenticeship to shoemaking was passed, as the idea of it had been given up by those who had me in charge.

Then another adventure came. There had been a separation of the pair. This done, John Tovey, now going by the name of John Gaily, spent his nights in the taverns that would accept so poor a patron. There he saw a man wearing narrow striped ribbons of red, white and blue in his hat and in the buttonholes of his coat; he was generously bedecked. Conversation was had between "John Gaily" and this be-ribboned officer of some kind, and an affair patched up which was to result in my becoming a drummer boy in the British barracks near the place, the enlistment to continue until I was twenty-one years of age. The shilling as an evidence of enlistment was passed, the ribbon was fastened on my coat, who the next morning was to be delivered at the army barracks. Then followed separation for the night. During a restless night again the voice which had spoken to me on the previous occasion—which I shall call the soul-voice—said: "If you are enlisted as a drummer boy, you will never see your mother in America." Formation of the same resolution to run away came: the same stealing out from the uncomfortable pallet carrying my clogs in my hand, getting to the doorstep, putting the wooden clogs on, and the same running away. In a distant town I knew of an old Scotchman who was a shoemaker and who sometimes had gone with John Tovey on his preaching exploits. After long and purposeless wandering about, the old Scotchman was found, but somehow he got into communication with the Toveys and told of my being with him. Soon afterwards Tovey came to take charge of me. It was about this time of being returned to the Toveys that there was some shifting from one town to another to find employment. The old gentleman had gone ahead to secure the job, and old Mrs. Tovey and I followed after.

The journey led through a beautiful country side of England, through green lanes hedged with blackthorn, occasional trees stretching up in the midst of the hedges. It was in the summer time, and the weather was sultry when the journey on foot was made. Along about midday old Mrs. Tovey was very tired and sat in the shade of the hedgerow to rest. Down in the deep-cut road from the foot of the hedge, two or three pages of a newspaper fluttered. I rushed out and gathered them up and brought them to the old lady, begging her to read to me. And here should be said that this matter of the old lady reading to me was something of a passion with me. She read the scriptures to her husband when evenings were spent at home and on Sunday morning to enable him to memorize the scriptures he used when preaching. Naturally I listened, very often entranced. Sometimes the church paper called the *Latter-day Saints' Millennial Star* was read. Somewhere about this time an anti-Mormon book was published in England, Samuel Mosheim Schmucker's *History of the Mormons, or Latter-day Saints, – Their Origin to the Present Time*, etc. Smucker was a Master of Arts, the author of *The Rise and Reign of Catherine II, Nicholas of Russia*, etc. It is not known when the first edition was published, but it ran through a number of editions. The time of the first is not remembered, but it is usually conceded to be the fairest anti-Mormon account of Joseph Smith and the religion he founded that existed up to that time. His discussion of the martyrdom of the prophet at Carthage, Illinois, was vivid as also were the engravings illustrating it. This was a choice section of the book to me, and I pleaded frequently for it to be read to me. Old Mrs. Tovey was kind enough to do this.

These readings made me quite familiar with historical personages of the church. The names of Joseph and Hyrum Smith, of Brigham Young and John Taylor, were familiar to me in my boyhood as well as the incidents connected with the Carthage murder and other striking events of history. In the case of John Taylor, it became almost a case of hero worship. I did not know at that time I would become the biographer of this hero of Carthage and the third president of the Church of Jesus Christ of Latter-day Saints, but it turned out so in the years that lay ahead of my strange boyhood. I admired greatly the courage that prompted this man Taylor to stand by his chief at the opening door as the guns were thrust through pressing their deadly messages into Carthage prison. He deliberately parried the guns, drawing them out of range as they blazed their death messages into the chamber where the prophet and his friends were confined. And from these impressions of the strength and manhood of John Taylor in that issue was fed some of the spirit and power of the future biography.

Familiarity with New Dispensation Scriptures also formed in those days and the spirit of that dispensation was engendered, which the impressions of later years have deepened. Perhaps there was no more fruitful period of mind training that came to me than in those hectic days of my early boyhood.

On every occasion when there was an opportunity, my one plea was to be read to. Hence the fluttering sheets of the newspaper were captured and were brought to the old lady, and hence the oft-repeated petition to be read to was made. The reading, however, on this occasion was very brief, for the weariness of Mrs. Tovey and the heat of the day soon induced a snoring sleep. I sat alone with the paper and my thoughts, marvelling at the miracle: that a paper could speak to one if he only had the power to read it. On this thought I dwelt in my mind, and after some time lapsed, I spoke out loud:

"Will the time ever come when books and paper will speak to me? Will I ever read books." Then a peculiar silence, and the soul-voice said: "Aye and you'll write them too."

Then all things seemed to be swallowed up in an immense and wonderful silence. I had no inclination to move or disturb the silence. It seemed as if the whole universe had become an ear and a voice. A slight trembling shook my frame as I listened to what might be called the very vibrations of silence. So I sat entranced a long time. How long I do not remember. I was merged in that silence, until my old lady companion groaned and awoke, and the journey was resumed. I made no reference to my strange experience, never through the many years, and for many years it was forgotten.

CHAPTER 3.

The Voyage

During the winter of 1866, word had been received by the authorities of the church in England that the Roberts children were to be brought to America that season. Consequently such steps were taken as would prepare my sister and me for sailing in the first ship to leave England that season, the date of which was set for April 30th. The details of the arrangements, of course, were not known to either of us, but in some way the instructions were complied with. At the Liverpool branch on Sunday, the 29th of April, great public meetings were held and great rejoicings had by the large number of emigrants that were preparing to go. All the forenoon of Monday, April 30th, small boats carried passengers from the shore to the ship *John Bright* lying at anchor with signals flying, announcing an early departure. Up the side steps of the vessel the throng of passengers made their way until the decks were reached and they were distributed to upper, middle, or lower-decked, according to the nationality, price of passage, etc. In all there were about 764 adult passengers, how many accompanying children is not known. It fell to our good fortune to be located on the first deck under the main open deck, which for pleasantness of passage was better than the other two.

It was a varied crowd of passengers milling on the main open deck before the sailing of the ship, and there were both tears and laughter in the matter of saying goodbye, since many of those who came aboard were relatives of the passengers. I noticed that my sister Mary was for most of the time in tears, and it was a matter of wonderment with me why she should be crying. For me the secret thought was that I was now on the way of fulfilling the promise I had given my mother, that I would join her in America, Zion to the Saints. That thought filled me with very great satisfaction. Although nothing was said between us on that head, I could only account for my sister's tears by supposing that she was afraid that the ship might go down. While clinging to her hand as she went among her friends bidding them goodbye, I stamped firmly on the strong open deck, and finally getting her attention, I said, "Polly, (for that was the family name for Mary) Polly, this ship won't sink." She gave tearful assent.

Some time late in the afternoon, the vessel was cleared of visitors, the anchor "weighed," and the ship started upon her voyage. It was the time now for songs of farewell, and among them I remember what to me was a familiar hymn:

> Yes, my native land I love thee
> All thy scenes I love them well—
> Friends, connections, happy country,
> Now I bid thee all farewell.
> *Refrain*
> Yes, I leave thee, glad I leave thee,
> Far in distant lands to dwell.

Also the gathering hymn:

> O Babylon, O Babylon, we bid thee farewell,
> We're going to the mountains of Ephraim to dwell.

There were several verses of each, and they were sung by a strong congregational chorus at this departure and often repeated through the long voyage. It was growing dark as the vessel drew away from the Liverpool harbor.

Days passed, and somewhere out from the coast of Ireland, a tremendous storm arose which lasted for three days. The roughness of the seas compelled the shutting down of the hatches, and as all the people were compelled to be mewed up below decks, life at sea was gloomy, and the tossing of the vessel made nearly all the passengers heartily seasick. Food could not be served, and there was much pounding of dry, hard sea biscuits, which were washed down with water already becoming putrid. Late in the afternoon of the third day, the hatches were opened, and the steps leading to them were thronged with people all but panting for fresh air. I was among the many children who pushed their way up to the top of the steps and got a glimpse of the restless ocean as it was being thrashed by the winds. After the hatches had been turned back, I observed quite a large ring in the farther edge of the hatch and, pushing my way round the side edge, seized upon it. Nearby within my reach was still another ring. This too I grasped, and by means of these rings, I could lie upon my back and hold on amidst the restless pitching and rocking of the vessel. Way off at the horizon, I could see the sun beaming through the clouds, giving promise of a better day on the morrow. Everywhere on every side, the sea was raised into high though choppy waves that presented the sea in its wildest aspect. This I enjoyed, though once in a while waves leaped over the low sides of the *John Bright* and drenched me. The joy within my soul, however, rose to meet the boisterous ocean, and it was remembered as an experience of supreme exultation.

It was not long to continue, however, as a sailor, who it seems had been designated to watch over the children and keep them from mischief and danger, came by with a rope in his hand. Because he was swarthy and had very black eyes, he was known among the children, whom he sometimes disturbed, as "Blackeye," and he took means to dislodge me from my place of vantage. There was a wild scramble for the entrance to the stairway, and in the wild scramble for the entrance to the stairway and in the wild dash, I won first place and slid down the side banisters of the stairs of the gangway and escaped. I had good reasons for getting away from "Blackeye," because some time before the storm broke, I had invaded the forbidden regions of the "rattlings." These ran from the side of the ship to the vast cross beams which held the main sails and thence on up from cross beam to cross beam to the "top sail." On this occasion I reached the first cross beam, when "Blackeye" saw me and, swinging on the under side of the rattlings, came up hand over hand almost catlike. For one vain moment I tried to escape by climbing still higher up the rattlings, but it was no use. "Blackeye" had followed me and, being on the under side of the "rattlings," was in excellent position to use his rope. I had started to scramble down, but I suffered from the cuts of "Blackeye" 's rope end, until he could drop on the deck and escape. After that "Blackeye" was something of a terror, and hence when the sailor made for the hatch to which I clung, there was hustling in hot haste to get to the deck below, where escape was made.

All the days, however, were not so stormy nor all the scenes stamped with sadness. Many of the May days were cloudless and the air balmy. There were frolics on deck, games and group singing. There were many beautiful voices in that list of passengers—English, Welch, Scotch—for they had been gathered from all the scattered branches in those countries, some of them noted for their music. There was dancing, also games for the children—among others, marbles for the boys when the ship was steady enough for the marbles to stay in the rings until shot out by the players. Of course, there were childish quarrels and violence too. I remember one which arose over the dispute about giving up of marbles that had been lost to me in the play—for the game was generally for "keeps." The boy with whom the quarrel arose was of dark complexion, swarthy skin, a hard face, it would have been called, because of its desperate earnestness and the fury with which he held up the fight of his quarrel. First blows were struck; but "Blackeye" was at hand and soon separated the boys. The dark complexioned boy's name was John Gibbs, and as he and I were held apart by "Blackeye," there was great anger registered on each face. Strange the meeting of us two under such circumstances. Twenty years shall not have passed when John Gibbs will have become a martyr to the faith of the Latter-day Saints, and I, presiding over a mission in the southern states, will take some risks in bringing John's body from an unsatisfactory burial to send it home from Tennessee to friends in his own home town in Utah. The identification of each other and the relation of the circumstance to our lives took place during our missionary experiences together. It cannot often be prophesied what future relations quarreling boys will have to each other. This was one of the strangest.

So far as remembered, the officers of the *John Bright* were very fine, and they watched with serious care over the welfare of their passengers. This is true of all of them. Perhaps one exception was the first mate, who was a "grouch" both towards the crew and the passengers. Maybe he was a splendid officer too, but he shouted out his words in a deep guttural or husky voice, and always he had the appearance of having got up feeling mad about something. One mid-afternoon, he gave a gruff order to "Blackeye" to go and bring him some bread and butter and a cup of tea. He was on duty and wanted this refreshment. Presently "Blackeye" came back with some choice, thinly-sliced white bread and butter laid together like sandwiches. The mate appeared angry that the slices of bread had been cut so very thin. Without any apparent reason, he shouted at "Blackeye" as he threw the bread and butter over the side of the ship into the ocean, "I told you to get some bread and butter, not wafers." And when I recall the sea fare of the passengers, which did not include delicately cut bread and butter, it was with no slight indignation that I witnessed this action of the first mate. "Blackeye," however, went to the cook's quarters and soon returned with bread thick enough to please the first mate's taste. But if ever the ocean was begrudged a thin bread and butter sandwich, it was when it received that double sandwich from the hands of the angry first mate of the *John Bright*.

The days of the voyage went on, and one after another the days passed. It began to be whispered among the passengers that we should in a few days begin to see land–American land. The rumor of it was remembered as thrilling, but it was not to be realized until another fierce and unlooked-for storm. The clouds gathered, which the officers and sailors spoke of as "angry," as they rushed about carrying out the orders to reef sail and lash every loose thing fast. Passengers were ordered below; preparations were made to shut down the hatches. One man remarked to a companion as he stood by the door of the cabin (for there was a cabin and a few special and apparently wealthy passengers among the emigrant companies that occupied it) and took a glance around the horizon from which in all directions the entreating storm seemed to be arising, "By G-d, I wish we were in New York Harbor."

I wanted to see this storm, but the emigrants were ordered below deck, and several sailors were hustling them down the hatch steps. I lingered near the penthouse on the rear of the deck, where the emergency compasses were and where subordinate officers were stationed to assist in steering the ship. On the bridge across the west of the ship, I could see the helmsmen being lashed to the frame of the steering wheel. Evidently there was going to be a wonderfully interesting time. I crouched down out of sight behind the penthouse until all the others would be fastened below, while I would be free to see what happened on deck. I did not have to wait long for the happenings to begin. A fierce wind gathered up a spiral of water, a water-spout in fact, and soon it was crossing the pathway of the *John Bright*. The ship was caught in the outer edge of the swirling waters, which carried the vessel far, far out of its course, and the wildest scene of lashed ocean and swirling water occurred. How long it lasted was not known, but before the vessel was entirely free from the influence of the raging column of the water, night was falling, and even I was glad to escape from the side of the penthouse and join the passengers under the hatches.

After this adventure, the location of the ship—its longitude and latitude—had to be ascertained by soundings taken of the ocean bottom. The storm and water spout had taken the vessel far to the north of the direct line of its proper course, and the talk on shipboard was that it had been brought up towards Newfoundland. Several hours, perhaps half a day, were taken up in these soundings, after which the vessel's course was once more in the direction of New York Harbor. On the sixth day of June, as noticed in chapter 1, the *John Bright* came to anchorage in upper New York Bay, and its passengers were temporarily lodged in Castle Gardens, waiting to be loaded upon the low-lying steamboats which would take them up Long Island Sound to New Haven. From there the journey by rail and river boats would proceed into the middle west of America.

It was an extremely zig-zag and indirect course which this company followed. It cannot be understood how it was that the journey from New York was made by boat up the Long Island Sound to New Haven; thence to Montreal in Canada; thence up the river to Fort Laurence; thence to Niagara by train. The recollection is distinctly impressed upon my mind that the train halted upon the Niagara Falls bridge with the falls in full view. There was some talk among the emigrants of one Blindell walking a tight rope over the falls, his feet encased in baskets to make the feat more difficult and exciting.

Another incident of the journey helped to fasten upon my mind the halt on Niagara bridge. This was an attempt of the woman who had gone insane at Castle Gardens to destroy herself. She had escaped from her guards and rushed from the car in which she had been installed and made an attempt to leap from the car and bridge into the river below. Her guards, however, succeeded in recapturing her and taking her back to her car, which was the same in which my sister and I were traveling. These cars were of the cattle-shipment type, and before the cars left the bridge halt, the exits were locked. This enraged a good Welch brother by the name of Williams who in some way exercised a sort of guardianship over my sister and me. He was a short man in stature, a typical Welchman of the excitable kind. His eyes were black and fiercely bright, the mustache was clipped rather short and stood out bristlingly, and generally it was remembered that his beard was seldom shaved and contributed to the ruggedness of his features. He was readily excitable and bitterly resented being locked up in these cattle cars. As chief guard of this poor insane woman, he wore an ancient rapier buckled about him in a leather scabbard, which he occasionally drew. It was supposed to add importance to his position as guard. At one point of the journey, he undertook to cut his way out through the deal or oak door of the cattle car. I remember how he smote repeatedly the door with this light-plated rapier, doing no other damage than loosening a splinter or two, until he satisfied even himself that his assaults amounted to nothing. He was poppery tempered, and in later years, as my extensive reading was well on its way, he reminded me of Shakespeare's Welchman known in Prince Hall's Glendower, who could call up spirits from the vastly deep, and Prince Hall's taunt of, "So can I, and so can he, and so can anyone, but will they come when you do call them." Williams's assault upon the impregnable door with his slight steel blade was something of the same order. At any rate this fiery Welchman was a source of amusement to me, on the boats and as one of the rear guard of the covered train.

The same night, after leaving Niagara bridge, our unfortunate insane woman again escaped from her guards and for a time ran wild in the car, leaping over benches and sitting upon the sleepers variously stretched out on the benches that were supplied in the cattle cars. I have a distinct recollection of her coming and sitting on my head as I was asleep. As soon as I recognized her from her screams and wild laughter, I let out a yell that would have awakened the "Seven Sleepers," which scream only increased her hilarity and clapping of hands. At the first yell she bounded up and then dropped back again on my head with renewed force. This went on for some time with alternating bouncing and screaming. At last the guards, who had fallen asleep, were aroused and succeeded in capturing the woman and relieving me. After that my sister and I avoided contact with the poor woman and succeeded until reaching Camp Florence on the Missouri. The journey was then continued to Detroit. Entering Canada, the baggage underwent an overhauling by the customs officers of that Dominion and again at Detroit. The red coats of the British military uniform brought vivid recollections and something of a pang about having left England.

The journey was continued through Chicago, thence to Quincy, Illinois, where much of the conversation among the emigrants turned to Joseph Smith and Nauvoo. From there we traveled to St. Joseph and up the Missouri to a point called Wyoming, a little to the south of Council Bluffs. Arrival was made on the 19th of June. Here the emigrant mule trains and ox trains were met that had been sent from Utah, chiefly by the Perpetual Emigration Fund Company, an organization for the gathering of the Saints to Zion. The means were advanced by this company to trustworthy members of the church, with the understanding that the means advanced for the emigration would be refunded with a very low rate of interest. When the object of the company was taken into account, it was one of the most unselfish and practical arrangements that could be made – and beneficial with all, both to the emigrants and also to the newly and sparsely settled valleys of Utah. Thousands by this means were delivered from limited conditions in Europe and given the opportunity of becoming landowners in the far west, many of whom attained unto independent conditions of prosperous middle-wealthy people and constituted the wholesome men of affairs in their new homes. It was a cruel blow to the prosperity of the common people when the government of the United States in later years abolished this system of mutual helpfulness between the poor of Europe and those developing Utah resources. Further notice of this will be taken when coming up to the period of the abolishment of the law. It was largely through the operation of this wisely planned institution that my sister and I were able to be brought to America. Both of us in later years met the obligation for our emigration by repayment—Mary through the man whom she married and I by working on the Utah Central Railroad, the road that connected Salt Lake and Ogden. The church trains to meet the incoming immigrants in the year 1866 numbered ten, with, of course, ten plains captains, 456 teamsters, 40 mounted guards, 89 horses, 134 mules, 3048 oxen and 397 wagons and 62 other wagons; 50 oxen and 61 mules were added by purchase. All this for the emigration of church members that year, which was one of the largest emigrations conducted by the church.

Nearly a month was spent at Wyoming, fitting out the trains and dividing them into groups for crossing the plains and going over the mountains. The movement westward from Wyoming could not begin until the 13th of July. Departures would continue through the summer into the middle of August. Captain Abner Lowrey's train left Wyoming on the 13th of August—the last train to leave. This train did not reach Salt Lake City until the 22nd of October, which was dangerously near the storm season of the mountains east of Salt Lake. In order to guard against calamities of the later contingencies, precaution had been taken to send out relief trains under Captain Arza E. Hinckley. This relief train extended eastward about 450 miles in order to meet the last company of Saints that year.

CHAPTER 4.

The Covered Wagon Journey

A month's encampment at Wyoming from the 19th of June to the 13th of July was a restful and glorious period in the emigrants' continental journey. The time of the year was hot during the day time with cold nights. The site of the encampment close to the Missouri River with rolling hills westward for some distance was good pasture for stock. With food plentiful, it afforded fine recuperating opportunities for the travel-worn emigrants. The adult portion of the emigrants with the robust teamsters and guards from Utah were engaged in making necessary preparations for the 1,000-mile journey across the plains and over the mountains. The children of the encampment were let loose for frolic and games.

These, however, were not especially attractive to me, who was inclined to quietness and retirement from the throngs. I found my amusement in bathing along the banks of the Missouri and fishing. One day I hooked from the river what was called a turtle of terrapin species, rather large and quite disconcerting for the reason I could not get the fishhook from the mouth of the beast. No sooner was it placed on the sand than it drew its head under the shell taking the hook and a portion of the line with it. There was nothing to do therefore but to wrap the fish cord around my hand and start for camp. This drew the head and neck from the shell and I so entered camp, the four feet of the beast clawing the air. Passing through one section of the camp towards the wagon to which I had been assigned, I passed a group, a middle-aged woman bathing two girls in a tub. My appearance seemed to create some excitement, and presently the screams of the girls rent the air. This woman was the one who had gone insane at Castle Gardens, and she was raking the back of the girls with her claw-like hands until red streaks appeared on their backs, and on the shoulders blood was oozing from the scratches. Past remembrances of her and her antics made me break into a run into my own wagon some distance away still holding on to the turtle.

Arriving at the wagon, one of the boys from Utah hacked off the head of the turtle, after it was drawn over a wood chopping block. Removing the shell exposed the meat deposited underneath. This was cut into small steaks, placed in the frying pan, and was eaten for supper, though I failed to relish the rich over-fat meat. Moreover, I could not get over the idea that the turtle was still alive, so persistent seemed to be its life, and I desired to catch no more terrapins.

The cruel antics of the insane woman I witnessed as I came through the camp was the last I saw of her, for that family was assigned to a different train of covered wagons than that in which I and my sister Mary made the journey. I never heard of her fate or her place of residence.

Captain William Henry Chipman's train was the company to which my sister and I were assigned for the journey. He was from American Fork in Utah County. The company was one of the largest leaving Missouri that year and made an imposing trail of covered wagons as it started over the long and adventurous trail. There was much cheering and cracking of whips by the teamsters and shouting of warwhoops in imitation of the Indians by the western men as they passed through the immense encampment of wagons which were to follow later in similar groups. There was a thrill in the departure for the long journey. All were rested up by the stay at the Missouri encampment, and all were eager for the march.

Day followed day in the slow creeping movement of the camp. Strict instructions had been given as to lingering behind the rest of the wagons or preceding the front ones. Each group of the encampment was supposed to march by the side of the wagon to which they were assigned, and sometimes several families were assigned to a wagon. Mary and I were assigned to a wagon that usually traveled in about the middle of the train. Beside us, there were two other families, man and wife and several children of mixed ages—one of them our heroic "Glendower Williams" of the Niagara incident. The arrangement was that at night the women slept in the wagon under cover; the men and boys met such arrangements for sleeping as they could under and beside the wagon.

Soon the lack of preparation for my sister and me became manifest. Of course our clothing was sparse and by now worn and not suitable to the journey. Our mother in distant Utah had sent with a young teamster who came from the settlement in which she lived—Bountiful, Davis County— gloves and a shawl and stout walking shoes for Mary with heavy quilts, homemade, for bedding and a little money such as she could manage to scrape together. But all these comforts that would have been well-nigh invaluable for us, never reached our hands. The teamster to whom our things were entrusted claimed that he could never find us in the Missouri encampments on the journey. However, some time afterwards in checking up our movements, Mary had been once hailed by this teamster, and carrying a bucket of water to the camp, he drank of the water she was carrying. This neglect on the part of those who were placed in charge of these travel comforts left us without any provisions for bedding. The only night covering I had was a petticoat that my sister Mary slipped to me after retiring into the wagon. This night covering I caught with eager hands, and I curled up under the wagon and generally shivered through the night.

This continued through the weary months of the journey to the Salt Lake Valley.

In a few days—how many is not known—the covered wagon train came to the banks of the La Platte (The Flat) River and slowly wended its way along its winding course towards the mountains. It seemed to take a long time to make the journey up this river. About its treacherous sands and the general health of the running water it supplied in unfailing quantities much had been said. The immigrants were cautioned about using stagnant water from holes along the bank, and we were urged to get water from the stream, but this was generally so muddy that it had to stand some hours before it could be used for drinking and culinary purposes. Solitary Indians some-times appeared in the camps about the Missouri, and part of the instruc-tions of not following behind the train or preceding it were issued as a precaution of safety against Indians and their likelihood of attacking from the front or the rear of the march. In spite of all instructions, some children and even adults disregarded these injunctions. Sometimes wild fruit was to be had along the banks of streams flowing into the La Platte.

On one occasion, just how many days out is not remembered, I and a boy about my own age had become interested in some ripening yellow currants along one of the banks of the stream and lingered until the train had passed over a distant hill. Before we realized it, we were breaking camp regulations, but still we lingered to fill our hats with the luscious currants we had discovered. The caps at last filled, we started to catch the train and were further behind it than we realized. Coming to the summit of a swale in which the wagon road passed, we saw to our horror three Indians on horse-back just beginning to come up out of the swale and along the road. Our contact with the Indians about the Wyoming encampment had not been sufficient to do away with the fear in which the red men were held by us, and it could be well imagined that the hair on our heads raised as we saw an inevitable meeting with these savages. Nevertheless, we moved on to the right and the other to the left with the hope that we could go around these Indians, but nothing doing. As soon as we separated to go around, the Indians also separated—the one to the right, the other to the left, and the third straight forward. There was trembling and fear that we were going to be captured. Many a time Captain Chipman had warned us of the possibility of such a thing, and indeed it was something that had happened in previous years along this route, that white children were captured from the trains and carried away. Some returned by ransom and some never returned. It was, therefore, with magnificent terror that we kept on slowly towards these Indians whose faces remained immobile and solemn with no indication of friendliness given out at all.

I approached my savage knowing not what to do, but as I reached about the head of the horse, I gave one wild yell, the Scotch cap full of currants was dropped, and I made a wild dash to get by—and did—whereupon there was a peal of laughter from the three Indians. They say Indians never laugh, but I learned differently. As the race for the train continued with an occasional glance over the shoulder to see what the Indians were doing, I saw they were bending double over their horses with their screams of laughter. Finally we saw just over the swale of the prairie the last wagon of our train. The running continued until each of us had found his proper place beside the wagon to which he was assigned. The fright was thought of for several days at least by strict adherence to camp rules about staying with your wagon.

In a few days the covered wagon train was approaching what was spoken of as the "first crossing of the La Platte River," the anticipation of which was fascinating. One evening in camp there was announced that the crossing would be reached early the following day. The temptation to be first at the crossing was too much for me, and so by dawn the next morning, I crept from my uncomfortable huddle in Mary's petticoat, which I threw into the wagon for her. I slipped out as silently and as unobserved as possible and followed the dim wagon trail beside the La Platte. The sun rose, such a sunrise as you can have along the La Platte River: the retreating shadows of the night, the crimsoning of the sky gradually changing to gold and purple until the night shadows were driven away before the rising sun, which bathes the earth in its sweet mellowness. Evidently the crossing was further off than descriptions had seemed to warrant, and so I trudged along the road hour after hour until nearly noon was approaching.

At last a sudden right turn of the road dipped into the margin of the river which seemed immensely wide. The stream was divided by sand bars running lengthwise with the stream. But the wagons had not shoved into sight. Up the stream, probably one quarter of a mile where a side stream dipped into the La Platte, clumps of willows grew, and as the sun by now was burning hot, I thought of the grateful shade that could be reached by going that far above the point where the road dipped into the river. I went on and soon found a comfortable place where I could recline and dropped into a sound slumber that had been denied me the night before on account of the cold. I slept on and on, and not all the shouting of the teamsters and emigrants nor the lunging of the wagons into the river awoke me. In fact, when I did awake, the last wagon of the train was just pulling up the opposite bank of the river, where the road led into the cottonwoods and other river trees, and was winding up the opposite bank of the turbid stream. Shouting at the top of my voice and rushing down to where the road met the river, I attracted the attention of Captain Chipman, who sat upon his horse on the opposite bank watching the last wagon as it was drawn from the river bed by its long line of yoked teams. Cupping his hands the captain shouted to know if I could swim and was answered in the affirmative.

In fact, I did not know the time when I could not swim. My earliest recollection of the feat was at the canals in the town of Wolverhampton where in the cool canals of the place I had learned to paddle and swim in very early boyhood. When the captain knew I could swim, I was directed to "come on then." With this, my old clogs from England were shuffled off blistered feet and left on the sand bar. Slipping off my coat—made as will be remembered from an old suit of a policeman, thick and heavy—with only shirt and barn-door trousers left, I plunged through one stream after another between the sandbars until I came to the main stream which surged to the north side of the La Platte above which on the bank sat Captain Chipman. Here was formed the main stream, which, however turbulent it looked and the current swift, was not wide. Without hesitation I plunged into this last stream to be carried down very rapidly. Apparently Captain Chipman felt uneasy and drove his horse, well practiced, into the stream and came swimming to where I was struggling for the further shore. The captain slipped his foot from the stirrup and bade me take hold of it and the horse without being turned upstream swam down until a suitable landing place was reached, and all three of us came up from the river together. The Captain held in his hand a light horse whip and as I let go of the stirrup and scampered up the bank to reach the road, the captain felt it evidently not unjust to give several sharp cuts across my pants, which stung sharply, but no cry was uttered and I felt that I was well out of a bad scrape.

Poor Polly was greatly excited at the disappearance of her brother and hailed me in camp that noontime with very great pleasure, shoeless and coatless and soaked though I was.

Of course, recollection of the sequence of events can be followed, but not with any certainty of their location. However, some time after this incident, another river happening occurred. The La Platte must be crossed again, and this time as the river crossing was shallow, strict orders had been given that all must wade, men, women, and children. As the wagons began driving into the river bed I observed one of the teamsters of a freight wagon, which, by the way, was the wagon next back of my own. A young lady was being crowded through the rear opening of the wagon cover, and I thought that if a young lady in her teens, probably her later teens, could be smuggled into a wagon, contrary to the captain's orders, there was no reason why I could not get across in like manner. A dash was made for the same wagon opening, and I tumbled into the wagon among the bags of light brown sugar, side bacon, and hams.

All went right until about the middle of the river bed was reached. Then the captain's first lieutenant rode up and ordered the driver to unhitch the teams from his freight wagon and go to the assistance of an emigrant wagon which had met with some quicksand and needed more team strength than it had to be drawn out. This was in the middle of the afternoon, and it was the last I saw of the teams taken from the freight wagon until next day. Other emigrant wagons were found to be in distress, and the freight wagon team was used over and over again to help these wagons across. Of course, the young lady in the wagon and I began to be a bit uneasy as night was coming on and no return of the team seemed likely, so I began to get outside the wagon with a view of finishing the crossing in order to get to the main camp by nightfall. At this the young lady in question began to cry quite aloud and plead with me not to go, for she felt that she would have to wade out, which she declared she could not do, or spend the night in the wagon, which she was equally afraid to do. The vibrations of the wagon standing in the stream of water indicated that it was settling in the sands, and so I gallantly consented to stay with her until the team should return.

It did not return until the next morning, and all through the night the vibrations of the wagon in the sand were continued until the water reached and sipped into the bed of the wagon and soaked the sugar bags. Hunger, of course, asserted itself, and how to satisfy it for the time was a question. But I was carrying as my most precious possession a four-bladed pen knife, a gift for my mother, which had been purchased with money coming into my hands in England. In addition to the four blades there were a pair of pinchers, a nail file, and some other contrivances that made it an amateur tool chest. The knife was used to slit a hole in one of the sacks of sugar; one of the pieces of side bacon was uncovered in the same way, and pieces of raw bacon or ham were hackled off. Upon these the young lady and I feasted.

While cutting the bacon, the knife slipped and dropped into the turbid water of the La Plate and was never found, and the treasure which had been bought for my mother, who was remembered to be a seamstress and to whom the complex knife and other implements would have been useful, was gone forever.

The next morning teams were brought to the relief of the freight wagons, of which there were several, which had been left in the river bed from the day before. It was always a matter of regret that the young lady's name was either never learned or else not remembered.

It was the season of the year when the prickly pear plant had bloomed and the buds of it had ripened. These were quite sweet and resembled somewhat in taste the pomegranate and were a choice morsel for the youngsters of the train. This led to little side excursions to find them and bring them to camp for eating, but unfortunately it also took the searchers for the fruit through prickly pear growths. Those who were barefooted suffered immensely from contact with the spines. I was among those who suffered much. My feet by dint of water, sand, and sun heat had now become black and hard and cracked, through which cracks sometimes the blood oozed. The addition of prickly pear contact brought me to camp very often with great feet-suffering. It was Polly's self-imposed task before nightfall to pick out the spines, and now that the knife was lost with its useful tweezers, the task was difficult and often accompanied by tears falling upon the smarting foot. Above all things else, my sister was noted for the quality of her tender sympathy, and it is not every brother's feet that were moistened by the tears of a fond sister.

The scenery of the covered wagon march began to change. Mountains appeared on the western horizon, and off in the distance away to the north, the range of the Wind River mountains was to be seen on clear days and were talked of. Sometimes night drives had to be made to reach certain streams for the benefit of the trailing teams. These night drives were a terror. It was bad enough to struggle on through the day, but to go on after dark was excessively wearing. At the end of one of these night drives, the train encamped by the side of a very large Indian encampment of tepees. The train was now in the region of country inhabited by the Sioux Indians, the Cheyenne branch of it, and the Arapahos, but word was passed along that the government guaranteed the peacefulness of these Indians and that covered wagon trains might make their camps in the immediate vicinity of their great encampments. The assurance was given that they were peaceful and so red encampment and white lay side by side.

Early the next morning of this particular day mentioned, the camp was astir by daybreak, and I having no special duties resting upon me wandered about among the Indian tepees, which were not far from the wagons of the train to which I was attached. I saw a group of Indians sitting in a circle at the top of a gentle mound-shaped hill passing a peace pipe from hand to hand, each of the circle taking a light puff from it. This was a curiosity, and I climbed the hill and sat beside the grim-looking warriors. The smoking went on for several rounds without any attention being paid to me, and then something happened.

I with nearly every other gamin of the camp had been persistently infected with lice, or lousy, from the time of shipboard until the journey began across the plains. Some of the Utah teamsters learned of my condition and snipped off the thick head of tousled hair with the sheep shears until nothing more could be snipped, and hence I was practically bald. Presently the Indian close by whom I sat, perhaps a chief, raised his hand, apparently to smooth back the long plait of his own black hair. Suddenly bringing his open hand with great force on the top of my head, he yelled as the blow was delivered, "No scalp!" I felt my short neck driven hard upon my shoulders, and with an answering yell to that of the savage's, I bolted for my camp. The complaint of the chief was that not even a scalp lock had been left on my head at the place where the scalp ought to grow. It was all mystery to me, but I felt a sense of relief as the great Sioux encampment was left behind.

The freight wagons' stay over night and settling in the river brought the water up into the wagon bed and soaked the sugar bags which lay in the bottom of the wagon with side bacon and hams stacked above them. They therefore became water soaked, and for many days much of the sugar was converted to syrup which dripped through the crevices of the wagon box. This attracted both flies and children to this particular wagon, where they lay under it catching the dripping syrup on finger ends and carrying them to their mouths. Of course clothing was dripped upon, and my shirt and trousers appeared to be the most visited by the dripping syrup, which with the accumulation of dust upon them converted them into stiffened clothes. It often occurred to me that my trousers were so heavy and sticky that they would have been able to stand alone had they been given the chance.

Another incident happened which greatly added to this condition. As already stated, the freight wagon followed next to the wagon to which I and my sister were attached. The young man from "Battle Creek" who was the driver had a kindly disposition to help several of the young ladies in their march by linking his arm in theirs and guiding them over the rough walking beside the wagons. Early in the journey he had turned over the task of keeping the teams close up to the wagon ahead of me, so that I became at least part driver of the freight wagon team, which was drawn by four yoke of oxen.

On one occasion a night drive was necessary, and the young man was entrusted with the freight wagon team. The young teamster was unusually devoted to helping the young ladies, especially on this night, so I ran in behind the ox on the near side and climbed up on the seat that had been arranged in the front of the wagon by the regular teamsters. This seat consisted of a broad plank placed across the open head of a large barrel. The day had been hot and the hours of the journey long, and I was decidedly tired, nearly unto exhaustion. Fearing that my riding, which was "agin" the law, would be discovered, I slipped the broad board from the barrel head and conceived the idea of dropping down in the barrel, secure from the eyes of those who might oust me from my seat in the wagon if I were found. To my surprise, if not amazement, I discovered when I let himself down in the barrel that my feet went into about three or four inches of a sticky liquid substance which turned out to be molasses. The smarting of my chapped feet almost made me scream with pain, but I stifled it. Too tired to attempt to climb out, I remained and gradually slipped down and went to sleep doubled up in the bottom of the barrel, with such results as can well be imagined. It was daylight when I woke up, and there began to be the usual camp noises of teamsters shouting to each other to be prepared to receive the incoming teams driven from the prairie by night herdsmen. As I crawled out of the uncomfortable position and with molasses dripping from my trousers, I was greeted by some of the teamsters and emigrants who caught sight of me with yells and laughter. I crept away as fast as I could to scrape off the syrup which added to the weight and thickness of shirt and trousers, for there was no change of clothing for me, and so bedaubed I had to pass on until dusk and drying somewhat obliterated the discomfort.

About now I had another item of experience. A worn-out riding horse of one of the night guards had its bridle tied to the rear of the freight wagon next to my own, and as there were strict instructions that nobody should ride in the wagons who was able to walk, here was an opportunity to climb into the saddle of this poor worn-out horse, poor in flesh to the point of being a mere shack of bones. Here was a chance to ride really without infringing the rules, and so I climbed up the side of the saddle and onto the horse and was relieving myself from the weariness of dragging through the hot day beside my wagon or driving Tom's freight team. How long I rode I never remembered, but Captain Chipman's first lieutenant came by. He was a tall gaunt man who had joined the church in Utah some years before as one of the discharged soldiers of "Johnston's Army," who came into Utah in 1857-58. He was a coarse, overbearing, and vicious-tempered man. Riding the length of the train as occasionally seemed his duty, he came upon me mounted upon the horse and shouted for me to get down. He accompanied his shouting by several cuts of his riding whip across my pants as I scrambled out of the saddle at the demand of Charleston. Then the first lieutenant hunted up "Tom" the teamster of the freight wagon and abused him, which abuse was accompanied with threats of what would be done to him if he permitted such a thing to happen again.

This attack upon "Tom" was a matter of conversation of the teamsters for and aft of the wagon, and I distinctly remember that it was said in these recitals and discussions that it was a good thing Charleston had not made such an abusive attack upon "Jesse." If he had he would probably have been laid out, and I heartily regretted that the attack had not been made on "Jesse" that the laying out process might have taken place. "Jesse" became an object of interest to me and was sought out from among the teamsters. He proved to be Jesse Crockston, who had come from Logan, a sturdy, stocky-built young fellow with red hair, blue eyes, and the best wrestler among the teamsters. I in my shy way tried to cultivate him, hoping that some day he would break Charleston in two, but it never happened.

At the edge of the entrance into the perceptible mountain region, the train cattle were stampeded by the Indians at a noon encampment, and something over a hundred head of stock were permanently lost to the train. The encampment had been made on a gently sloping hill that declined to the northward where the train moved into its two half crescent-shaped sides. Some distance down the gentle declivity, springs of water oozed out and, in cutting their way gradually through the rich soil, were collected into quite a large stream which meandered on northward, how far is not known.

Undoubtedly this place of encampment was chosen because this stream afforded excellent watering places for the stock. Willows grew upon its banks, and wild pea vines were entangled in the willows and formed fine forage for the hungry cattle. The lads in the train were always in search of swimming holes in such streams, and so they scampered down through the willows in search of bathing places. I and a comrade more venturesome than the rest went some distance down the stream until we found a swimming hole that was admirable. The water had washed out a hole on the west side of the creek with quite a deep clear collection of water under the banks held up by the willow roots. Here we began our bath. Cattle were on both sides of the streams when suddenly a strange rattling sound was heard, followed by intense hissing and hissing. Looking out of the swimming hole, we observed three Indians riding up the bank of the stream. One of them had a dry piece of rawhide in his hand, which by shaking produced the rattling noise. All three, following the rattling of the rawhide, hissed intensely. As they did so, the cattle with loud bawling rushed out of the willows to the open prairie which rolled off in successive hills. Pretty soon it seemed as if the whole herd whose thundering hoofs could be heard were stampeded, their mad race accompanied with bawlings. The thundering of their hoofs would have waked the dead.

As soon as the Indians and cattle had reached the creek bottom, we, naked as when born, ran for camp full speed. We found Captain Chipman seated on the tongue of his wagon and made our report of the Indians among the cattle, apparently stampeding them. The Captain laughed at us and advised that we had better find our clothes before we went into camp. While saying this, he climbed upon the tongue of his wagon and opened the lid to his bread box in front, making an improvised seat of it. As he did this it enabled the captain to see over a line of willows, and he beheld the whole herd under stampede, followed by the three Indians. Crestfallen, we left the captain on our way back to secure our clothing. All at once a cry arose from the encampment, a number of whom now saw the cattle under stampede. Then there were attempts of mounting in hot haste and seizure of firearms and a rush made to follow the marauders. Captain Chipman, however, stood at the west entrance of the encampment and commanded all to remain where they were until he could give his orders. We two boys meantime, humbled by the humor of Captain Chipman, wended our way back to the swimming hole where we obtained our clothing.

Captain Chipman here proved himself a real plainsman captain, and the thought nearest his heart was care for the emigrants bound on their way to Zion. He ordered the men to roll up the wagons into solid corral formation, namely by pushing the wagons together in such manner as to have the forewheel pushed up and interlocked with the hind wheels of the wagon before it. The corral became an improvised fort with the men and the women of the camp and such stock as remained huddled on the inside. After this the three remaining horses of the encampment were brought out and saddled, and three men mounted and went after the Indians to bring back as many of the herd as would be possible. By this time the greater part of the Indians and the herd were lost to view.

The three men who had been given the honor to pursue them passed quite a large number of the cattle that had fallen out of the mad rush of stampede. Some three or four miles distant, they came to a hill top from which dipped down steep slopes until a ravine was formed. Here the herd of the stampede was in the bottom, guarded by quite a large number of Indians. On the opposite side of the ravine on the prairie level westward from it, a large number of Indians (several hundred) were encamped, and as the three horsemen of the covered wagon train appeared on the hill overlooking the ravine with the cattle in it, the Indians on the opposite side set up a great cheer. Throwing buffalo robes and red government blankets on the muzzles of their guns and in some cases swords, they waved for the white men to come on, accompanying their motion with great shouts of derision. There was nothing then to be done but for our three horsemen to turn back and gather up the scattered remnants of the herd and slowly drive them back to the train encampment.

It was a straight loss of over 100 head of our strongest and best cattle and some six or eight riding horses. There was no moving further that afternoon, and guards on all sides of the camp were flung out to resist possibly approaching Indians bent on the destruction of the camp. As night came on, Captain Chipman selected his second lieutenant, generally called "Joe," to ride back through the night to give information to trains in the rear of the apparently increased hostility of the Indians. There was almost a protest in camp against this night ride of the second lieutenant, for he was greatly beloved by all the people, a fact which stood in marked contrast to the indifference and hostility manifested towards Charleston. The esteem of the camp and the contrast in this matter of likableness was as great between the men physically. "Joe" was rotund in stature, smiling and good natured, while the first lieutenant was sour faced, extremely dull, which was a good accompaniment to his disagreeable personality. Protests, however, were in vain. For the welfare and security of trains in the rear which would pass this point, Captain Chipman felt it his duty to warn them, and whenever it became a matter of duty to Captain Chipman, it was always strictly adhered to. "Joe" made the lonesome journey through the night until he overtook the rear company and delivered the message and in a few days returned to his own train.

CHAPTER 5.

Chimney Rock – A Plains Landmark

Chimney Rock is a well remembered landmark. Situated on the south side of the Platte River not far from the present boundary line of Nebraska and Wyoming, it marks about half of the journey between Wyoming and Omaha. Also it is about half way from these points to the Salt Lake Valley. The column so named rises from a conical elevation about one hundred feet high, and from this apex arises a shaft about forty feet high like a chimney straight up into the blue.

It was for the weary travelers of the covered wagon period a famous place, because it marked about half way of their journey as already stated. It had a peculiar attraction to Mary and me because it was at this point that our baby brother, Thomas, who had been carried from the Missouri River in the arms of our mother to this point, had died and was buried. To us it was, in a way, his monument. The child had been afflicted from its birth with water on the brain, and the head had grown large with the progress of the disease. He was peevish and during the whole journey did not permit anyone to touch him but his mother, and here this burden had ended.

There was a pathetic painful incident in his burial. Morton B. Haight was the captain of the company in which my mother made the journey in the year 1862. The grave for the baby was dug between Chimney Rock and the Platte River, and the babe wrapped in a blanket, a bed sheet, and lowered into the grave. Then came the dropping of the dirt upon the body. This was too much for my mother, and with a groan she sank beside the grave in a dead faint, as she heard the clods of dirt fall upon her baby's body. "Hold on," said the captain, beginning to feel the grief, "this is too much for me." He went to his wagon and took out the bread box in the front end of it and came back with it to the grave. Then the body was taken up and comfortably placed in the bread box and in this improvised coffin was again lowered to the bottom of the grave, which was then filled in and covered with cobblestones gathered from the surrounding hills to afford protection. Ever after, of course, the name of Captain Haight was an enshrined memory in the Roberts house.

After days of travel the covered wagon train came to the banks of the Sweetwater and in sight of Independence Rock. In the middle of the forenoon when the train reached the first crossing of the Sweetwater, an incident happened which I clearly remember through all the years of my life. I had been entrusted to keep the team of the freight wagon following the one to which I and my sister were attached. Somehow I failed to do this, and a considerable distance was between the two. I came to the beautiful clear water of the stream. I remember it was in sharp contrast with the turbid boiling muddy water of the Platte. So transparent was it that I could see the sand bottom of the little river. Thinking it was only a foot or two deep, I headed the leaders of my team at the head of the four yoke of cattle into the stream. That yoke becoming unruly, I entered into the stream to straighten them out. I was amazed to find that I was in the water up to my neck, being deceived as to its depth by the transparency of it. But I succeeded in making the crossing by my own exertions to the apparently pleased astonishment of those who had meantime gathered up to the banks of the crossing. In this achievement I had become drenched but was happy and soon brought my team to the proper place in the line of march.

The next great natural monument in the journey was well remembered. The significance of Independence Rock and its name meant nothing to me, to whom it appeared only as some immense monster object, rising abruptly out of the plain beside the windings of the Sweetwater. A night encampment was made close to it and also the beautiful Sweetwater stream. This afforded an opportunity for an early morning visit to its summit, from which could be seen the beautiful mountain scenery of this region. Years and years afterwards on the occasion of an historic visit, where a great gathering of nearly five thousand boy scouts met, this rock brought to mind this early visit of my boyhood. Now I was an old and broken man, but I remembered and told the story of my little adventure in passing the Sweetwater ford.

A few miles beyond this was the remarkable cliff in the range of outcropping stone formations known as the Devil's Gate, through which the Sweetwater passed. It is described in Orson Pratt's journal as being a chasm nine hundred or one thousand feet in length and one hundred and thirty feet in breadth, with perpendicular stones, one of the most picturesque landmarks on the journey. Here it was buzzed about the camp that many of the handcart pioneers of previous years' emigration had died and were buried.

I well remember South Pass because the water somewhere adjacent had to be reached by a night drive and I was sorely overcome by weariness that usually attended upon all night drives. I had expected some marked rugged mountains and perhaps narrow buttes through some high mountains as essential to "South Pass," but the crest of the continent was really a slowly ascending plain; it was not perceptible just when the summit was reached. The encampment was made that night near some streams on the westward side of the divide.

It was the custom of the emigrants to gather and carry in their arms, or else in the rear of their wagon, dry sticks gathered from the bushes or else "Buffalo Chips" from the plains for the evening camp fires. "Buffalo Chips" were the droppings of cattle and buffaloes that once inhabited the region in certain seasons of the year, and these "dried chips" made an excellent smoldering fire that gave out a great amount of heat. Before dark, I had gathered my quantum of such fuel. Then the train was drawn up in such formation as the usual corral. I wandered outside the corral a bit and back up the sloping plain of the divide until I found two boulder stones which I rolled together. Between the two I lighted my fire, carrying a blazing buffalo chip from another fire with which to ignite this fire. After it had burned down a little, I curled myself about the two stones with the fire between, and in the warmth sleep soon overcame me. In the early morning when I awoke, to my amazement I was covered with an inch or two of snow which had fallen through the night and which had covered me and my now dead fire, as with a white blanket. Shaking off the snow, I made my way to look for breakfast, grateful for this long night of pleasant and apparently warm covering until the sharpness of the morning hour made me shiver again with cold.

After the Indian raid upon the cattle of Captain Chipman's train, the team power was considerably reduced, and the distance covered per day was less. Also the rations of food were cut down in prospect of the remaining part of the journey being prolonged, until it was inconveniently scanty and at the last reached the finishing point. For several days all the food depended upon amounted to the game secured by the camp's hunters. This consisted of sage hens, rabbits, mountain hares, and occasionally antelope. But the game was always pitifully scant. A company, however, of relief wagons had been started from Salt Lake eastward as soon as the catastrophe threatening Chipman's train was heard of and came in time to rescue the train from absolute starvation. But there had been an entire absence of bread and meat rations, save for the game before mentioned. This game, as it was brought into the camp, was sparingly distributed, and teamsters and emigrants alike could be seen with a small portion of game meat, or joint of it, split upon sticks, held roasting in the fire, and then eaten without salt.

I cannot trust myself where the event happened, but a few days, perhaps a week, after the theft of Captain Chipman's cattle, very early in the morning as camp was waking up, some of the night cattle guards came with the information that they had discovered two men in charge of quite a cattle herd some three or four miles beyond the feeding ground of their own cattle. They reported them as making unusual efforts to keep the cattle in the prairie swales and around the corner buttes and in the shadow of buttes shooting out into these swales. Upon this report Captain Chipman directed several to go out and find these mysterious men and cattle and if possible to bring both in. This was accomplished before noon. The men avoided giving direct statements of their presence, where they came from and what they were doing with these work cattle. Since no satisfactory statement was made by them, he placed them under arrest and in custody of two or three guards and took the considerable herd of what were evidently work cattle into his own possession and yoked them in his depleted teams and renewed the journey late in the afternoon.

Some two or three days after this, Captain Chipman's train came upon an encampment of United States soldiers, their wagons backed up to a stream of water that passed through the little valley where they were found, this to afford protection from assault on that side of the stream, and the wagon tongues extended out into the direction of the road passing the encampment. Both horses and cattle of the camp were gone, and some of the trainsmen were out in the hills searching for them. It was soon discovered, after the soldiers identified their cattle with those picked up by Captain Chipman, that the two mountaineers had raided the camp's stock and were running off the greater part of the herd for some market. Of course, Captain Chipman made his report to the soldiers' captain and other officers, and the cattle he had taken from the mountain thieves were thus restored to the soldier's encampment. The two men that were taken prisoners had during the night since their capture made their escape from the guards, and nothing more was heard of them. After the soldier's camp, cattle were soon separated from Captain Chipman's company, and the incident largely forgotten.

So the covered wagon train crawled its slow way along through the mountains and passed old Fort Bridger, where the camp fire gossip in the cold evenings detailed the adventures of Johnston's Army invasion of Utah some ten years before. I discovered an interest in myself over some of these incidents, because I had heard them already by the old lady Tovey in my English boyhood recollections.

It cannot be expected that exact succinct recollections of the sequence of incidents of the journey would be remembered by me, but about ten years of age, yet the winding of the road through the mountainous country that was now approached had a wonderful fascination to me. I have some recollection, however, of Coyote Canyon and the crossing of Yellow Creek just before the journey dipped down into Echo Canyon. Echo Canyon had long been an objective of the journey, made so by the teamsters' weird stories of the echoing qualities of the canyon. Soon it was reached, and as the train wound down the red creek and in, the shooting of cannons and the cracking of whips with Indians' warwhoops imitated by the teamsters set the echoes flying over the rugged cliffs that rose, perpendicularly for the most part, on the right hand of the stream. Wonderful accounts of the defense of this gateway into Utah territory during Johnston's Army invasion were told and of the hoax played upon Governor Albert Cummings. The appearance, disappearance, and then appearance again of the same company of wild Utah Militia, who would deliver again the flamboyant speeches he had already heard several times, and the appearance of monster campfires made him believe that the mountains swarmed with mountaineers and troops resisting the approach of U.S. forces under command of Colonel Johnston, who was there to install him (Cummings) as the governor succeeding Brigham Young.

At the mouth of Echo Canyon, the emigrant road turned southeastward up the Weber, and this brought the wagon train to the first Mormon settlement, Coalville. The settlement was composed chiefly of log houses and dugouts along the hillsides and was decidedly a straggly settlement at that time. The place received its name because coal had been discovered in the vicinity, and the mines were being opened by coal miners from Wales and other sections from England. The mines were valued as a fortunate addition to the spare amount of timber for fuel in the country. The place looked ragged enough, with its irregular scramble of soil-covered cabins and the smoke issuing from its chimneys, but, forlorn as it was, it was a grateful sight for the emigrants to see something once more like settled life. The "dugouts" spoken of above consisted of small drifts on a level floor into the hillsides, and these blind trenches were covered over with timber and willows covered with dirt. They made perhaps all in all the most comfortable kind of living quarters for the settlers, and they abounded in other settlements of Utah as well as here on the outskirts—Coalville. They were valued for their warmth. Life and living in Utah, even at this time, was primitive enough and simple.

Parley P. Pratt had the enterprise to discover this route into the valley via Coalville and made a road through his "Parley's Park" and down Parley's Canyon into the Salt Lake Valley, which he named the "Golden Route." Possibly he was trying to make it attractive to or to flatter California emigrants taking that course to the golden state of California. It was over this route that Captain Chipman's train passed in 1866.

Owing to the journey drawing to a close, the impatience of the returning teamsters to get home and of the emigrants to arrive at their objective point created a spirit of restlessness, which the slow movement of the ox train severely tried. I remember that I thought what was called Parley's Canyon never would come to a close. Every once in a while a side dip of the spur of a mountain into the canyon seemed to close the vista beyond which the train could not go, and yet by the winding of the road, that spur would be passed only for another to arise in the distance. There had been an expectation created that the close of a certain day would find the emigrants landed in Salt Lake City, but it was turned to disappointment. It was growing grey in the evening when the slow-moving caravan moved out of the mouth of the canyon and off in the distance, the Great Salt Lake with some mountain islands rising above its surface came into view.

But Captain Chipman decided to make his encampment out on the bench several miles from the city and make an early morning drive into the long-sought end of the journey. I remember that the encampment was a rather gay one that night, and some variations were allowed from the usual close corral formation. To react to the greater sense of freedom from plains and mountain encampments, the wagons were scattered promiscuously along the foothills for quite a distance, and camp fires more numerous and larger than usual were soon ablaze in the advancing gloom of the night. Teamsters mounted upon the tops of their wagons and gave their peculiar war whoops, so common on the journey, to make the inhabitants of the distant city aware of their arrival. Captain Chipman and some others prominent among the leaders of the train rode down to the city that evening and left the encampment in charge of the lieutenants. It is doubtful if there was much sleep in camp that night. All were too excited: the teamsters in that they were returning home and would tomorrow begin to meet their friends; the emigrants in that they had at last arrived in "Zion" in the midst of the mountains that they had sung about and prayed about and longed with anxious eyes to see.

In the morning everybody seemed to be up with the first streaks of the light of day over the eastern mountains and in great haste in preparations to take up the journey. Breakfast seemed to be neglected, and there was not much to eat anyway. Before the sun rose, the train, falling into its old line, swung down the low foothills until they struck a well-defined road leading into the city.

This entrance proved to be via Third South–then and long afterwards known as "Emigration Street," now Broadway. When Captain Chipman's ox team swung around the corner of Third South into Main Street, I found myself at the head of the lead yoke in that team, walking up the principle street of the city, the rest of the train following. Here the people had turned out to welcome the plains-worn emigrants and were standing on the street sides to greet them. Some horsemen dashed up the street swinging their cowboy hats, the customary cowboy handkerchiefs around their necks as if they were in from the ranges.

Along the road, perhaps nearly half way from the mouth of Parley's Canyon to the city, I as I strode on ahead of Captain Chipman's team saw a bright-colored, dainty, charming little girl approaching me in the middle of the street. It was a strange meeting, we two. My hair had grown out somewhat. But three months' journey over the plains and through the mountains without hat or coat or shoes for most of the way had wrought havoc with my appearance. My hair stuck out in all directions; the freckles seemed deeper and more plentiful and the features less attractive than when the journey began. Shirt and trousers barely clung to my sturdy form, and my feet were black and cracked but now covered by the shoes I had taken from the feet of a dead man at a burnt station. These I was wearing in compliment to my entrance into "Zion." Also my face had been more carefully washed that morning.

But try as I would, the shock of hair was unmanageable, and so no wonder the dainty little lady was somewhat timid in approaching me. She had on her arm a basket of luscious fruit, peaches, plums, and grapes. These she extended to me, the "ugly duckling" of a boy from the plains, and asked me if I would have some peaches. The answer was to gather up several which I strung along in the crook of my arm, and as soon as I had obtained what I supposed a reasonable portion, I wondered how I could get this fruit so wonderful back to Polly and at the same time retain my place in the march up Main Street. Pondering this question, of course unknown to the young girl who had brought me such a treasure, I finally turned back as best I could to the wagon where Polly was concealed under the wagon cover because of her being a little ashamed of her appearance. Running behind the wheel ox and climbing up on the tongue of the wagon, I called to my sister, handed to her the fruit, and then scrambled back to the ground and ran for my place at the head of the train and marched on until the head of Main Street was reached.

This then was the old tithing office behind the high cobble walls with its half round bastions and through a crude gateway on the west side of the block leading into the stock corrals of President Young, where most of the wagons of the train were driven and placed under the many straw-covered sheds that then occupied the place where the Deseret Gymnasium now stands. The cattle were soon freed from the yoke and seemed delighted with the straw and hay brought them. Across the way on Temple Square block, the foundations of the temple rose above the general level of the surrounding ground and seemed to be an object of interest to nearly all the emigrants, many of whom were permitted to go within the wall, and view it. By and by there were numerous meetings in various groups of people, friends of the emigrants, parents and sweethearts, and perhaps in some instances wives of the teamsters that had returned. There seemed to be an air of cheerfulness in all this meeting of people on the arrival of this large emigrant train of Saints.

Mary and I seemed to be so little part of this excitement and joy, because nobody seemed to come for us. Mary remained concealed under the wagon cover, and I lonesome and heartsick sat upon the tongue of Captain Chipman's wagon, my chin in my hands and elbows upon my knees, thinking "Zion" was not so much after all, if this was all of it. The spirit of sadness, if it was not forlorness, settled upon me.

Presently, however, approaching from the west gate, I saw a woman in a red and white plaid shawl slowly moving among the hillocks of fertilizer that had been racked from the sheds and the yard. She seemed to be daintily picking her way, and there was something in the movement of her head as she looked to the right and to the left that seemed familiar to me.

The woman was moving in my direction, and the closer she came the stronger the conviction grew upon me that there was my mother. I would have known her from the dainty cleanliness of everything about her.

I stood until she came nearly parallel to where I sat; then sliding from the tongue of the wagon, I took a few steps, which brought me near to her and, plucking her gown, I said: "Hey Mother," and she looked down upon my upturned face. Without moving she gazed upon me for some time and at last said, "Is this you, Harry? Where is Polly?" Of course Polly was in the wagon, and I led my mother to where she was hiding, and when mother and daughter met, there was a flood of tears on both sides. At last I joined them, making the trio of the united family. It seemed difficult for our mother to realize that we at last were her children after more than four years of separation, but once in a while, a smile would break through the tears and she seemed to be extremely happy. A neighbor of hers, Brother John K. Crosby, a New Englander, had driven her from Bountiful to the city to get us children, and it took but a short time to leave the remaining emigrant teams and people to find this wagon and make the start for home, Bountiful.

There was one thing remembered in this reunion, and that was on my part. I felt that I had arrived, that I belonged to somebody, that somebody had an interest in me, and these were the thoughts that were in my mind as I sat in the wagon on the drive home to Bountiful. I had heard incidentally that my mother owned her house, and that, of course, for English people, who among the poorer classes were all renters, meant a great deal to me. Now I was going to my mother's home – her own house.

As the wagon drew near to Bountiful, its clear-cut New England meetinghouse with a tower upon it seemed to loom large among the homes surrounding it, and before getting to it, I wondered if that was my mother's home. When the wagon passed it going eastward, without anything being said about its being her home, of course, I was sad with disappointment. I experienced a sense of great humiliation. Two blocks beyond it on the east, we came to the site of a log house with a dirt roof on one part of it and another part adjoining on the south that had been built up to the square with logs unchinked without a roof, and this, my mother turned to explain to me, was her home. But soon mother and children climbed out of the wagon and went into the house, and Brother Crosby drove away.

No one was at home when the little group entered, much to the disappointment of the mother as to the children, for, of course, we were anxious to meet our other sister, "Annie," who was remembered lovingly by us. Our mother seemed annoyed, for she had expected her other daughter at home, perhaps with supper ready. It was only a short time, however, until "Sister Annie" came in and what a charming thing she was – bright, blue-eyed, fine long hair combed back from her face. Everything about her seemed so perfectly clean and wholesome, and to my eyes she was beautiful too, and spritely. She seemed to be everywhere about the house at once, and the meal that our mother had expected was soon under way.

Meantime there were certain preparations made in the unroofed, annexed part of the log home, for presently my mother with a pleasant smile and a twinkle in her blue eyes took my hand and said, "Come with me my son; I haven't washed you for more than four years." After she got me into the open addition to the one-room cabin with hand bowl and towels, she stripped off that one shirt that had done duty for so long a time and started in to give me a scrubbing, which led me to believe that she was under the impression that I had not been washed since the last time she had washed me four years before.

What was left of the day was the wonderful meal prepared by Annie. Not much variety of food, for our mother was desperately poor, but what there was, was fit for princes—just white light buttermilk biscuits with butter, clear water from the creek, and dark, sweet, sticky fluid called "Molasses." It was heartily enjoyed, Mary and me furnishing the principle appetites. How long the talk of the reunion lasted is not remembered, but it must have been far into the night. With the awakening of the next day, my life in Utah had begun.

CHAPTER 6.

Life in Bountiful

It was a crude sort of society that existed in Bountiful, Davis County, about that time and for that matter all through Utah, as conditions were about the same all over. Schools were of the crudest kind and not systematically organized. The teachers were not professors, for most teachers were taken from other walks of life and were supposed to be competent if they could read or cipher or write ever so little ahead of their pupils. Sunday schools existed, but they were undeveloped and taught the ideas of the Mormon faith in a very primitive manner. High schools there were none, and higher institutions of learning, while existing pompously on paper, had really no existence in fact. The community had reached a stage where it was a struggle for physical existence, food, clothes, and in the winter, heat. Timber was scarce and high up in the mountains – made almost inaccessible by the snows that filled the great depths in the higher reaches of those mountains. Roads into the canyon were crooked, almost impassable, and everywhere cleanliness abounded. Money was scarce. The community had to learn to live by barter of commodities.

Children ran wild and for the most part uncontrolled even by parental authority. My first contacts with boy companions in Bountiful were a couple of chaps not quite as old as I in the immediate neighborhood. These were boys named Joseph and William Holbrook, which turned out ultimately not to be their names. They were Joneses, but they lived with an old lady next door to us who was a plural wife of Judge Holbrook and had taken those boys to rear. The old lady Holbrook was truly a village character, and it will be necessary to mention her again later.

Meantime curiosity brought these two boys and me in contact with each other. I doubtless was a strange semi-savage to them, and they were an odd pair of Utah's crude product to me. I, of course, brought with me my Lancashire dialogue from over the seas and across the plains and mountains, and they made much fun of the strange speech. Much of it they could not understand. They took to trying to mimic me, and this to me was a caucus belle. Driven to impatience by the fun they made of my dialect, I at last blurted out, "I'll have none of your sauce." They mimicked this, and, of course, a fight followed with both of them – the first of many such encounters. But being small boys, our fights ended in little damage. There were no knockouts and they usually ended in a draw. These experiences, however, were interspersed with some boyish pleasures and good nature, and the fights grew less and less in number until they practically died out.

But there were many mock battles, for I had quite a recollection of Indian stories that I brought from the plains, and these with the attacks upon emigrant trains were often re-enacted by us lads. The Holbrook boys generally acted as the emigrants with their trains and defended themselves with rocks, while I played the part of the Indians, with my bow and arrows made by me personally from cane growths, which came to my hand, and a bow I made from a straight oak stick from one of the many oak bushes that grew in the wilderness about my mother's home.

Sometimes the rocks of the "emigrants" took effect on the "Indian" as I approached their mimic encampment, and sometimes my arrows punched the ribs and backs of the "emigrants." But all this was good-natured boy-play and provoked no real quarrels.

Aunt Hannah, the guardian of these two boys and a school teacher from Nauvoo, Illinois, by the way, who knew personally the prophet Joseph Smith, was a frequent caller at my mother's humble home, and I gradually became aware of the fact that I was under her scrutiny. From the first I felt that my mother had received a shock of disappointment when we first met in the stockyards of Brigham Young in Salt Lake, and now she was seeking the judgment of this mother in Israel as to what I might become in my growth and development. Aunt Hannah could not say much, of course, from my appearance. But I remember one remark she made after conceding there was much against me from my appearance. Yet, she said, there was something in my eyes that reminded her of "Anson V." and that if I should turn out to be like him—and somehow in the odd relations that existed at the time this "Anson V." was in some way supposed to be a grandson of hers, which he was not—but if I should turn out to be anything like him, then I would be worth my weight in gold.

This brought on a natural desire on my part to meet "Anson V." It was a long time before we met, for "Anson V." was something of an aristocratic youth in this crude community, being a grandson of Anson Call, a veteran in the church, and reputed to be rich. Also his father, the son of this aforesaid rich man, had died upon a mission while in England, and in the course of a few years, the body of his father had been shipped from England to a resting place in Utah. However, "Anson V." and I subsequently met.

The former was some two to three years older than I and was a progeny in his educational development. The grandfather had seen to it that he had the best advantages in schooling, being sent from Bountiful to special schools here and there in Utah, that his education might be developed. Among the accomplishments accredited to him, he was reputed to have committed the Constitution of the United States to memory. But for all that, I learned in the developing years that came afterwards that he did not know much of anything about the Constitution. Committing it to memory had resulted in nothing as to an understanding of it.

Strangely enough, the two lads with one or two of his brothers became fast friends and formed something of a boyish clique in the new scraggly settlement of Bountiful, which by the way was a Book of Mormon name applied to this first offspring of the larger pioneer settlement, Salt Lake City. It was so near its birth that its name had not become a settled reality, as it was also known as Sessions' Settlement, supposed to be the first settlement in that place. Afterwards at the advent of the railroad stations at that place, it was known as Woods Cross, but finally it settled for many years to simply Bountiful, except for a time on one occasion when Brigham Young referred to it as Scantiful—this owing to the slowness with which they completed their principle public building, the Bountiful Tabernacle.

Meantime such were the exigencies of my family's struggle for existence that I had to find employment at ever so little compensation with the farmers wherever it could be found. This in that first fall consisted in stripping cane at the molasses mills or in husking corn, which some of the farmers cut from the field and hauled to the yards of the farmers. Compensation was in molasses for stripping cane and the seventh or tenth bushel out of every seven or ten. Sometimes the pay was in apples, sometimes in flour, which in those years was from $6.00 to $8.00 per hundredweight. Sometimes pay was in side pork or ham or potatoes—anything that could be used to eat or make clothing—and so it continued through many years. After a time a brick maker came from England, and the bricks out of which the Z.C.M.I. was made were manufactured by this brick maker, and I got a job from him. Money orders were issued upon the Bountiful Coop, a branch of the parent institution, which was established in Salt Lake. Here a mischief arose for me. I was learning to use tobacco, and the workmen on the brickyard could obtain alcohol at this branch store, and it was so obtained, diluted by them and used, sometime to their disgrace.

I was eleven years of age when I learned my alphabet as the first stepping stone to learning to read. This was taught to me in the private school which Aunt Hannah Holbrook conducted in her home and which was sustained by voluntary tuition, there being at the time no tax-sustained schools in Bountiful or, so far as remembered, in the state. By the time I had arrived at thirteen, I had acquired the mysterious art of reading from the simple textbooks. Papers and magazines there were none in our home, but sometimes I did struggle painfully through reading a chapter of the Bible. About then there came one of the semi-public schools, which began to come in fashion in Bountiful, taught by an old Scotchman by the name of Finlayson. "Wilson Readers" were made textbooks for the reading classes. These contained Bible stories, the story of Joseph in Egypt is remembered, and some of the religious poems of N. P. Willis, an American poet, now too much forgotten but included because of the excellence of his treatment of biblical subjects.

Here at this school I began to win my first victories. It was the custom of the old teacher to have the reading class stand in a row like an old time spelling class, and at the close of the reading lesson, questions would be put to the class. Perhaps they were provided in the textbook on the subject matters of the story. These questions were put first to the head of the class and then ran the length of the row to the foot. He who would stand at the head of the class must take his place at the foot the next day, and as the questions were submitted, if an incorrect answer was given by the pupil but answered by the next in line, he took his place ahead of the one who missed until he worked himself up to the head of the class.

It was my good fortune to be able to answer these questions, which brought me very frequently at the head of the class, and I began to feel the thrill of superior capacity in remembering the subject matter of the lessons. This might be referred to as the dawn of my victories and their encouragement. There were only two of these schools, however, and then an end of them. The poor old gentlemen Finlayson was so mocked and abused by the larger boys of the school that it was no longer possible for him to continue, and he moved away from Bountiful. In after years I learned of his living in Panaca, a frontier settlement of the state of Nevada, some distance westward of the scene of the Mountain Meadows massacre.

It was in 1870 or 1871 that the connecting line between the Union Pacific Railway from Ogden and Salt Lake City—known then as the "Utah Central"—was constructed and one Seth Dustin, who meantime my mother had married, took contracts from somewhere near Farmington into Salt Lake City. He had been quite an extensive contractor on the Union Pacific road through Echo Canyon and had large amounts of railroad material, scrapers, mule teams—hence was prepared for contracts on the Central Railroad. From somewhere there was an ox team in his paraphernalia, and it, because of my knowledge of handling such teams, was turned over to me. Because the team was large but manageable by me, I took his place in the circling teams of scraping for the grade and for buildings. The work was made easier for me because I could, with an ox team guided by voice and whip, use both hands for the scraper, and it was possible for me to do the work of a man. My wages from this work finally repaid the Perpetual Emigration Fund for advancing my passage from England to Utah.

CHAPTER 7.

The Youth

The marriage of my mother to Mr. Seth Dustin was not altogether a fortunate circumstance in my life. Mr. Dustin had a number of grown-up sons who were ignorant in their manners, boisterous in their conduct. As they were brought to live in my mother's home, the unfinished part of the log home was roofed in to accommodate them. The home life became less and less attractive. Besides my sisters Mary and Annie had meantime been married and, of course, had withdrawn from home, and for several years home life was considerably interfered with.

Mr. Dustin, however, had at various times prospected for coal on the west side of the Wasatch range, and I accompanied him in these enterprises until silver mining developed out in the Oquirrh range of mountains west of Salt Lake City in the Ophir mining district. Soon there began to be talk of new finds of silver more especially in Dry Canyon adjacent to Ophir. A number of well-to-do farmers in Davis County conceived the idea of getting rich by silver mining and organized a company which tendered employment to Mr. Dustin. He took charge of the company's prospecting and was induced to leave the search for coal and prospect for silver in Dry Canyon.

In contemplation of this movement, I was sent out with a company of men to begin this work. My first trip to Dry Canyon was merely to learn the route by way of Salt Lake across the intervening plain between the Jordan and Black Rock and so through Tooele City and beyond to Dry Canyon. Unfortunately the main part of the company of men were of very irregular habits, and in Salt Lake a large amount of whisky was obtained and drinking was freely indulged in. As we made progress in our spree, every occasion I stopped to get a drink I was urged to partake of the fiery stuff with which they had supplied themselves. Compliance, together with the idea of impropriety of drinking whisky, led me to decline until towards the close of the day, near sunset.

I then yielded to the solicitation and drank a half tin cup full of the fiery liquor. Its effect upon me, unpracticed in that kind of beverage, can be imagined. I was soon in the swirl of intoxication, with a reckless dare-devil spirit that had been awakened. I was mounted at the time upon a scarcely broken three-year-old colt, and now with me senseless, there was wild riding, putting the colt through his paces, circling the wagons, conveying the miners to the west, challenging them to a race, etc. At last as the sun was setting, the great round crimson ball behind a film of clouds suggested the insane notion of riding out to the sun and overtaking it, and so I put the horse on a dead run for the blazing objective. That was the last I knew.

From my companions I learned that the horse, slowing up and entering upon a straight, bucked to get rid of the rider and seemed to succeed, and I was picked up unconscious and placed in the wagon. The next remembrance was a dull aching body slowly awakening amid the bedding and kegs of whisky in the wagon and entering into something of a quarrel and fight with the man on the front seat. The company was making a night drive to reach the springs of water at the south end of the Oquirrh range, close to the shores of Black Rock. As this water was brackish and my drink of whisky had created a tremendous thirst, the drinking of this water through the night only increased the thirst and brought on an illness. The next morning the rough mining crowd urged me to take some more of "the hair of the dog that bit him" as a cure. Needless to say this was declined; I had had enough.

The journey was made to what was after known as Shoofly Hill in the middle of Dry Canyon. There was no road at that time up the canyon, only a deer trail that had been followed by some packers to reach the region of prospecting for silver. Arriving at Silver Hill, some of the partners of Davis County companies had opened a prospect that was called the "Empire." On the arrival of the new recruits to the enterprise, they were about to fire a blast that they had put in during the morning, and I begged the privilege of lighting the fuse. This was consented to, and the rest of the miners went to the tent encampment back of the Empire prospect, having cautioned me about lighting the fuse and especially that I must yell several times, "Look out below," so that anyone coming up the narrow winding trail would have time to get out of the way before the blast went off.

All this, of course, was a very necessary and sensible precaution, but the trouble was that I lighted the fuse and started to run up the hill to get away from the explosion before I thought to yell, "Look out below!" I then stopped and let out the warning in frantic yells, fearing that an accident might happen, and just at that point I saw a man riding a white mule directly below the sputtering fuse and charge. The mule in addition to the rider was loaded from neck to tail with bundles of ax and pick handles and several other large bunches of tinware, milkpans, and breadpans. The man began belaboring his mule to get beyond the probable shower of stones, and then, mule-like, the beast stopped and would not budge, leaving the rider under the now soon-to-be-exploded blast. The blast exploded, and the whole canyon, to me, seemed to be filled with the shower of dust and stones of various sizes.

The next I saw of the mule and rider was a white streak breaking up the opposite side of the canyon through a grove of quaking aspen, scattering the tinware as he went. Nothing was said of this misadventure of the mule and his rider, but in about an hour he came into the Empire prospector's camp inquiring for the d[amn] f[ool] that let off a blast before he could get out of the way. He had been severely stoned, and the mule from his ears to his tail bore a number of pealed-off patches of skin, which showed his experience had been quite serious. I confessed being the d[amn] f[ool] inquired for, but the whole thing was so laughable when it was related that good nature obtained, and the unfortunate rider of the mule was reconciled to my omission to give proper warning. What the mule thought was not expressed.

Dry Canyon was properly named, for no stream of water trickled down either its main gorge or the side ravine opening into it. The drinking water for camp use had to be packed on burros some distance over the summit at the head of Soldiers Canyon, which Colonel Wall of Salt Lake had taken up as a stock ranch. From the springs upon his ranch, it was my job to convey kegs of water daily for the use of the prospectors camp. My two jacks were loaded with two barrels on each animal, becoming the little train that made the daily journey for water.

Three years were spent by me in the rough mining camp bearing the name of the canyon. Midway from its mouth to the summit rose Jacob City, a new mining town and one of the roughest and most reckless of all the mining camps of Utah. Here drifted from Montana and Colorado and Wyoming all prospecting miners of almost every degree of intelligence and desperation known to that element of the mining population. Saloons sprang up in large numbers and became the center of gambling, with numerous roadhouses where reckless frivolities were indulged in.

During my three-year sojourn here engaging in various jobs of camp cooking, prospecting, water carrying and the like, I absorbed much that was injurious to character building. Men were vile, and I witnessed some of the deepest criminality that it had been my fortune to meet with so far in life.

It had so happened that a neglected prospect of the Davis County company had been abandoned for some time, and a party was organized to jump the claim. They held it until a compromise was effected, and the jumpers and the original owners entered into a reconciliation and agreed to work the prospect together. This threw me into the association of one of the jumpers, Ben Maynard, a Texan and a man who rather deserved the title of "desperado." Maynard was familiarly known as "Big Ben." He was the son of a Texas planter and occasionally received heavy remittances from his home. This was generally thrown night after night into gambling dens until it was all lost. But a strong friendship grew up between "Big Ben" and me. Ben insisted on taking me to the gambling joints, where I was presented as the Texan's mascot. Night after night was spent in this association, where fights and gun play were frequent enough to create intense excitement.

Something of a feud arose between "Big Ben" and a man whom he heartily despised. At last in a meeting of the two on Main Street, Salt Lake

City, immediately in front of McKimmon's Livery Stable on the west side of main street, it came to a showdown. Bad blood had existed for some time between them. Meeting at the place designated above, "Big Ben," whose manners were always excessively polite and his voice soft and low, made the statement to his enemy that he had heard some ugly rumors of things alleged to be said and done by him. He said he was calling this opponent to account. Maynard deliberately permitted the man to make an attempt, and he did draw his revolver, but Maynard was too quick for him and shot him through the heart before his enemy could fire. Maynard did not move from his tracks but waited until a policeman appeared on the scene, and he coolly surrendered the pistol to the officer and willingly accompanied him to the City Hall. The hearing on the case was sufficient to absolve Maynard from the charge of murder, and a verdict that he had killed the man in self defense was rendered.

Maynard returned to Dry Canyon and took several occasions to make the first attempt to start a grave yard in it. He was the hero of the camp; and even I confess to something of pride in accompanying him to saloons, which were also gambling dens, as his mascot. I had a boyish reverence for the desperado. What finally became of Maynard I never knew. For three years I had contact with an awful life and rough frontier camp experiences instead of high schools and college training. Under the above circumstances schooling was utterly neglected in the way of preparing me for the life that was to be in the years ahead.

CHAPTER 8.

The Learned Young Blacksmith

After these three unfortunate years, I paid a visit to my mother in Bountiful. She called my attention to the trend of a life that was not chosen by me but in a way forced upon me by circumstances. She expressed a wish to me for a change of things and spoke to me about learning a trade or getting into some regular order of life. She mentioned the fact that my grandfather and a number of his sons, including my own father, Benjamin Roberts, were tradespeople in Kent, England, and held an honorable station among them and suggested that it would be a fine idea to perpetuate the line of their industry through their representatives here in America. She expressed a desire that I should call on a young man who had been reared in Bountiful, James Baird, then living in Centerville. He with a Mr. Henry Rampton were now establishing an independent shop of their own in Centerville.

The idea struck my fancy to perpetuate the trade of my ancestors in America. The interview with the young man referred to, one James Baird, resulted in my becoming an apprentice regularly installed to take up learning the blacksmith trade in three years of service in Mr. Baird's shop. Provision was made that three months in the winter of the first year should be granted to me for attendance upon school. It began to look as if something like a decent and respectable home life was opening to me. But it was not without its difficulties. My mining encampment life followed me, and, at least by the good boys of Centerville, I was looked upon askance, and they withheld association from me. There was, however, another element, irregular and somewhat lawless, that had centered in a vacant house in this good hamlet of Centerville, where some of the finest "characters" from among the Utah pioneers had located. These gave me, the "young blacksmith," as I began to be called as soon as I entered the shop, a hearty welcome, and I found somewhat congenial associations among them.

Among other things I became nearly betrayed into the gang of horse thieves who were located at this place and associated with one Ben Tasker, a somewhat noted Utah outlaw, who had a station here. He was known to possess large ranches somewhere southward in Utah on which bands of horses were raised. It was supposed that he was shipping these through northward to Evanston, Wyoming. But in addition to the horses from his own ranch, he shipped stolen horses and kept up a regular transportation of these from the south to Evanston. One of his stations was located in the mouth of Bingham Canyon, where his henchmen, a family of Cottons and another by the name of Butcher, lived. These people both received the horses brought into their neighborhood and passed them on, generally using night riders, to this other station in Centerville. These Bingham people were desperados and quarreled with each other and nearly wiped out the existence of both groups.

The manner in which I came dangerously near being mixed up in this affair is through my friendship with the irregular roughnecks of Centerville. A woman by the name of Crawford was undergoing an intensely desperate delivery at childbirth. Her husband was located in one of the Little Cottonwood mining camps doing team work, and it was necessary to get word to him to come to the extreme, dangerous illness of his wife. There were no telegraph or telephone means of communication in those days, and the quickest way would be to drive up to the encampment in Little Cottonwood and bring Mr. Crawford home.

Mr. Baird, my employer, assured some of his brethren of the church that if a team could be obtained, he was very sure that I would undertake to drive the team and bring the man home, and so the hamlet was canvassed for a team to perform this journey. At first none could be found. Centerville had a postmaster at that time who kept a very fine team and spring wagon or carriage. They were practically idle, since they were only used by the postman, who was the county assessor and collector of taxes, but he would not accommodate his neighbor. At last a team was obtained to make the journey, but the man who owned it preferred to drive it himself rather than trust it in my hands.

The next day at the blacksmith shop, village idlers being assembled there, comment was free about this postmaster's action in refusing to allow his team to be used for the journey to the Cottonwood mining camp to bring Mr. Chris Crawford home to his wife. The thought was freely expressed that such a man did not deserve to have a team—I joined in. Towards evening when the loafers left the shop, the gathering place of gossips and idlers, one young fellow remained, and when alone with me he said, "So you think the postmaster does not deserve to have a team." I assented. "All right," said his remaining visitor (he was one of Tasker's men and helping to run his station from the hamlet of Centerville), "let us run it out of the country; I can manage it." And so it was agreed upon that the team should be taken from its stall and run out of the country the night of the second day from then.

Although I did not know it, an installment of horses from the mouth of Bingham Canyon was to arrive at that time and pass on for Evanston. But the Bingham installment of horses came in the night before the night appointed, with orders to rush them through, and the tax collector's team was not taken at the time appointed. It was, however, taken from his stable, led to an adjoining village, and put into the stray pond. And even so simple an arrangement made a three-day hunt for them necessary before he found them. The next time I contacted the would-be horse stealer, Tasker, I learned all the facts, the plans being carried on in Centerville in aid of Ben Tasker's horse running schemes, and, of course, the relationship was dropped at once and forever.

Then came a peculiar personal struggle. The good boys, having learned of some of my irregularities, would have nothing to do in the way of fellowship with me and held themselves aloof from association with me as far as possible. I cut the tether between myself and the roughnecks, and hence I had to stand alone.

Through the influence of Mr. Baird, to whom I was bound as an apprentice, I did after some difficulty become a member of the Young Men's Club of Centerville, as it was called. This was a company of young fellows who were banded together in their association to encourage reading and meeting at stated periods—usually once a week—and to retell the stories of their reading. There was an entrance fee to pay of $2.50 and after that a monthly payment of $.50 for membership, all of which was turned into books. Also if there was any failure on part of a member to attend meeting, there was a fine of $.50 for each offense. As the association had continued through several years, the accumulation had amounted to considerable sums of money. The number of books they purchased therewith was considerable for a country hamlet and made a rather considerable library for boys.

Into the work of this association, I projected myself in full cry of its objectives, and, as retelling stories was something of a gift of mine, I secured a standing in the group. In the course of a year or two, I became its president. Under my presidency the conception of building a public hall as a meeting place for the club, which had hitherto met in private homes, was considered. Stock was subscribed by the members, and the Young Men's Hall began to take form and was finally completed. Soon the Young Men's Club would be transformed by the movement which began throughout the territory of Utah in 1877—the Young Men's Mutual Improvement Association of the LDS church.

I remember vividly the coming of Junius F. Wells to Centerville to organize this church association. Young Wells had received an appointment from the great Mormon leader Brigham Young to institute these organizations. Finding the Young Men's Club in existence when he began his work in Centerville, early in the Mutual Movement, he proposed the transformation of that organization into the kind of organization he had been commissioned to establish. To his astonishment there was strong opposition in the membership of the Young Men's group to this proposal, but I was favorable to it and agreed to preside at Junius Wells's meeting to hear his explanation of what Mutual Improvements proposed. There was open, direct rebellion against my taking the presidency of this preliminary meeting, and

I was notified by some of the leading members of the Young Men's Club that if I consented to preside at Wells's meeting that a move for my impeachment as President of the Young Men's Club would be proposed at the very next meeting. Of course, this made no difference to me. I presided at the Wells meeting and at the conclusion pledged myself to bring the matter before the Young Men's Club at their next meeting and consider the transformation proposed.

Before the meeting of the group, however, Thomas Hull, who had just returned from England as a missionary, visited Centerville and supplemented the efforts of Wells to create a Mutual Improvement Association. I was called upon also to preside at this meeting, which I did, and unfortunately Thomas Hull seemed to be so impressed by my manner that he did not only urge the Young Men's Club but also urged me as its president. This was rather embarrassing to me, but when the Young Men's Club convened, I reported what had taken place in the village meeting. Strangely enough it had created widespread interest and excitement. In spite of all opposition, the transformation took place.

Although the effort was made to impeach me, it failed, and I was elected president of the first Mutual Improvement Association in Centerville. I also persuaded the now-vanishing Young Men's Club to change their club hall into the Y.M.M.I.A. Building. As construction had not yet been completed, this change was effected, and in the west gable of the structure was placed the stone carved title, Y.M.M.I.A. Hall. It became noted as the first building erected by the Y.M.M.I.A. specifically as a meeting place for that organization.

A week or two later after this achievement, I attended by request the general board meeting of the church in Salt Lake City for this association and reported the organization effected in Centerville and the change of the Young Men's Club Hall to a Y.M.M.I.A. building. Elder John Nicholson, so long identified with the development of the intellectual life in Utah as editorial writer of the *Deseret News* and also author of books, was the secretary at the time of this general board. His recital of my appearance from Davis County to make this representation before the general board and the uncanny silence which prevailed while I made my report was one of the features for a number of years at the general board's proceedings.

It was during these years of separation from the good boys on the one hand and my refusing to associate with the irregular elements that I turned to my prodigious reading program, which was omnifarious rather than general. I had access to the now-forgotten but substantial *Chamber's Encyclopedia*, a cheap copy of which I purchased, also a set of eighteen or twenty books known as *The Library of General Knowledge for the People*. The Young Men's Library also afforded some substantial works, among them Hallam's *Constitutional History of England*, McCaulay's five volume *History of England*; also the two volumes of *Blackstone's Commentary* on the English Law. For these books, including also eight volumes of the *Rise and Fall of the Roman Empire* by Edward Gibbon, I made some exchanges of other books for possession of the above. Later, of course, there came other readings of like subjects, including McCaulay's five volumes of *Miscellaneous Works*; John Fiske's works, forty-two volumes of the Christian Fathers, a product of the Oxford movement in England early in the ninth century; Kabder's ten volumes, *Credibility of the Gospel History*; Rollins's six volumes of *Ancient History*; six volumes of the *Christian Religion and Church*; Mosheim's three volumes of *Ecclesiastical Histories*; Calvin's two volumes of *Institutes*; Milner's four volumes of *History of the Church*; two volumes of Shedd's *History of Christian Doctrine*; two volumes of Stebbin's *History of the Christian Church*; four volumes of Milman's *Christian History*; Priestly's two volumes on *Corruptions of Christianity*; Brueck's two volumes on *History of the Catholic Church*; Jortin's two volumes of *Christian History*; Daubigne's *History of the Reformation*; Dowlin's *History of Romanism*; and Edersheim's two volumes of *Jesus the Messiah*.

I also read various authors in the same line of historical treatment of Christianity, both Catholic and Protestant, with an unabridged *Bible Dictionary* by Smith, and all of Renan's works, also Thomas Payne and Robert Ingersol. In fact, there were included Christian writers together with numerous philosophical works of Plato, Aristotle, Spinoza, Descartes, Rousseau, Bacon, More, Campanella, etc. Harvard's *Classics* and a number of other miscellaneous classics were included in my readings.

However, I always suffered from vicious pronunciation that often was humiliating. In even some of the higher schools in Davis County, I had teachers who warped my pronunciation. For instance, the teacher taught me to pronounce lunatic asylum as luna'tic a'sylum, Penelope as Pe'ne'lope', together with almost endless other vicious pronunciations, the handicap in all my subsequent readings and speaking. Also I never learned to spell. During the years in which accurate spelling is usually acquired I did not even know my letters or the most basic primers for reading exercises. This, too, proved a handicap in my subsequent efforts at writing and was the source of much humiliation.

I remember quite well my earliest efforts at composition. There was in the Sunday school of the church, which I irregularly attended, a prize offered for a composition on the life of Joseph Smith, the Mormon prophet. In my visits at Aunt Hannah Holbrook's home seeking the companionship of the two boys of whom she was guardian, Joseph and William Holbrook, I discovered that Aunt Hannah was laboriously writing out quite an elaborate article on this subject, which would be presented by the two boys as a collaboration on the life of Joseph Smith. The prize was to be $1.00 and to be received by the successful competitor. Of course, these boys were really making no contribution of an idea or even copying Aunt Hannah's manuscript. By this time I had learned to read the Doctrine and Covenants and there found the account of the martyrdom, which appealed to me as a rather fine summary of the prophet's life, mission, and character. Therefore, since the Holbrook boys were to present a paper not theirs, I concluded if they could do that it would be all right to present this article, which I copied out and filed with the committee in the Sunday school awarding the prize.

Strangely enough these two papers were all that were filed with the committee, and they held them for two or three weeks before making the award. In the report made, it was decided to divide the $1.00 prize between the two contestants. They stated the excellence of one of the compositions was that it began logically with the birth of the prophet and completed his life. The second paper (which was mine) began much later, but the beauty and power of the composition rendered it equal to the other. No one recognized that it was a plagiarism pure and simple from the Doctrine and Covenants.

In later years I gave my views of plagiarism in an admonition that is deemed worthy of reproduction here from the *Seventy's First Yearbook* (p. 233):

"I desire to call the attention of our seventies and missionaries to the fact that the ugly words 'stolen,' 'theft,' 'stealing' are used as describing this act; and in literary ethics the act is just as despicable as those acts in commercial life that go under similar descriptive titles, 'stealing,' 'theft,' 'robbery.' And indeed, there is more excuse for such acts in commercial life than in literature. Of all despicable characters in the literary world, the plagiarist is regarded as the most contemptible, and yet there have not been wanting among us in the ministry of the Church (due to their ignorance of the ethics of literature, of course), those who have advocated the appropriation of sermons and lectures prepared by others; and have advocated the repetitions of these stolen sermons in the preaching of the gospel. I know of nothing that should be so completely repudiated by the seventies and missionary class work and their subsequent ministry as this course, or anything that smacks of it. It is as bad as wearing stolen clothes. It is asking one to shine not even by borrowed, but by stolen light. It will result in mental laziness. It is a confession of one's own inability to think for himself and work out from the mass of material that lie before him in the revelations of God, the deductions and conclusions that make for the establishment of faith and righteousness in the lives of others. A few ideas hammered out on the anvil of one's own thought, even though they be crudely and haltingly expressed, if they are one's own, that is a better beginning and more hopeful that the most glowing declamation of the sermon that has been stolen from another, or plagiarized from some book or tract. I beg of you to adhere to this counsel. Of all things have you discourses honest before God and before man."

This lesson for me began with the sense of shame that attended upon what I always thought my first and last act of plagiarism in the production of thought.

Meantime I had made provision for each year of my apprenticeship for three months of schooling, which were obtained at very inferior mixed common schools, but it helped some. During this time of apprenticeship, I formed a very dear relationship with Elder Nathan T. Porter, Sr., a naturally gifted man of fine spiritual character. He was of the swarthy type, deep-set and dark hazel eyes above which loomed a marble-like forehead, back from which was a fine black head of hair of almost silken texture. His nose and mouth and chin were shapely and tapered to a pear-shaped pointed face. He was somewhat noted as a local orator, and I used to imagine a great similarity to some of the finer portraits of Patrick Henry of Virginia. In his speeches, which were always extemporaneous, he was fervid, even passionate, and under the spirit, he rose to real heights, apparently both in knowledge and the expression of it—especially in matters involving the interpretation of scripture, of which he was a severely logical and impressive interpreter. In fact, in this little mountain hamlet of Centerville, there was gathered quite a number of gifted men with what passed as "oratory." Nathan Porter was the chief shining example.

There was a weekly meeting of the "Centerville Debating Society," which invited like societies from Farmington and Bountiful. The subjects of government ethics and relations were handled fiercely if not logically and classically. In these debating societies, I was always an observer, critique, and admirer, though perforce a silent one because I was not a member of these societies and therefore did not participate in them in any respect except as a listener from the sidelines.

There had drifted into this community school teachers both from the Union and Confederate states, and the discussions sometimes included "Had the South Succeeded in the Late War?" and "Had a State a Right to Secede?" These teacher representatives from both parts of the Union threw into the debates some of the hot passion which some of them had felt when the battles were really on and the questions live issues. I remember with what "precision" they insisted on the statement of the case, and these definitions frequently gave the slight advantage which sometimes determined the effectiveness of the argument. I remember how genial, generous George Chase would deal with those matters in defining the ground of the controversy. With impressive fixtures he would draw the *Webster's Unabridged Dictionary* across the table to himself, where he would pompously open its pages, saying, "Well, lets see what Uncle Dan'l has to say about it"—evidently under the impression that Daniel Webster was the author of the dictionary, which bore the Webster name. In fancy I imagine he could see Noah Webster turning over in his grave. Just the same, they were great debates and did much to develop the local talent on expression on which it broke itself.

CHAPTER 9.

The Bear Story

In the spring of 1877 my contract as an apprentice to James Baird after three years duration came to an end, and for some time I had exhibited a restlessness that came from the restraints imposed by my indentures as an apprentice. The desire for change had been long coming to my consciousness. Rather favorable conditions for a partnership in the blacksmith shop were offered by Mr. Baird, but others advocated a sort of journeyman's tour in the trade to pick up wider experience before settling down to business.

However, a more attractive offer in employment came from a ranch and dairying company up in the mountains east of Ogden and above what is generally regarded as Weber Canyon proper. This offer was from a company of dairy ranching organized at Centerville, which that spring had enlarged its business by purchasing a ranch higher up in the mountains. Always a lover of outdoor life, I finally concluded to take this chance for riding the range and participating in the ranch and dairy business. Early spring therefore found me on these ranches with the business to be responsible for the dry stock and also to bring in of an evening the dairy cows belonging to the ranch. For the work I had a pair of riding horses, one of which was a roan mare I had broken from a colt. It was during this summer that I had my adventure with a grizzly bear who when dead weighed about 550 pounds. The adventure was published by request in the *Improvement Era* (April 1921).

Farther back in the hills, two miles above the Centerville Dairy, a California company had been running a cheese factory on what, for a time, was a large scale. But the California company had been meeting for years with reverses of fortune. The business had been badly managed; and the man whom the company had brought from the east to run the factory, a very good cheesemaker, also, by the way, and a gentle, good man, too, had unfortunately become mentally unbalanced and incapable of running the business except as directed by his good wife, one of the most patient and excellent of women.

The misfortune made the California company anxious to sell out their ranch, stock, and cheese factory, and the Centerville Dairy company became willing purchaser, which so increased their need of hands that when it became known that the "young blacksmith," as I was familiarly called in those days, intended to break away from the shop, the manager of these now consolidated companies urged me to take employment with them and ride the range for them that summer. The offer had its attraction among which was the fact that a dozen or more of the young people of the village, boys and girls of my own acquaintance, had been engaged for the summer for the same company, so that there was then prospect of merry times, song and laughter and joy unmeasured, things, which in those days had their appeal. Then there was the promise of freedom and the big out-of-door life–the life I had always loved, and which before apprentice-ship days was the life I had always lived. So I accepted the employment to ride the range that summer of 1877.

The job yielded me all the pleasure I had anticipated. The days of April and May and the days of all the summer months were golden; and all the nights, sleeping in the open–for I scorned the bunkhouse–were glorious. In my earlier reading, I had learned the names of some of the great, fixed star groups, and somewhat their relations in space, and now I could mark their rising and progress across that great "inverted bowl" called the sky and marvel to my heart's content upon their beauty and majesty and glory–with now and then a flashing thought upon the greater majesty and glory of him who must have created them, his very handiwork.

All this with the fresh mornings and thin sunlight tinting the snow-clad peaks of the Wasatch mountains; likewise the sultry noons of the midsum-mer months; the frugal meal from the saddle bags, eaten in the solitude and the silence of the mountains while the horse, relieved of his saddle and bridle cropped and munched the tender mountain grass with evident delight. Then there was the return to the ranch, the shouted welcome as one approached it, the jest, the courteous retort, the joy of being young, without being quite conscious that you were young, and not knowing really that that was the source of your joyful exuberance. Such the setting of this story.

Starting off early one morning, for what was to be a long day's ride in search of stray cattle missed from their accustomed range, I saw in the dusty road of the canyon two miles above the ranch house the tracks of what must have been a very large bear. They were sufficiently fresh to cause me to keep a sharp lookout for bruin myself, and I thought I noticed an unusual restlessness in the roan mare I was riding, which I attributed to her scenting the nearness of the brute whose tracks were so plainly visible in the road. These, after a bit, turned off from the road into a red willow swale on the right, and I rode up the canyon a little relieved that I had not come up with the owner of the tracks.

An earlier find than I had expected to make of the stray cattle I was in search of and an easy drive of them over a low divide to their accustomed range enabled me to return to the ranch early in the afternoon. Riding down the canyon road, over which I had passed in the morning, I noted again the bear tracks and the point at which they came down from the hillside into the road, from the left as one would face the head of the canyon. About a mile above the ranch house of the company for which I worked and several hundred yards from the canyon road was a strongly built stake and rider corral made of quaking aspen poles. Indeed, the corral had been made in an aspen grove where the poles had been cut, some of the stumps unwisely being left standing at the height of from two to four feet. People from the valley settlements had made the corral into which they might drive their range horses, capture the ones they might need for work purposes, and turn the band loose. A few days before this bear incident, a band of horses had been driven into the corral for the above named purpose, when, in racing among the stumps, a two-year-old had struck on one of them, ripped out his entrails, and died. Remembering this I turned from the road and went to see if the bruin had nosed about the carcass and found that it had ripped it wider open and tore away the fleshy parts, though I could not see that he had eaten very much, if any of it.

Reporting to the ranchmen what I had discovered during the day created quite an interest and led to a very general desire that the bear might be killed. Especially was this so with one member of the ranch force, one Alma Peterson, familiarly called "Al" and son of the man after whom the settlement of Peterson in Morgan County had been named. "Al" was about thirty-three and an odd character in many ways–very interesting, however, because of the Indian stories he could tell of early days in Morgan and Summit counties. The memory of his family, and his own, too, as I recall, went back to the days of Chief Wanship and Little Soldier and their bands, which were wont to range through these mountains of Wasatch and Summit Counties, with an occasional visit from Chief Pocatello and other Shoshone braves from Idaho. Also Al's brother was the hero of a hand to hand fight with a wounded grizzly bear. While the bear had been killed, Al's brother always carried the marks of the fight on his face and neck, and the flesh from his right shoulder had been cruelly torn away. Some of the glory of this fight, one way or other, seemed to be reflected upon Al.

Al was also interesting on another account–not because of his beauty of person, but contrariwise. He was among those few men one meets who were ugly enough to be positively attractive. He was built on the ramshackle order of loose, big-jointed men–tall, gaunt, with big hands and big feet. His frame was topped with a huge head, on which grew bristle-like hair with disposition to sprawl out in all directions; it knew no parting. All the features were large and ill formed. This was true of the big and spreading nose, the mouth, the large and outstanding scars–his face was badly marked from a severe case of small pox–and the eyes so turned that you could never be sure in which particular direction Al was looking.

But for all this rough and uncouth exterior, one could not help liking Al; perhaps it was because the innate gentleness and patience, the really sympathetic nature of the man was in such marked contrast with all the outside of him. At any rate, all at the ranch liked Al, and especially companionable did I find him to be.

Well, the remembrance of Al's odd personality flashes upon me; he of all the ranch force was anxious to attempt the killing of the bear whose tracks I had seen. He pointed out how this could easily be done by several of the men going to the corral, wherein lay the horse carcass which would doubtless be visited again by the bear, and likely this very night. The party could lie outside the corral, and when bruin arrived and proceeded to amuse himself with the carcass, they could shoot him deliberately from their place of concealment, and with entire safety to themselves.

It happened that I was the only one to whom Al's plan of battle appealed, so about ten o'clock, when darkness had well settled over mountain and canyon defile, we took our departure for the scene of action, with many good wishes for "good luck" from the rest of the ranch folk. Half a mile from the corral, we proceeded with utmost care lest we should startle the quarry, if he had already arrived at the proposed place of meeting. However, it was our theory that very likely he would not arrive until towards morning. Silently we reached the corral. Bruin had not yet arrived, so we chose a point for our ambush nearest the carcass and settled down to wait for our victim. Hours dragged our slow length along, but no sign of bruin's coming. After the passing of several hours, I fell asleep; so, too, I thought Al did, but he always denied the guess.

When I awoke, the stars in the east seemed to be growing brighter, and by that token I knew the dawn was approaching. "The thin, grey line that frets the east as heralds of the day" soon appeared and gradually grew broader until daylight was unmistakably coming down from the mountain, and Al was confident no bruin would now put in appearance, and so we slowly, and with disappointment plainly visible, returned to the ranch to meet as best we might the gibes of our friends.

That morning my day's ride took me again up the canyon and past the corral. A short distance above the ranch, and yet before coming opposite the horse corral, I was surprised to see bear tracks in the dust of the road heading up the canyon, and from their size they must have been made by the brute whose tracks I had seen the day before farther up the canyon. The peculiar bellowing of a cow, off in the direction of the creek bottom at the right, attracted the attention, and I turned off to see what her distress meant. She was rushing here and there wild eyes through the thickets that fringed the creek. I could find no cause for her alarm, unless she had been startled by Mr. Bruin. The half remains of a young calf found a day or two later was generally accepted as the cause of her alarm; bruin had killed and eaten part of it.

I followed the tracks up the road until they turned off on the side in the direction of the horse corral, and I traced them for a short distance through the sage brush up the hillside. A late start for my day's ride through the hills made it necessary to cut short the trailing and get on my way. Back into the canyon road and well past the corral, I saw again bruin's tracks in the dust and reached the conclusion that during the night the bear had come up the road after his attack on our calf corral, and having scented Al and myself at the horse corral–a thing he would most likely do, since a breeze came nightly down the canyon–he had merely walked around the corral and then came back into the road, and so to his daylight wallow in the willows.

I did not return to the ranch this day until after dark, and interest in the bear hunt seemed to have subsided. Discussing my report as to what was evidently bruin's movements during the night before, it was thought that the best plan would be to let him get to the horse corral first and to its carcass and then open fire upon him as before planned. But how to find out the time at which bruin would likely visit the carcass was a problem. It was the consensus of opinion that he would not go there before early in the morning, and someone suggested that the alarm clock might be set for about three in the morning, and such "Nimrods" as might be disposed for the adventure could undertake it. Most of the ranch hands had no stomach for it. Neither had I, at that hour in the morning–three o'clock–and especially after the previous night's experience, its loss of sleep, and the long ride of the day.

It was now eleven o'clock of the night, and some remarked that bruin might even be at the corral now. "That is so," I responded, "as likely there now as at three o'clock in the morning. Al let's go." "All right," said he, and with that we picked up our guns and left the ranch. Al carried a breach-loading Ballard rifle, such as were once used by the U.S. Cavalry. I had an old English rifle–a musket–in common use during the Civil War. I had bought it some years ago and after cutting off a few inches to the barrel had used it as a shot gun in hunting mountain hares and geese on the Jordan bottoms. It was loaded literally for bear, however, on this occasion. I had put in two ordinary charges of powder, the regular infield slug bullets, two slugs cut from the end of a bar of lead, and some buck shot. It was a matter of good-natured banter at the ranch, among those who knew how it was loaded, as to which would be the most dangerous end of the gun when fired.

The night was intensely dark; the sky was overspread by clouds; there was no moon; not a star could be seen. As we came into the canyon road, Al muttered something about a couple of fools going out on such a night hunting a bear–perhaps a grizzly. But then one does such things when he is young–when he is twenty, else how would there be adventures?

On we went. We were approaching the corral and left the road for the hillside and the brush clumps. Cautiously we drew near, creeping slowly and breathlessly for silence sake. A few rods from the corral we halted to listen beside a clump of bushes. I dropped to one knee. Al remained standing. I heard what I thought was a movement through the bushes immediately above in front of us. The air, or else I, was tense. Al laid a hand on my shoulder and whispered, "I think he is coming." "Be sure it's not a calf," I whispered back, for even now I thought of the possible ridicule to which we might be subjected, in the event of shooting a calf for a bear.

Just then I saw an object move above the tops of the sage brush and quickly raised the hammer of my gun. The loud click, click, the hammer as it went to half and full cock, startled his bruinship, and he rose to his haunches with a tremendous "whoof, whoof." Two rifle reports rang out at the same instant (though Al always contended that his barked a hundredth part of a second before mine roared). The shots were answered by such mingled screams of fear, rage, and pain as I had never heard before and would not care to hear again. The huge form literally fell at our feet, or so close that I could have touched him with the point of my gun, and then bounded down the hillside which here was rather steep.

Bruin landed in a clump of bushes, and we could hear him crunching there as he twisted them off with his teeth in his rage and agony. His screeching had now lowered to deep, low growls. I noticed Al slip his gun through his hands, clubbing it, and then I remembered that on the way up he had remarked that he had forgot to bring any cartridges with him, so that he was limited to his single shot. So, too, was I, for I had not more than half thought we would meet bruin. Then, too, my gun was muzzle-loading, and it was night. But noting that Al had clubbed his gun made me sense that there might still be a fight, and the thought flashed through my mind that I could do better with my belt knife at close quarters than by clubbing my gun, and so I drew my knife. By now the growls of bruin had grown fainter, but we could not see just where he was nor judge the state of his helplessness. But Al at this moment spoke to me, still in a whisper, "Don't you think we had better get out of this?"

"You bet I do," was my prompt answer, and with that we sprang to the left and a few leaps and bounds brought us into the road. Al's feet caught a root as we gained the road, and head over heels he went rolling. I remember thinking that it was well that I had not fallen, as I still carried my belt knife in my hand and might have been severely cut if I had so stumbled and fallen. The road gained, we stopped and listened a while but could hear no more of bruin's movements and so went on to the ranch, where we detailed and discussed our adventure.

With daylight all the male hands of the ranch went with us to the scene of the shooting; and there, sure enough, lying square on his back and all four legs straight up in the air was bruin, stark and stiff in death. An examination showed that Al's shot had passed through the lungs, while mine tore through the groin and hips of the brute, perhaps hitting him just as he sprang in the air and rendering use of the hind limbs impossible. From the clump of choke-cherry bushes into which he had rolled after being shot and which he had broken off with his teeth as if they were straws, he had dragged himself by his front paws to the place where we stood when shooting and there died.

Bruin was a large grizzly. I was accounted as broad shouldered in those days, but when I stretched myself at full length on the carcass, my shoulders between the brute's front legs, there were several inches between my shoulders and each foreleg—so broad was he across the chest. A drag litter was formed with small quaking aspen poles and brush, onto which bruin was rolled and dragged by lariats and ropes hitched to saddle horses and so taken triumphantly to the ranch. On the scales he tipped the beam for more than five hundred and fifty pounds.

The only thing of value about him, at this season of the year—it was August—was his hide, and upon this, of course, Al and I had equal claims. It was decided that we would fix value upon the hide, the half of which we would either give or take. The price fixed, I sold my claim to Al, as I felt that I could ill afford to buy. I have always regretted selling, however, for what would I not now give for that trophy of my young manhood days? But, during the summer on the range, the determination had been slowly forming in my mind to attend the then Deseret, now Utah, University for a year at least, and this made it necessary to augment my savings through the years of my apprenticeship. Certainly I could take nothing from my savings to buy shares in bear skins, while selling would add a little to them, so I sold.

I have always regretted the selling of the skin, however, and all the more so because of the bad use Al made of the bargain, for he sold the skin at a few dollars in advance of the value we had fixed upon each other, and the man buying it cut it up into housing for the harness of a pair of horses of which he was rather proud. "To such bad uses do things noble sometimes come, Horatio."

The summer of 1877 was remembered on the mountain ranges for excessive drought. The pasturage from the milk herd was early dried up, and the seasons run in cheese and butter making seemed to head towards disaster. The question as to what should be done under such circumstance was frequently debated on the ranch between managers and the employed. The thought occurred to the management that a range over the Weber River and on the north slopes of the Weber River offered very much better prospects for feedings. This, however, was the home range of a little Mormon settlement, and an emphatic protest was made by the people against this invasion of their settlement range, which they depended on for pasturage for their milk stock. The reasonableness of this protest appeared on the very surface of it. However, the determination of the management of the mountain dairies constantly increased, until there was a settled policy fixed upon to invade the summer range of the good local people.

During this discussion by the dairy companies, I urged their and my own objections on the ground of the injustice of it. When it seemed at last concluded and the large herds were to be driven across the ravine to this range, I rebelled and told my employers, the managers of the ranches where I worked, that I would take no part in moving the herd to the north side of the range, and that if the settlers would resent this invasion of their rights, I would stand by them. I would consider every hoof of the large herds that crossed the river as trespassing and would favor shooting them down and resisting to the limit this injustice.

This threatened resistance, of course, created something of a sensation, and I was threatened with dismissal from the company's service, all of which made no difference. I persisted in my opposition, and as the settlers themselves were determined to offer this resistance, the project of the ranch management was abandoned, and the range herds were driven further into the mountains, notwithstanding the inconvenience of it. Here the feed was better, with increasing results of more milk production.

CHAPTER 10.

A Student of Deseret University

It was while working at this ranch that the offer came to me from the Davis County authorities for me to become a normal student at the University of Deseret. The Salt Lake Council House, which had been the first public building of the State of Deseret and Utah territory and had stood on the south corner of Main and South Temple Streets (where the university had met for several years), was destroyed by fire, and the university had to seek new quarters. The only building available that year was an adobe story-and-a-half private house. By the adjustment of the entrance and stairway it was improvised and used for the new quarters of the university. The building was known as the old "Doremus House." It stood and now stands among a clutter of buildings on the corner of 1st North and 2nd West St.

The curriculum of the university in those days was as humble as the quarters in which it was lodged. My own department—the normal school for teachers of the territory—was the humblest of its divisions, scarcely equal then to a high school curriculum of today. How humble it must have been will be learned from the fact that I completed the two-year course in one year and graduated at the head of the class and by virtue of that became the valedictorian of commencement exercises at the close of the school year.

Of course, this matter of coupling up the work of two years into one was with the sanction of that most influential teacher of Utah, Dr. John R. Park. Notwithstanding the humble lodgings of the institution and the very limited curriculum, he made it a university in spirit. Indeed I thought that if the school had been only one log room, it would nevertheless have been a university. Rightfully he is ranked today as the father of Utah's chief higher educational institution of learning, now known as the University of Utah. Despite all talk and effort to establish a University of Utah, previous to his entering the field it was chiefly a paper institution. He imparted the spirit of the university to the institution in Utah. In proof of this, it is only necessary to call attention to the principles he laid down at the time of inaugurating his own connection with higher education in Utah. His report to the chancellor and Board of Regents made on conditions existing in 1882-83 was as follows:

"No institution that contemplates such a broad field of instruction and usefulness as a university can be successfully carried on without ample and permanent means of support. Such an institution should be placed beyond the inimical influence of personal whim, popular gossip, and the uncertainty of fickle, or temporary patronage. The university needs a sure support, and its patronage should be well established. Both of these conditions are essential to its purpose and prosperity. No hand to mouth existence will ever create confidence in the institution or enable it to carry out successfully any plans for thorough instruction."

Undoubtedly it was Dr. John R. Park who breathed into the mere name and mere community aspiration for a university the breath of its life. Years afterwards when writing the *Comprehensive History of the Mormon Church, Century II,* I made these comments on the school system of Utah:

"The school system of early Utah, of course, suffered from the limitations of pioneer conditions which obtained. From the isolation of the respective communities imposed by the long distances separating them both from each other and also from the more populous centers of east and west; from the imperfect territorial system of government enforced upon the people of Utah far beyond any reasonable time for its continuance—forty years at least beyond such time; for there can be no question but that Utah, by 1856, was prepared for and deserved statehood by reason of her population, wealth, real and potential, and by her heroism in making conquest of a desert wilderness and proved ability for self government."

The lodgings selected by me in which to live in Salt Lake City while attending the school were of the humblest character and enforced upon me living entirely alone and separate from all social connection. To relieve my loneliness I conceived the idea of having some musical instrument with which to beguile the time. As I was not ambitious about mastering music, I purchased a flute but never succeeded in connecting a dozen notes together and finally gave it up in disgust.

I soon discovered that the summer wages I had mostly saved would not be sufficient to carry me through my year's attendance upon school, and hence in the way of economy, I gave up my lodgings and for some several months walked daily eleven miles from an improvised home in Centerville to the university in Salt Lake, arriving usually on time when class exercises began at nine o'clock. The journey back home was usually tramped over the country, and almost daily I was picked up by the returning teams which had hauled hay into town. I was a sort of "hitchhiker," but the conveyance that picked me up was usually an empty hayrack instead of an automobile, but at any rate, it got me to school and back and that was the main thing.

Then for a time when spring came I arranged to live with some stone cutters in a little loghouse which stood across the street northward in a lot immediately opposite the 17th ward chapel near a cluster of adobe houses, where the colored families and their descendants lived who had come into the valley with the first pioneer company. It was a studied effort on my part to leave the university at the end of each school day a little before the day's dismissal in order to keep the knowledge of my living quarters from the students. Pride even under these humble circumstances attended upon me still, and I was under the impression at least that my abiding place was not known. I shared these humble quarters with three stone cutters working on the temple block, who were sustained in wages provided by the people of Centerville – this being their contribution to the building of the temple at that time. These with me were all too poor to afford a fire, and therefore on reaching the humble log cabin, I rolled myself up in the bed clothes of my nightly couch on the floor to keep warm and stretched out to study the lessons for the next day. Such were the conditions under which I completed the remaining time of my attendance upon the university, under which I won my class standing and received the appointment of valedictorian.

Of course, this sort of existence precluded all contact with the other students of the university and was a grave defect in the very lame and inadequate education that this brief attendance at the university entailed. That was a defect and always was a vacant spot in my so-called education, and I desire it laid down now that such limitations from contact with fellow students is a great lapse in the education furnished by higher institutions of learning. I never recovered from that defect but suffered much from it and even now suffer from it. It was a lopsided experience for me, that is to say, one-sided as an education, if education it could be called.

Finally the day for graduation came – and the valedictorian address. If there ever was a time perhaps when an address should have been carefully written out it was then. But somehow the disposition to commit my thought to writing did not impress me, and I ventured in that rather august assembly, for some of the leading officers and citizens of the state crowded into the humble assembly hall of the limited building, to speak extemporaneously. A few leading items were first in my mind, but the reliance upon the fitting expression of them rather broke down. I was overwhelmed with a sense of failure and longed most of all for the silence and solitude of the log cabin in which I lived. I withdrew from the hall before the closing of the services and made my escape. In doing so, however, a ray of sunshine was put into the gloom in which I was invested. As I passed by Joseph F. Smith, who was in attendance and counselor to President John Taylor of the LDS church who was also present, Mr. Smith laid his hand upon my arm and said with a twinkle of humor in his serious eyes, "Them's my sentiments, too." That remark cheered my mind through many dark days when I thought upon the crudeness and failure of my valedictorian address.

The choosing of the valedictorian for the normal class that year was not without interest. Doctor Park had appointed a meeting of the class in which to make the announcement of choosing the class representative. I was not present. Perhaps the good doctor had arranged it so that I might not feel embarrassment of it. When the purpose of the meeting was announced, some popular and prosperous-born young ladies immediately nominated and the nomination was seconded of a very popular beaux ideal of a student for the honor. The action was taken so rapidly that the rather slow-moving deliberate doctor was outrun, and he was under the necessity of saying that a popular choice was not the usual method of determining the valedictorian but rather class standing, and the examination best determined who was at the head of the graduating class. And when several voices asked who was head in graduation, the doctor informed them that the student from Davis County held the highest graduation marks and by all means should be made the one to deliver the graduating address. This was followed by a few moments of silence, I was informed, and then a prominent young lady voiced perhaps what was the feeling of her group that he would never do. When asked why, she said, "Why look at his clothes." His appearance would be against him, and another added, "It is certain too that he will buy no other." This circumstance alone justified the wisdom of Doctor Park arranging for my absence.

All through the attendance of the school, my clothes had really been mortification to me. I remember it was a brown sack suit, the first venture in tailoring of a relative who had taken about six lessons in cutting after the Curtis model. As a matter of economy, I had allowed the apprenticed hand to practice on this suit. The thing was a misfit throughout, and the cut had the wretched habit of puckering up the back. However after hearing this casual remark on my misfit suit, I did contrive, notwithstanding my poverty, to purchase a new hand-me-down coat and vest, which in the end was not much better suited for such an occasion. But I did get rid temporarily of the ugly misfit I had worn through most of the year. The new coat was called a Prince Albert in style, but the flimsy materials of it soon disclosed that it was too long waisted and the tails were too long. This was sought to be remedied by cutting the tails shorter and stitching the raw edges. Its ungainly appearance was a sore temptation even to go back to the brown sack suit of the previous winter. Consciousness of unsuitable clothing was one of the tortures that attended the graduating exercises of that day. The claim that clothes do not make the man may be all right as a theory, but I aver it to be my testimony that they have much to do with distressing uncomfort.

Among the foolish things done while attending school was to contract a marriage without any forethought or scheme looking to the maintenance of that relationship with dignity and reasonableness of successful negotiation with the consequences involved in such relation. I had been engaged before the opportunity for attendance at the university had come to me. It was an engagement that I could not reconcile myself to ignore after the opportunity to attend school had come to me. It therefore happened that I undertook to fulfill the engagement without proper preparation to meet the obligations. It was with a sense of being bound in honor to that obligation that I undertook to fulfill it. Of course, it resulted in multiplying my problems in life.

CHAPTER 11.

Mission to Iowa – The First Call to the Ministry – A Seventy

After graduation I was under obligation to the county, of course, to teach school for at least two years to fulfill this obligation. I accepted the appointment to teach in the county and discovered in myself some aptitude for that class of work, and an educational career threatened for a time to be my life work. Meantime, however, I had been ordained to the office of Seventy and had joined the 19th quorum of that organization. James Townsend, proprietor of the rather celebrated Townsend House, a hotel in Salt Lake City, was the Senior President, and Brother Nathan T. Porter, Sr., before mentioned, was also a president of that quorum. I therefore was thrown more immediately under his benign influence.

The Seventies quorums in the LDS church are general quorums of the church and are especially devoted to be the witnesses of the Lord Jesus Christ and engaged in the preaching of the gospel to all the world. In fact the most immediate and proper body of propaganda and the increasing interest which I felt in relation to the New Dispensation naturally threw me into an intense love of the work, which it was the special function of the Seventies to discharge.

Within a year or two after graduation from the university, word was received from the general presidents that the 19th quorum had been appealed to by the general authorities of the church to provide several missionaries from this quorum. Therefore, President Nathan T. Porter at the request of the senior president called a meeting of all the Seventies in the Centerville Ward, presented the request of President Townsend before that body, and called for volunteers for the mission field. No one, however, of the school of men in attendance volunteered. President Porter said, "If you brethren do not feel that you ought to volunteer and that for some reason or other you cannot go, or if any of you feel that if you were able to go you would be willing, then make that desire known under these circumstances." He concluded by saying, "How many of you would like to make a mission if your circumstances would admit." Even then there was absolute silence; no one took the liberty of saying that they would even like to go if they could. Finally one of the members of the quorum at last said – and the remark is important because it represented the feelings among the rank and file of those upon whom this responsibility rests—"Brother Porter, I reckon you will have to take the responsibility of telling some one to go." This responsibility Brother Porter declined but still said he would like to be able to say that some of the seventies in Centerville who had reported at the meeting said they would be glad to accept a mission if it were possible for them to go. Thus admonished I arose and made the statement that if I could see my way clear and had the means supposed to be necessary for the mission I would be glad to go. I was converted to the necessity of Seventies fulfilling the functions of their office and there the meeting closed.

However, it was immediately noised abroad that I had volunteered to go upon a mission. My mother heard of it and was heartbroken because she was satisfied that it meant long separation and would defer the task that both I and my wife had set before ourselves to establish a home. That meant, of course, the provision of a site and the erection of a home, and tears and disappointment came of this misrepresentation that I had volunteered to go upon a mission. In any event the matter was now reported to the First Council of the Seventy, and my name was sent to the missionary committee of the Apostles and listed among those who were prospective missionaries, who would likely be called at the spring conference of 1880. A letter was received from those making up the list at that time. I wrote to the missionary committee stating how my name had perhaps reached their list on an entirely misapprehension, and I felt myself, and had so reported, unable to go. A small amount of savings from my teachings had been in a way consecrated to the establishment of a home, and I could not fulfill this engagement without an entire abandonment for some length of time of creating the home which had been contemplated. I therefore asked for a reconsideration of the matter based upon my own representation to those who had made inquiry about missionary service in the quorum. The result was a release from the obligation to go upon a mission, and so I resumed activities for the home building project.

During the apprenticeship my expenses had been very light, and the small salary allowed me while an apprentice had been accumulated to my credit with my employer Mr. Baird. This gentleman owned two vacant lots in Centerville. I made a bargain for these, turning the accumulated apprentice wages on the purchase and giving my note for the remainder. Straightway that spring of 1880 I began digging a basement by hand for the two-roomed cottage home contemplated. I was about half way through with excavation when a letter was received from the First Council of Seventy reproving me with an effort to avoid missionary service for the church. It contained a notification that they would still regard their call for me to go upon a mission as standing good.

For some time while digging the excavation, with every shovelful of earth that I threw out on the growing embankment, would come a silent voice, "You will not complete this building now; you will not complete this building now." These two things, the letter of reproof and this voice that had been my guide, prompted me to make an unqualified acceptance of an appointment to the mission. Then the bishop of the ward got busy and told the Council how utterly impossible it was for me to go upon that mission and maintain myself while I was gone. In a few days I received word that my mission was cancelled again.

The rumor of the vacillation on the part of those managing this matter appeared to have reached the ears of President John Taylor, and he sent for the bishop and, in his good-natured way which nearly always included his relapsing into Lancashire dialect, said, "What's this I hear about Young Roberts going on a mission? What's the matter with him? Is it anything wrong that would prevent his going on a mission that would make him unworthy?" The bishop answered there is absolutely nothing wrong with me. I was in every way worthy to go upon a mission, but I could not possibly maintain my family and at the same time meet the expense of a mission. To this President Taylor replied, "Well, Bishop, what do you suppose we have bishops in the Church for? If the young man could not maintain his family during his absence, why don't you undertake the job and assure him that they shall not want?" A new light came to the bishop apparently, and so he withdrew his objections and at the April conference my name was read off for a mission to the Northern States Mission.

The notion was inculcated in those days that in the main missionaries would travel without purse and script in the United States at least, and this situation I prepared to meet. I turned over what means I had to my wife to live upon during my absence, and I myself took only means sufficient to pay my way to my field of labor, which was finally determined to be the state of Iowa beginning at Sioux City.

Other experiences occurred in this year of beginning of the mission. There had been born to my wife and me our first babe. She was a beautiful child but stricken at one time in infancy with a very serious illness that threatened her life. Strangely enough, it had been decreed, apparently in my life, that I had a special gift of healing the sick. It was so designated in my patriarchal blessing, much to my own astonishment, for while I had administered to many sick and there had been remarkable cases of healing, yet I had never thought upon it as being anything special until that patriarchal blessing named it. But for clear understanding, this must receive some explanation.

The Church of the Latter-day Saints has in its organization a line of men holding the special office of patriarch, which is supposed to give inspirational power to these men to confer blessings upon the membership of the church. It consists in assuming that they have the power to designate the tribes of Israel to which its members belong and then speak forth those things which come to them in outline about the spiritual properties to which they may attain.

In keeping with this idea I had determined when about twenty years of age to seek a patriarchal blessing at the hands of the Presiding Patriarch of the church, who at that time was John Smith, the oldest son of the martyr Hyrum Smith. The right to this office was proclaimed by the prophet of the New Dispensation to belong to his father, Joseph Smith, Sr., and from him it descended to his son Hyrum and then to Hyrum's eldest son and so on down the chosen line.

John Smith, the patriarch, was in some respects a peculiar man, but since the gifts of the patriarchal office were his, I determined to obtain a blessing at his hands, which I received in Salt Lake City on August 24, 1877, and which here follows.

"Brother Brigham Henry Roberts: In the name of the Lord Jesus Christ, I place my hands upon thy head, and pronounce and seal a blessing upon thee, which shall be a guide and a comfort unto thee in time to come: For thou art of the House of Israel, numbered with the Sons of Zion of whom much is expected: therefore, seek to inform thy mind, for the day is not far distant which thou shalt be called to labor in the ministry.

"Thou art of the lineage of Ephraim, and entitled to the blessings of Abraham, Isaac, and Jacob with the gifts of the Priesthood.

"Therefore, be prudent, and listen to the whispering of the still small voice of the comforter, for through that source thy guarding Angel will warn thee of events to come and give thee power over evil and unclean spirits; and thou shalt realize that the hand of the Lord is over thee for good; and that He has preserved thy life in the past for a wise purpose. He hath also delivered thee from among thine enemies, therefore, give praise unto whom praise is due.

"And thy days and years shall be many; and thou shalt become a mighty man in Israel and assist in gathering the honest in heart from among the nations of the Earth. Wisdom shall be given thee that thou shalt counsel in righteousness among thy brethren and shall exhort the Saints to repentence. Be faithful in keeping the commandments of God, and thou shalt preside over a stake in Zion. Thou shalt also be prospered spiritually and temporally, and shall feed many with both temporal and spiritual food. Thou shalt also fill up the measure of thy creation, and thy name shall be handed down with thy posterity in honorable remembrance and written in the Lamb's Book of Life.

"Thou shalt also be mighty in healing the sick by laying on of hands, for this shall be thy special gift through prayer and faith. Therefore, be firm in thy integrity and all shall be well with thee, notwithstanding thou shalt witness many changes and see trying events among the people. This blessing I seal upon thy head and I seal thee up unto eternal life to come forth in the morning of the first Resurrection a Savior in thy Father's house. Even so. Amen."

The blessing in the main was unsatisfactory and greatly disappointing, but there were two things which stood out prominently in it that attracted attention and constituted in the main its value as demonstrated in the experience of the recipient. One was the fact that my special gift in the priesthood and ministry of the church was to have power to heal the sick, and the other was what must have been a prophetic statement that "the Lord hath delivered you from the hands of your enemies." Aside from these two things, all was commonplace and as before noted disappointing.

Well this promise of having power to heal the sick had, of course, become known, especially in my family. On our infant's illness my wife had appealed to me to exercise that gift. I doubted my spiritual strength to rise for the occasion and therefore left the sick room and walked out into the orchard, where I engaged in very serious and earnest prayer. I conceived my unworthiness to undertake such administration as had been called for, and at the conclusion of my struggle in prayer there seemed to be a voice outside myself who took me to task for carelessness and on the weakness of my human nature. But in conclusion it told that my daughter should live and grow up into beautiful young womanhood on condition of my own faithfulness. Her life was left in my hands. And with these reproves and promises vividly implanted in my mind, I returned to the sick room, and when the anxious mother extended her hands and welcomed my return—as she suspected what I had been doing—she asked: "Well, will she live?" Remembering the obligation, I answered, "Yes, she shall live." With that I administered to her, and her recovery began and was completed. She fulfilled the prediction that she would grow into a beautiful young woman and has now long since passed that period, well beloved by all who know her. She has become a tower of strength and example to those she has contacted in her life. We shall have to speak of her and the exercise of this gift further on.

The time had now come to depart for the mission. On the 29th of March 1880 there was a large gathering of my friends at the home of my father-in-law, President William R. Smith, president of the Davis Stake of Zion. It was made an evening of lively conversation, the singing of hymns, and finally the more sober word of admonition, counsel, and advice to me and the family I was about to leave. Also there was a small contribution of means to help me on his journey. I was being sent by the apostles of the church to the state of Iowa and was to commence my labors at Sioux City in that state.

The place had been visited a few months before by a returning missionary from Michigan and Minnesota by the name of Hintze, who had reported some interest in the place in regard to Mormonism. At that time there was no organization of the mission in Iowa, although it was counted as being in the Northern States Mission. Cyrus Wheelock of Mount Pleasant, San Pete County, Utah, exercised at least a nominal presidency of that mission, but he had not visited the Northern States Mission for quite a number of years. This was the Cyrus Wheelock who visited the Prophet Joseph in Nauvoo, just previous to that prophet's martyrdom, and left with him the six-barrelled pistol with which the prophet had made his spirited fight in defense of himself and his brother and other associates.

There was a gathering of forty-two elders at the Old Council House on the northeast corner of Main and South Temple streets, the building since occupied by the Deseret News Building. We forty-two elders were set apart by two of the apostles and the senior president of the Seventy's organization, Joseph Young. The apostles were Orson Pratt and Wilford Woodruff, and the proceedings were conducted under the direction of Wilford Woodruff. Joseph Young was mouth in my case, but the two apostles joined him in the ceremony of laying on of hands. My ordination came near the close of the occasion, and, incidentally, I noted that forty out of the whole company of forty-two were promised a safe return from their missions. Two did not receive this promise, of which I was one and another brother, whose name is now forgotten. It may be said to have been customary for such pronouncements to be made upon the heads of departing missionaries. I noted the omission in my own case and naturally wondered if it were significant.

Some of these missionaries were bound for European countries such as England, Scandinavia, Germany, and Holland, and it was in their company that I made my journey as far as Omaha. Among the few elders assigned in the United States at that time was one William M. Palmer of Sevier County, Utah. He had been on a previous mission in Michigan and was now returning to that state with an understanding more or less that he would act as the president of the Northern States Mission under the direction of the above-named Cyrus Wheelock.

The company of elders from Ogden to Omaha were assigned to a special car, and I was startled on the way down when the passengers in the pullman car sent in word that they would like an elder to present to them the message of the Mormon company of emigrants being taken to various parts of the world. Elder Palmer, who was my seat companion, was chosen as being a man of some experience to go into the pullman and deliver this message. Lightning seemed to be striking close to me, and I wondered how I would have felt or appeared had the choice been delegated to me. There was an awful feeling of blankness when that thought asserted itself, and I made a hasty movement for a Bible to find out some text that I could use for such an occasion.

Surprisingly Elder Palmer, who was more experienced and momentarily at least president of all the northern states, regretted the fact aloud that I, who was very young and utterly inexperienced in missionary work, was to take up my labor in Sioux City. Much to my astonishment, Elder Palmer began to propose that he should accompany me for a few days in missionary service before leaving me to pursue his mission as had been appointed. What was still of deeper wonder, he represented to the companies of missionaries that he could not stop off even for a few days in Iowa unless means should be donated by the company of elders for that purpose. As a result he took up a collection which amounted to a few dollars and decided to begin the Iowa mission at Omaha.

Accordingly we two elders left the main party at Omaha and searched out a brother by the name of Gibbs in Omaha, whose presence and prospective openings in Sioux City had been reported by the aforesaid Elder Hintz. At the home of this Brother Gibbs, who was on the point of making a journey from Omaha to Utah by wagon with a number of his sons-in-law and their families and who had already assembled his teams and his people for the journey, it was proposed that a meeting should be held before his departure since a Sunday would intervene before the time set for beginning the western journey. Palmer and I only had one day in which to notify the people of such a meeting. Dodgers were printed, and with a bucket of paste and an armful of notices of the meeting, we placarded the town, giving notice of the meeting. It was a new feature of missionary work to me, and it was something of a trial for me to be found with paste pot and bills placarding the town. As the last bill was being stuck onto a telegraph pole by the wayside, I remarked aloud, "Whosoever is ashamed to acknowledge before my Father and all the holy angels . . ." As this was quoted, Brother Palmer spoke up and said, "I thought of that passage at every place we have stuck up a placard."

Sunday night came and the deserted parlor and kitchen of the Gibbs home, its furniture already packed in wagons to commence moving on Monday, was crowded. Here resulted an experience, chiefly for Elder Palmer, that became instructive to me. Saturday evening, the night before the meeting, had been spent with Brother Gibbs and his family in studying the scriptures and asking and answering questions. Brother Gibbs was a man of considerable experience in so-called Mormonism. He had been a member of the church at Nauvoo and was led away by the sophistry of a man who sought to build up a section of the church. His name was James J. Strang, whose following was called the Strangites. He had led the people to an island in Lake Michigan and there found what was called "The Kingdom." He claimed to have received authority from Joseph Smith for his work, but he was generally discredited and was shot down by his opponents. After this his following, among them Brother Gibbs, scattered, and the faction was broken up. Elders passing through Omaha had come in contact with Brother Gibbs, and he and his wife and one of two children had been baptized, but the greater number of his company preparing to go to Utah were not members of the church.

In this evening's conversation Brother Gibbs launched some of the ideas of Strang having to do with Genesis 49:24, speaking of Joseph, the son of Jacob of Israel. There it represents that the "archers have sorely grieved him, and shot at *him*, and hated him: But his bow abode in strength, and the arms of his hands were made strong by the hands of the mighty *God* of Jacob; (from thence *is* the shepherd, the stone of Israel)." According to Brother Gibbs's idea, this "stone" whence is the shepherd of Israel, etc., was interpreted to mean the "stone box" in which the Book of Mormon was found. This was greatly elaborated until that old Nephite stone receptacle of the Book of Mormon was given an importance which in no way could I be led to understand. But Elder Palmer seized upon it as a wonderful new thought and announced to the small company present that he would take that for a text the following evening and elucidate.

Before retiring that night to bed, Elder Palmer and I took a walk along the bank of the Mississippi, which flowed close to the home of the Gibbs, and I ventured to bring up this passage that had been the matter of conversation that evening. I inquired if Elder Palmer really intended to make this passage his text for the next evening's subject. He reavowed his intention to do so. I asked if he was not jumping at a conclusion rather suddenly. Had he not better consider it awhile before making it a text? I further ventured to say I could see no connection between this passage in Genesis and the Nephite stone box, and I did not believe that there was anything of special importance, any vital principles of the New Dispensation, associated with that old stone box in which had been concealed the Book of Mormon. I suggested that I thought it would be wise to give further consideration to it before accepting a hasty conclusion. "Oh no," said Elder Palmer. "There is no use waiting when the Holy Ghost discloses a truth to you; it can be accepted and used at once." I replied, "Yes doubtless, if the Holy Ghost discloses or gives it to you."

With this, the subject was allowed to rest until the time for meeting on Sunday evening occurred, and Elder Palmer true to his expressed determination read the text and started to make his connections and prove its significance in the message he and I had to deliver to the people. But soon his ideas began to run into confusion, and after about ten minutes of floundering and making nothing of what he was trying to say, he suddenly stopped. That left the rest of the meeting to be occupied by me, his younger and less experienced companion.

What to do I did not know, and my mind seemed all confusion when I arose to complete the meetings. Then I remembered Joseph Smith's story of how the New Dispensation opened, and taking that circumstance I related it in the most simple manner. As soon as my mind cleared and I got possession of myself, I felt a reaction from the congregation. It gave me confidence to feel that I had struck the right line of approach, and the people listened with rapt attention.

At the conclusion of the services, there was a long lingering of the people asking questions concerning this subject, and considerable time was spent in answering these questions. I elaborated some portion of the great events which Joseph Smith's first vision introduced and the consequences growing out of it. After the congregation took their departure, I observed the absence of Elder Palmer, and as soon as the house was cleared, I went out into the night and found him lying full length face down on the bank of the river and plucking up the grass in an agony of spirit. His discourse in which he felt he had failed had produced in him this agony of soul. I sought to comfort him and advised against the indulgence of great mental suffering. The next morning, much to my surprise, six adults of the Gibbs Company preparing to go west, who had not been members of the church, offered themselves for baptism. They were the first fruits of my missionary services. They were baptized in the Mississippi River, and in the afternoon the company of Mr. Gibbs made its departure for the west. What came of them or where they located, we never learned.

The experience of Elder Palmer was not the end of his dealing with the passage from Genesis alluded to above. He kept on for some years elaborating the idea of the connection between the old stone box containing the Book of Mormon and the opening of the New Dispensation. It resulted at last in the production of what was supposed to be a poetical effusion which linked together perhaps a half hundred of scriptural passages or allusions with the citation of them marked in the margin of the so-called poem. Elder Palmer by the time this publication was issued had become president of the Northern States Mission. The poem was published over his name and his position in the church.

This led to a rather marked embarrassment on the part of Elder George Q. Cannon, through those years the congressional representative of Utah Territory. Returning home at the close of one of the sessions of Congress, he was engaged in conversation with a number of gentlemen in the pullman car when some aspersion was made by one in the group about the ignorance of the Mormon community in Utah. President Cannon attempted the defense of his people, whereupon the gentlemen referred to drew forth from his pocket a folded copy of this two-paged alleged poetry and prefaced his remarks, "Mr. Cannon, you appoint men to preside over your various missions in the United States and elsewhere. You undoubtedly select those of the highest intelligence—men of education and understanding. Now I will ask you if this poetry by the president of the Northern States Mission is any evidence of anything but ignorance." And then this poem was read. Brother Cannon repeating this experience in a company of church authorities where I was present stated that he was never so embarrassed in defense of his people than on that occasion, and this doggerel miscalled poetry was the occasion of it.

It was while in Omaha at the residence of the Gibbs that an experience came to me which lasted through all my missionary appointments. This came in the form of a very vivid dream, which was as real as life itself. I found myself returned to Utah without a proper release. I seemed to be conscious of my whereabouts when crossing the Centerville school square in the center of the town. I was making my way to the home of my father-in-law, President William R. Smith. My wife for the time resided at her father's home. The locality was extremely vivid. I noted the houses and the orchards so well remembered until at last I came to the story-and-a-half adobe house where my wife and child were residing. Through the window, I saw Emeline Smith, the wife of President Smith, and heard her exclaim, as she hurriedly left the kitchen of the house, evidently to go in search of my wife. I even took advantage of a board which had been broken from the fence surrounding the old homestead, which enabled me to make a shortcut to the kitchen door without going on a quarter of a block to get to the gate entrance. As Mother Smith left the kitchen for her daughter's room in the home, I heard her exclaim, "Well, if there isn't Henry come back." The words produced a peculiar shock in me. Presently my wife Louisa came from the further part of the house and met me in the kitchen. Putting her arms about my neck, she said, "I'm so glad to see you, but O I do wish you had stayed and finished your mission."

By this time I was nearly collapsed. The dream included the retirement, and then during the night I seemed to wake up and begin to realize the seriousness of having returned home without an honorable release. I began to speculate upon what kind of excuse or story I could fix up to tell President John Taylor, who was a boyhood hero of mine. What should I tell that battle-scarred hero of a half hundred missions, and what excuse could I offer for having left the post? Then I resolved I would not make a report to President Taylor but would undertake to get back to my place in the mission field and then began contact with innumerable obstacles. Having no money, I would have to beat my way back, and this I did by stealing rides upon freight trains and getting into all sorts of adventures, including hunger. I felt disgust for my unwarranted desecration of my field of labor, and so it went on until I began to approach the familiar regions of Omaha, which is a center of early pioneer reminiscences for the church.

I finally noted the moonshine penetrating into the upper chamber to which Elder Palmer and I had been assigned in the Gibbs's home. The thought began to slowly dawn upon my troubled mind that the experience might not be real but that I had dreamed the whole thing through. As I lay there, I recalled that if this thing had been really only a vivid dream, then Elder Palmer ought to be in a bed across the room from me and would be a means of helping me decide whether the experience was a dream or a reality. Accordingly I slipped out of bed, crossed the room, and sure enough found Elder Palmer in his bed not only sleeping but snoring. This, I report, was the most welcome sound I ever heard. Dropping on my knees at the side of my own bed, I thanked God that I had only been dreaming and again thanked God of this experience of what would probably happen should I desert my post and return home without being honorably released.

So acute had been my suffering and so real a counterfeit presentiment to my mind that it stood as a permanent lesson through all of the years of my missionary service and a security against the likelihood of anything happening of that kind in my conscious life. And it never did. It was only necessary to recall the suffering endured in this dream to put any such thoughts from my mind thereafter.

Elder Palmer accompanied me to Sioux City, which was where my real work commenced. Brother Palmer had discovered out of his recollection that he had a distant relative living there and so had continued his companionship with me up to that point. He only remained, however, a few days, and I was left on my own. It was about the time that I realized that I was truly without purse and scrip, all the money I had brought with me having been expended. But occasionally the way was marvelously opened, and I began the missionary experience of an elder in my church. The means came into my hands through a gift, and I was able to hire halls, print notices in the newspaper, and was excessively active through all this region of country.

Some months previously Ann Eliza Webb, reported as the nineteenth wife of President Brigham Young, had recently been in Sioux City and had poisoned the minds of the people there through public meetings held in sectarian churches. As a result only a very limited hearing could be obtained in the city. However, and just before the departure of Elder Palmer, a vacant store room in one of the largest buildings was engaged in which to hold meetings. An improvised pulpit was made out of an empty dry goods box, and planking obtained about the building provided the temporary seating of the hall. Several successful meetings were held. The arrangement in the long room brought the improvised stand or pulpit close to a rear door, and as I, following Elder Palmer, made a few remarks, there came a furious assault upon this door close to the speaker. Brick bats and what-not were hurled at it, and the door stood likely to be crashed through. My patience was too short for this kind of treatment, and it produced rather emphatic denunciations of it. In fact at one of these crashes which had interrupted me several times, I said, "D-- the door." Fortunately, however, this was not heard by the congregation, and I proceeded for some time with the unfolding of my message in that city. Then a mob assembled in front of the store room and crashed the windows with brick bats and clubs, and they appeared to be fixing an entrance to the meeting place. The police of Sioux City, however, got busy and soon dispersed the crowd. The rest of our activity in the neighborhood was carried on in the country surrounding Sioux City.

As no permanent opening occurred, however, the selection of another center took place, and such work as visiting homes and obtaining preaching places went on. As a sample merely of this work, I recite the following circumstances. The incident occurred in Wright County of Iowa, a short distance from Sioux City. I had taken the map of the state of Iowa and spread it out before me, following prayer for direction in the selection of the next place of a hoped-for opening. This resulted in the selection of the town of Rockwell, perhaps twenty-five miles north of Sioux City. Rockwell proved to be a town of some 1,500 or 1,800 inhabitants. Quite a number of stores of ordinary dimensions were found in such a town, where a fairly good business was transacted in the reception of the grains raised by the farmers for the exchange of goods of a great variety.

Among the public buildings of the town was a fine two-story school-house and a Union churchhouse built by the three Christian denominations represented in the place—Methodist, Baptist, and Congregationalist. Application was made to a Mr. Howard, the directing trustee of the school building, asking for the use of it in which to hold religious service. Mr. Howard was an infidel and readily gave his consent to the use of the schoolhouse, but the head teacher who was a Methodist took it upon himself at the close of the day's school to lock the door and carry off the key. He was heard to remark that he did not propose to see his school room used by a Mormon to preach in. As night was falling, I went to the house only to find it locked, but quite a number of people had gathered about the doors seeking admission. When it was found locked and the opposition of the head teacher learned, a party of young men called upon me to see if they might not make application to Mr. Howard to take the door from its hinges. To this I gave my consent, and Mr. Howard when waited upon by the aforesaid group of young men said that if the key could not be found, they were at liberty to take the door down. But by the time this party had returned, someone had found another key in possession of one of the janitors. The room was crowded, and I had good liberty of the spirit. Before dismissing the meeting, I gave out an appointment for the nearest evening. I also told the congregation that I was without purse or scrip and would regard it as a great kindness if someone present would give me lodging.

The people, however, filed out of the hall until all had gone save one old gentlemen, whom I contacted during the afternoon and with whom I had had a somewhat extended conversation. This man stopped after the retirement of the congregation to ask some questions, and the conversation was extended until eleven o'clock. "Where are you going to stay tonight?" asked the old gentlemen.

I answered, "I don't know. Didn't you hear me tell the people that I was without purse or scrip? That means without money."

"Then you won't stop at a hotel?"

"I reckon not," I replied. "It generally takes money to stop at a hotel."

The old gentleman said, "Well, that's too bad, but it's late, and I must be getting home. Goodnight."

After the man's departure, there was nothing for me to do but to commit myself to the Lord in prayer, make a pillow of a valise, and lie down to such pleasant dreams as might come. At early dawn I was astir and left the schoolhouse. Wandering out of town a short distance, I found myself behind a swale of prairie. Here I asked the Lord to open the way before me and direct me to a place where I could obtain lodgings during my stay in the neighborhood. On the way back to town, I noticed a large white farmhouse nearly surrounded by poplar trees. The spirit said that this was the place, and I started for it, entering the premises at a double gate. I overtook some men wheeling a large dressed hog from the direction of the barn towards the house. I asked the name of the person owning the place and where he could be found. One of the group answered that he was the proprietor. He owned the place, said he, and his name was Trapp. "What can I do for you?" He was then told by me that I was a servant of the Lord and wanted to stay in this neighborhood to present the gospel to the people of the town and vicinity and then: "Will you provide me food and lodging for about two weeks?" This request was as much a surprise to me, since no such thought had entered my mind until the moment of giving voice to it. Mr. Trapp also seemed somewhat astonished at the largeness of the order, but he finally answered in the affirmative.

It was singular that although I remained the full two weeks, I found no other place at which to obtain either food or lodging, and many wild rumors were set afloat misrepresenting both my people and mission. It was hinted that Mr. Trapp would likely regret his hospitality to the Mormon missionary, when his daughter, a very intelligent young lady just home from school, would likely be run off with to Utah—for which, of course, there was not the least likelihood or intention. Again it was rumored that I was the husband of four wives and about twenty children. This rumor had gone to the ears of Mrs. Trapp, and as I took my seat at the breakfast table that particular morning, I observed a coldness of this lady at whose right I had sat at the table through several days. After an awkward silence of some minutes, I at last turned to Mrs. Trapp and politely said: "Mrs. Trapp, what is the matter? What is troubling you?" And then she exploded and said, "Well, you might as well know that it is rumored in the village and neighborhood that you have boasted that you have four wives and at least twenty children, and I think that is too bad." Then there was silence for the space of I know not how long, but at last I mildly said, "Mrs. Trapp, don't you think that makes up rather a patriarchal family too large for so young a man as myself?" Whereupon the absurdity of the whole thing seemed to be so apparent that she broke out laughing, and good fellowship and pleasant relationship immediately followed. Nothing like that occurred again. In all, seven public meetings were held during the two weeks. But there being no prospects of a permanent field of labor being opened, I took my departure for a new center of operations.

I was led eastward. Here it may be well to explain that I had formed the habit, when scanning my field of labor, to spread out the map of Iowa before me. Seeking divine guidance through prayer, I indicated on the map the place to which I would next remove. This method at this time brought me to a district known as West Fork in Cerro Gordo County. A few miles away (ten or twelve) was the railroad and post office town called Sheffield. After holding several meetings in the schoolhouse at West Fork, I went to Sheffield to get my mail and remained in that town all night. During the night, it rained—no it poured down—and there seemed to be no reserve to it. If such had occurred in the Southern States, the people would have called it a "stump piler and gully washer." In this part of Iowa, really the lake region of the northern part of the state, there were many unbelievers in the Bible. They were especially skeptical about Noah's flood. But after that night's rain, their doubts began to grow weaker; they admitted Noah's flood was a possibility. On the flood question, they stood about seven to eight after that storm.

The following day I felt that I must return to West Fork, as there was an appointment out to preach tonight. All the creeks were swollen, and in every swale of the prairie, I found a muddy view of Cedar River, the main stream of the district. It had overflowed its banks. As I approached the river, a portion of the bridge could be seen, and I hoped that the bridge over the main flood water would be intact. I waded in backwater crotch-deep for several hundred yards before reaching that part of the approach to the bridge above water. On getting to this point, I found that the bridge had been torn away by the tumultuous flood, which now swept with angry rush between the bare abutments. What was to be done was the question. Should I return to Sheffield and cross again on the streams I had waded through all the day and miss filling my appointment? Or should I attempt to cross the vicious river and hold a meeting? The latter was decided upon.

On the lower sides of the abutment on which I stood, I noticed three two-inch planks. It occurred to me that if they were on the upper side of the abutment, I might stand on them. Then by giving a vigorous push towards the opposite shore, the stream would drift me over to the other bank. The planks were therefore carried to the upper side of the approach. I moored two of them in the still backwater, and my valise, books, papers, and clothing were then placed on two of the planks held together by my feet. The lighter of the three planks was used as a push car, and the improvised narrow raft of the two planks was headed for the opposite bank. At the point I gave the "mighty push" which was to carry me to the other shore. I soon learned that my plans began sinking into the water under the pressure of the push, and as the plank push car was heavy, I soon had to drop it about midway across. Here too I encountered the full force of the turbulent stream, and the planks, instead of moving sidewise of the stream, headed downward. It looked as if I was starting for the Gulf of Mexico.

The banks of the stream were gliding by at a tremendous rate, I thought, but I had no time to take note of the beauty, which perhaps adorned them. Wild flowers in every variety and in large profusion may have clothed the rolling prairie in a garment of many colors, but I had no time to admire them. The sweet songsters of nature may have made the stillness glad with their melodies, but I had no time to listen. The two planks on which I was standing manifested a disposition to separate, and it was all I could do to keep them together by holding them in that position with my cramped feet. They were awfully particular as to the amount of weight each should carry. If I happened to bear down a little more on one than on the other, it would begin to sink. I could boast for once that I was a very evenly balanced young man.

The stream appeared mad with delight in having me in its power. It played many pranks with my hopes and fears. I would be drifting towards the bank which I hoped to reach, and the thought of soon reaching "terra firma" would bring happy anticipations. Then I would be swirling out of them to the middle of the current. At last I came around the bend of the river and saw a large part of the bridge which had been carried away lodged in a growth of willow saplings. Towards this the plank drifted. As soon as I was near enough to the ruins of the bridge, I threw my valise on the drift, plunged towards it myself, and missed it. But a few rapid strokes brought me within reach. It was an easy matter from the drift of the bridge to reach the shore by wading several score yards through backwater, which was not, at least in any place I waded, more than neck deep. I came out on the right side of the river, opposite that from which I started. After wringing the water out of my clothing, I continued the journey feeling grateful that I had escaped so easily from an unpleasant situation.

As is usual here, we elders preached the gospel. The doctrine advanced in the meetings became for a time the absorbing theme of conversation throughout the neighborhood. In this case, it forced itself upon the attention of three ministers who resided in the district of West Fork, and during my brief absence at the post office town of Sheffield, a plot had been devised to attend my next meeting. As these ministers worded their intention, they would "tie up the young Mormon preacher" by submitting questions, etc., etc. I had adopted the practice of giving my hearers an opportunity of proposing questions at the close of each meeting on the subjects treated, and these ministers hearing of this said that would be their opportunity to expose Mormonism generally. Everywhere they went, they boasted of this intention. My friends, when I arrived in the neighborhood, disclosed the plans of the ministers, so at the evening meeting I knew what to expect.

That night the schoolhouse was crowded, not even standing room for all who came. The ministers were there and occupied the front seat facing the teacher's desk, from which I spoke as from a pulpit. The subject of the discourse was "The Affirmation that a Man must Be Called of God by Prophecy and the Laying on of Hands by Those in Authority to Preach the Gospel and Administer in the Ordinances Thereof." This theme was treated at some length, and the ministers on the front row were ready with their pencils to make notes. I stepped from behind the desk and stood in front of them, addressing them as a lawyer might a jury. I record that the spirit of the Lord was with me and loosened my tongue, and soon the ministers became tired of taking notes. It was proved from Holy Writ that God had always called men by prophecy and revelation when he sent forth men to administer the gospel of salvation. Then I turned to my message that God had again spoken from heaven and had called men by his own voice to be prophets and apostles and commissioned them to minister in things "pertaining to God." I myself was sent to them by that authority to call upon them to repent of their sins and return unto the Lord.

At the close of the remarks, the congregation arose and were dismissed. Then the announcement was made that the audience had the liberty to submit questions. All eyes were turned upon the ministers. They shifted uneasily in their seats, evidently uncomfortable. For them the supreme opportunity had come. They exchanged glances with each other and then settled back in their seats in a way which seemed to indicate that they had nothing to offer. Perfect silence was retained for perhaps ten minutes. Then a lady arose, who in some way was connected with this group of ministers. She spoke of my talents and announced that she intended to pray for me and ask that God would direct me to the real service of mankind through some of the orthodox churches. I thanked her for her interest in my welfare. Then again silence. At last some man arose in the rear of the audience saying, "I guess we can go home now." "Yes," I replied. "I am through for this evening unless some persons have questions that they wish to ask." As none was asked, the people filed slowly out of the house, the ministers being among the first to leave. Evidently they had changed their minds about "tying up the young Mormon." Men do sometimes change their minds.

Next day they were found visiting the members of their respective flocks, advising them not to encourage the Mormon meetings by their presence. By such methods, interest in my mission began to wane in the West Fork district, and I soon had to give attention to finding another field of labor. Thereby hangs a very remarkable incident in my missionary service.

One other incident happened in closing up the work in the West Fork neighborhood. While in the vicinity I had made my home with a very generous-minded farmer by the name of Slade–he and his family members of the Catholic church. One evening at the schoolhouse where I delivered a discourse, Mr. Slade was unfastening his team from the tie-rail at the side of the schoolhouse. Some genius for persecution stepped up silently behind me and very quietly turned a large dipper of cold water down my neck and back. If the wretch had only known how I shrank from contact from cool water, he would have had the satisfaction of knowing that he had annoyed me extremely, but I never moved, never even turned around to give the fellow opportunity of knowing that he had made me very uncomfortable. By this time Mr. Slade had driven his wagon to the front stoop of the schoolhouse, and I climbed in and was driven to the latter's home. While this incident of the dipper of cold water was kept to myself, someone else must have seen the act. In a day or two the local paper took the perpetrator of it, without giving his name, severely to task for such contemptuous treatment practiced upon a gentlemen of my evident standing.

The day following the meeting, the lady of the evening before who promised to pray for me called at the home of Mr. Slade, the Catholic, and we had a long conversation. I felt that she had kept her promise to pray for me but experienced no result or change of heart in consequence thereof.

CHAPTER 12.

The Rockford Incident

My opportunity for extending the field of labor in the vicinity appeared to be closed, and, growing restless, I decided to seek a new field. The map was again extended before me, and I gave serious consideration to a number of small towns, which are characteristic of the state of Iowa, but I seemed not to get the usual response. At last, however, using my own judgment in the matter instead of any inspiration that came, I selected Mason City, near the center of Cerro Gordo County, as being the most likely place for opening the work.

At that time Mason City was the largest town in that northern section of the state of Iowa, and I informed the Slade family of my intention to move and to try to find an opening in Mason City. As soon as this became known, the Slade family, following perhaps their Catholic custom with their priests, each seemed to arrange to give me a piece of silver money to help me on my journey. This very naturally I took as a good omen. Retiring on that day I made arrangements for Mr. Slade to carry me to the next railroad station, as the generosity of the Slade family had made it possible for me to pay railroad fare to the point designated for the new opening. As long as I had stayed at the family of the Slades, I had occupied a lounge, transferrable to a bed, in the parlor or sitting room of the home, and this night I slept soundly, due perhaps to a hopeful contented mind.

Waking as the day was dawning, I found myself with my face turned closely to the wall and somewhat cramped from lying in one position for several hours. Stretching, I turned over on my opposite side, bringing my face toward the spacious sitting room, and to my astonishment as I looked down upon the carpet, I saw the bare feet of some personage. Gradually looking up until the whole figure was before me, I saw standing there a young man, beardless, light complexioned. I noticed beautiful wavy hair, tastefully waved about a handsome face. This personage was truly noble in his bearing, erect, but not stiff—a graceful, subtle pose, which seemed quiet and native to him. I looked upon him for some moments, the fear passing and a beautiful feeling of confidence and pleasure clothing the circumstance. Then the youth bent forward smiling and said in a voice, the tenderness and beauty of which can never be forgotten: "You are called to Rockford." Then gradually the vision vanished.

Immediately arising and dressing, I walked out in the open prairie, which at that time existed in Iowa. This was a sparsely settled region, and there was still government land to be obtained by preemption or home-steading. There was a large growth of grass covering the plain, plentifully sprinkled with great varieties of wild flowers, and the dew was heavy, heavy enough for me to get wet feet as I walked about. Returning to Mr. Slade's house in time for breakfast, after which I was to start for Mason City, I found the family taking their seats about the table, and I took what had become my usual place. I inquired if Mr. Slade knew a place called Rockford. He answered that he had never heard of it. Neither had any of the family. Before the breakfast was finished, a man, whom Mr. Slade had employed a few days before to herd the milk stock of the farmers in the neighborhood out on the open and uncleared prairie and to bring them in and distribute them to the several ranges to which they belonged, came in to his breakfast. The question if he knew anything about Rockford was put to him. He stated, yes, that he did. It was the home of his parents, and he himself had lived there the greater part of his youthful life.

Meantime there had been passing through my mind the probable effect on the Slade family and others of my friends in the neighborhood who had learned that I intended moving to Mason City. It presented a case of vacillation of uncertainty and instability in my plans, and this might negatively affect me in the minds of these friends. This I so allowed to influence my judgment that I finally decided to adhere to my plan to go to Mason City and set aside the direction that I had received from this supernatural direction—a thing, which I admit, was very unusual. And so without saying anything to the family of what I had experienced as I awoke that morning, I was taken to the railroad station and went to Mason City. After paying for my railway fare, I arrived shortly after noon and resolved not to expend this money for food but keep it for lodging should an emergency arise.

Immediately I called upon the several ministers of Mason City and tried to get the use of one of their churches in which to begin my mission work, but each very sternly refused to open his church for such a purpose. I next inquired for the trustee of schoolhouses within the city and made applica-tion to several of these for the use of the schoolhouses of which they were directors, but not one would give me any hope that I could get any of these buildings for this purpose. By the time night had fallen, I had missed supper but found a cheap lodging house where I could get a bed for my left-over half dollar. Early in the morning I resumed my inquiry for some hall but failed altogether. Seeing the way so hopelessly closed against me, I resolved to go out into the country where I had nearly always been successful in obtaining the use of schoolhouses for my purpose.

I walked out eastward of Mason City, following a country road. I left the city about eleven o'clock, and as it was in the month of August, the sun poured down pitilessly upon me. Having moved my headquarters from Mr.

Slade's, I had with me my grip stocked with all my books and clothing. It was decidedly heavy and added to the burden of traveling about. Between twelve and one o'clock, I saw on the right of my road an apparently well kept schoolhouse and on the opposite side of the road on a swale of the prairie country an elaborate farm house, barns, stacks of grain, etc., looking very prosperous. To this house I directed my footsteps to make inquiry that would locate the responsible trustee for this schoolhouse.

As I was bidden to enter the main room of the building, which in this instance proved to be the dining room, I saw a company of men just drawing up their chairs to a bountifully supplied table, and it passed through my mind that it would be a fine thing for the farm owner to invite me to dinner. There was certainly a good opportunity for a feast, for the table was literally burdened with good things to eat and in great abundance. It seemed so at least to me, who in addition to the two meals I had missed the day before had also missed breakfast, and this abstinence with a general husky physique and whetted appetite made the prospect of dinner look good.

However, I had scarcely closed the door behind me when the farmer at the head of the table demanded to know what he could do for me. I had formed the habit of carrying with me the official letter of recommendation from the First Presidency and using it as a credential. I therefore unfolded this letter and approached the man that had spoken to me. He had no sooner glanced at it when he at least surmised its origin and so with very cold severe tones, he said: "Then you're a Mormon." I answered in the affirmative. "All right," said the man, who was the proprietor of the farmhouse with all its appurtenances, "the sooner you get out of my house the better."

This was rather rough treatment, and I began forming in my mind resentment of it. I explained, not knowing the name of the owner, that I had come to call upon this man to learn the whereabouts of the trustee of the adjacent schoolhouse. I had come in this neighborhood to preach the gospel of Jesus Christ and had an important message to preach to the people and to the man of the house included. "Of course," I said, "you have the right and liberty to reject me and drive me from your house, but I came to you with a message which God has sent into the world and would like to have had an opportunity to deliver it to you." The attention of all his working force, perhaps a dozen men, were very attentive during this conversation. Again he roughly ordered me to leave his house, and again he was told: of course, it was his right to reject me and my message, but, I said, with due solemnity, "You might know that you this day rejected one sent of God to you. I wish you gentlemen good day." And so I departed–but I confess with something of a heavy heart.

Back to the main road, I continued my journey eastward. A mile or so distant from the house, I passed a large spring of clear water sending forth a generous stream into a meadow. I remembered the Lord's injunction which directs that: "He who receives you not, go away from him alone by yourselves and cleanse your feet even with water, pure water, whether in heat or in cold and bear testimony of it unto your father which is in heaven and return not again unto that man. And in whatsoever village or city you enter, so likewise" (D&C 84:92-3). Climbing through the fence I stripped my feet and washed them in witness against this man and house for the rejection of me. This I recount as the only instance when I felt at liberty to attend to this ordinance of the washing of feet against one who had rejected me. I never returned to the house and never knew what became of it, but I left my testimony thus registered according to the commandments of the Lord.

This done I continued my journey eastward until the middle of the afternoon, suffering greatly from depression of spirits and weak from my long abstinence from food. Late in the afternoon, however, I passed a homesteader's shack and called for a drink of water. The inhabitants of the shack were a young couple making an effort to establish a farm and home. About the time I reached the boarded shanty, the young man drove in with his sweating plow team from the field, and his good wife remarked that I seemed weary and could she do anything for me. Whereupon I confessed my hunger, and she brought to me a ham sandwich, which was very palatable food. The pair regretted that they could not invite me to stay for the night. They pointed out at a distance of two or three miles the outer edges of a town and said doubtless I would be able to find lodgings there. Wishing my kindly host goodbye and from my heart leaving a blessing with them, I dropped on and shortly reached the town which must have constituted about one hundred houses or more.

Again I resumed my inquiry for those having charge of the schoolhouse in the town and was informed that the directing trustee lived a mile or two outside of the town, down the river, for the town stood on the river's bank. This was the Bur River which flows into Shell Rock River, thence on enlarging until it flows into the Mississippi. A scant two miles from the town, I came to the residence of the directing trustee, who, however, refused to grant the use of the schoolhouse for a Mormon meeting. He said that he doubted very much if the people of the district would be pleased with his granting such liberty. By this time darkness had settled over the country, and I asked if I might have lodgings with him that night. This request also the man refused to grant but said that back towards the town not far from the road there lived an infidel who had the reputation for hospitality. Perhaps he might be willing to afford lodgings to me.

This suggestion was followed and the infidel called upon. Many times I had found that this class of citizens was often willing to accord hospitality to me, because of the opposed antagonism which they felt must exist in the Mormon representatives towards the orthodox Christianity. This man's house was situated some quarter of a mile from the main road. He had traveled back in a meadow. As I entered the door which stood open, I could see in the living room a very large man stretched upon a couch. I approached into the middle of the room. The man hearing me sat up, apparently dazed from being awakened from an early sleep, and demanded what he could do for me. I stated my mission, referred to my possessing credentials for my standing in the community from which I came, and announced my desire to obtain lodgings for the night. This was all listened to in solemn silence, and at the end the man said, "On northward of here, if you saw the road, you will find a town, and in the town there is a hotel or tavern, and if you have money, you perhaps will find lodgings there. I will not keep you."

Nothing to do but to return to the road I had left a short time before. This time I took a direct course to the road passing through the meadow now wet with evening dew, and as I walked I soliloquized, "Well, it looks as if I might spend one night more on the open prairie." I began looking for a place where I could lie down, but then the thought came, "This man had refused me lodgings in his house. I will see him hanged before I will sleep in his meadow." So I went onward and climbed over the fence into the road which wound along beside the river. Something over a hundred yards along the road, I found a place which perhaps would be as good as any, and here taking my valise for a pillow, I stretched out for the night. Soon I discovered that the grass was full of spiders and bugs. Taking from my grip a large handkerchief, I wound it around my head, and through the night fought with crickets and other vermin for a little rest.

Towards morning I must have dozed off into a fitful sleep, for when I next became conscious, the sun was struggling through the mist to shine in my face. Rising to a sitting posture, my knees drawn up and hands over my knees, I began to review my experience of the past few days and then commented, "Well, this is a pretty hard way it seems to me to serve the Lord." Just then, as if in answer to my comment, the severe and clear reproving voice, evidently of the one who had visited me in the living room of Mr. Slade, spoke out, *"You were told to go to Rockford."* Rising like lightning I turned in the direction of the voice and cried out aloud: *"Then to Rockford I will go."*

The message received shed a flood of light upon my experience during the past few days. I found every door closed to me because I was not following the directions I had received. I resolved therefore to return to Mason City and thence back to Mr. Slade's, whence I had started to carry out my self-willed plans. About noon I reached the homesteader's shack that I had visited on the evening before and this time was served with a glass of buttermilk and a piece of dry bread, which an exceptional appetite made extremely palatable. Thence I walked on and reached Mason City, where letters that Mr. Slade had forwarded to me from Utah were found awaiting me. One was a letter from my wife containing a $5.00 bill, which a brother about a week before had given to her on meeting her in the streets of Centerville village. He had made inquiry as to my welfare. After reporting to him, he peeled from a roll of bills $5.00 and handed it to her to "send to Henry—It may be of use to him in a crisis." And so it had come just in the nick of time, for it enabled me to get something of a square meal and at the same time buy railway fare back to the Slade neighborhood. I took the train that afternoon and by eight o'clock at night reached the Slade home. The whole family seemed to be anxious to know what had happened that I returned so soon. I only answered that I had come back to make a fresh start and to really go where I was sent, which was Rockford.

Meantime I received word that Hyrum Jensen of Salina, Utah, had been directed by the authorities to connect with me and become my traveling companion. Elder Jensen was a young man who had left upon a mission at the same time I did and who had gone into Minnesota. I had already written to Elder Jensen to make his way to the residence of Mr. Slade in Cerro Gordo County and was expecting him to arrive any day. Following the day of my arrival at Mr. Slade's, I left word for Elder Jensen to remain at Slade's until I should return and then I started for Rockford. In the course of two or three days I arrived there. It was located in Floyd County. Just how to proceed, being without money, I did not know but called upon the proprietor of a public hall used for lecture purposes, etc., and engaged it for two public lectures the following Sunday. Also I called upon the county newspaper published in the place, *The Rockford Revelle,* and left an advertisement of the time and place of the meetings to be held the following Sunday.

This time I made a forced march back to the Slade home, where sure enough I found Elder Hyrum Jensen had arrived. We just had about time to return to Rockford to hold the meetings arranged for. These arrangements, the hiring of the Leigh Hall and advertising in *The Rockford Revelle,* had been undertaken in the belief that Brother Hyrum Jensen would have some money with him, as he had left home with several hundred dollars, but he was by this time as literally without purse and scrip as I was. How the obligation was to be met, of course, we could not surmise. Anyway we started for Rockford in the hope that something would happen to make it possible to fill these engagements.

Approaching Rockford on the Saturday afternoon preceding the Sunday of the appointments, I called attention to the fact based upon my experiences that it was easier to find lodgings among the farmers outside the towns than among the people of the towns. Hence I suggested that we find lodgings a few miles out of Rockford and then make an early journey on Sunday morning to the place of our appointments. It was also agreed by us, since this was our first journey together, that we would alternate in asking for places to stop at and thus divide that rather disagreeable part of our labors. We acted plum foolishly dragging along on the road. When I would suggest some house we were passing as a likely looking place to which to make application, Brother Jensen would have a weak heart and suggest that we pass it up. Then when it was my turn to ask for lodgings and Elder Jensen would suggest a likely looking place, I got cold feet and lacked the heart to go and make the request.

Thus it went on through Saturday afternoon until finally we found ourselves in Rockford, passing the railroad station of the town and starting down the main street. By this time evening was approaching, and I was frankly out of patience, mostly with myself and my companion at the childish way we had acted during the afternoon. While fretful under that impatience, I said crossly to Elder Jensen, "I think what we want, Jensen, is for somebody to note us walking down this street and come out of their house and not only invite us in, but propose to drag us into their homes to lodgings. Then I doubt very much if we would have sense enough to go with them even at such circumstances." Thus relieved of an impatient gesture, we resumed our journey down the sparsely settled end of the main street of Rockford and began approaching the business center of it.

Just then on the same side of the walk and coming toward us was a rather rotund happy-go-lucky looking sort of a fellow with his hat tilted on the back of his head and in his shirt sleeves. He was so rotund and fat that he seemed almost to waddle along towards us and, when he reached us, stopped suddenly and said, "Well, men, what train did you come on?" As there was no train due at that time of the day and we had just passed the railway station, I said, "If you were a little further west, I would perhaps tell you that we had just come in on Walker's train." That went over his head as he failed to find in the statement an account of our having come into town on foot. Then I explained that we were the two Mormon elders who had an appointment to fill in Leigh Hall the next day, and we had come to town to fill the appointment. "O," he said, "is that so? Well where are you going to stay tonight?" He was informed that was one of the problems not yet solved. We were without purse or scrip and preaching that way, which meant without money, and we had not yet found a place at which to lodge. Turning on his heel he pointed down the street to a large white building with a board running along the comb of the roof and printed on it was Beebe's Hotel, Rockford. "So you see that sign up there?" he asked. I was told it was plain to be seen. "Well," said he, "that is my hotel. Go there and put up." Without further word of explanation, he continued his walk in the direction of the railway station.

I looked at Brother Jensen. Elder Jensen looked at me. Shaking my head solemnly, I said, "I don't know whether I like that or not. It may be a trap to get us to run a bill there, and if we can't pay it, as certainly we can't, then we would be in his clutches." Elder Jensen said, "I guess we hadn't better go." Then a light flashed through the discussion. "Hyrum," I cried, "its happened, I tell you; it's happened. The thing which we a moment ago thought impossible has happened. Someone has come out on the sidewalk, stopped us, invited us to lodgings, and here we stand discussing whether we had better accept it or not. I told you not five minutes ago," I went on, "that if anyone should come on the sidewalk, confront us, and invite us to lodge, I doubt if we had sense enough to accept the offer. Here it all is and here we stand. Now, Hyrum, banish that woebegone look of yours, and let's go to that hotel and act as if we owned it, register, get supper, stay all night, and as long thereafter as the man will allow us to."

Accordingly we raised our heads and in a brisk walk were soon at the hotel and registered. It was an old-fashioned hotel. It had on the ground floor a common wash house, with basins strung around the wall and roller towels which from their appearance had been altogether too popular. But we were soon washed and preparing to go into the dining room, when the proprietor who had returned passed through the wash room, saying in his good-natured way, "Hello, boys. I see you are getting ready for supper." We told him we were ready, and just then the gong sounded and we were hungry enough to enjoy anything spread before us. We partook of food and had a long evening in which to make preparation for the next day's meeting.

Refreshed by baths and a change to clean clothing, we went to the hall and found it well filled with congregation, all curiosity. The meeting began with a brief talk from Elder Jensen, after which I spoke and rather unexpectedly drifted into the consideration of Judah's place in this New Dispensation. I referred to many prophecies. All tended to prove that God had not forsaken Judah and had for him a prominent part in this New Dispensation he was introducing to the earth. While the gospel was first to be preached in this New Dispensation to the Gentiles, lo afterwards it was to go to the Jews. Sometimes that name was used for the symbol of all the tribes of Israel. There was a strange quiet in the room while these descriptions of Judah's place in Israel were named. While no Jews were discovered to be in the congregation, it was learned afterwards that quite a large part of the congregation were of the House of Judah. In the afternoon the theme was discussed and very much enlarged upon, and again I felt the strange presence of an unaccountable silence.

With the dismissal of the meeting in the afternoon came the question of settling for the hall and also for the advertisement of the meeting. The situation was explained to the audience, but they paid no heed to it. No one volunteered to make the payment of these expenses. Meanwhile the proprietor of the hall was pulling down the windows and presently approached with a financial look in his eye. Elder Jensen was all a flutter and excitedly asked, "What will we do, what will we do?" "Well," I replied, "the thing to do will be to hire this hall for next Sunday, and we will have to be quick about it so as to notify the people before they all get out." Attention was called to the large attendance and interest manifested, and if he would consent to it, the proprietor was told that we would settle with him after next Sunday's meeting. He said, "Well, I reckon it will be all right, but we pay as we go." "O do you," I said, "well we pay when we get through." With that I sprang upon a chair and called the attention to all those remaining in the hall of the intention to hold a meeting in this same hall a week from that time. Then I rushed to the head of the stairs, called to all those that were slowly withdrawing from the hall, and gave out the notice. I asked them to pass the word on to those who had reached the sidewalk, and I felt relieved from an awkward situation.

There seemed to be little reaction on the part of the people to these successful public meetings, but the day following as I was going down main street of the town, a rather impressive-looking man stopped out on the sidewalk and with speech and action indicated that he was a Jew. He urged me to come into the store, whereupon the gentleman stated that he had attended both the meetings the day before and had become interested in the prophecies that had been referred to regarding Judah, some of which were new to him. He expressed a desire to compare the translation used with his Hebrew books to see if the translation agreed with the Hebrew. With this I was invited to go into the library, where there was a fine collection of books written in large character in the Hebrew language and each of the Books of Moses and also the Book of the Prophecies were bound separately. I reread the passages of the day before, and these were identified in the Hebrew books.

The investigation lasted about three hours, during which time the clothing merchant's brother, a skeptic by the way, entered and added somewhat in verifying the translations. He could not refrain, however, from passing his own unbelief concerning these prophecies relating to Judah. He had been in Palestine, was acquainted with the physical nature of the country, and held other doubtful views respecting the inability of the land of Palestine to sustain the very large population of the people in that land as described in ancient Jewish literature. He said that it was impossible as to the past and would be equally impossible for such a population to be sustained in the Promised Land. The country was a desert, and the resources for such a looked-for population were simply ridiculous. At this point the elder brother stepped to the middle of the room and bore a testimony to the land being sufficient for all that was said of it in the past to sustain all the people. He was also fervent in testimony that when the blessing of the Lord turned upon the land and upon the people, it would again be a land flowing with milk and honey and plenty for the sustenance of the millions to be gathered there. To that I added my own testimony relative to my confidence in God to make the land equal to the burden to be put upon it under his blessing. The infidel Jew was silenced.

It was a pleasant almost half day that I enjoyed at this meeting, and I obtained impressions and vivid testimony concerning the Jews, which ever afterwards stayed with me—especially about the part that they would take in the New Dispensation, the Restoration of Israel, and the redemption of Jerusalem as a holy city for their near future habitat. Now after more than fifty-two years from that event, I can refer my intense interest in Judah and the part that Judah will take in the New Dispensation to that circumstance of contact with this inspiring member of the Jewish race. From that time commenced my gathering and preserving utterances of Jews concerning the Christ and the redemption of the race. But I did not realize at that time that there was to be a future for me in contact with Judah, nor did I appreciate all that which this contact would mean in fixing in my mind undying interest in Judah. Indeed it never completely rushed through my mind how important this contact was until it was brought forth from the press fifty-two years later in my book, *Rasha, the Jew*. It was that book and what led immediately to its publication that joined together the closing as well as the beginning of this incident. It completed the electrical circle that made me conscious that for fifty-two years I had been subconsciously working on the problem of Judah and his connection with the New Dispensation of the Gospel. Those who are anxious to understand how important this was in my life mission will be able to discern it from the scope of this column completed in December 1932.

Meantime the problems of how to meet the payment for the hall and the indebtedness to *The Rockford Revelle* were pressing for solution. On Tuesday morning following the first Sabbath meetings in this hall, the proprietor of the hotel introduced us to a farmer who had come into the town and was looking for help to harvest his fast ripening wheat fields, for it was by now mid-July. A bargain was struck between us and this Mr. Darling to engage from ten days to two weeks in harvesting his fields, and accordingly we went to his home and prosperous farm. The machine he used was a McCormick harvester. The cut grain rolled on its platform as the machine was driven around the fields, and the bundles were dropped off at convenient distances to help in putting the grain in sacks. Mr. Darling's family was an interesting group—his wife, two girls, one of which was a school teacher. Both had come home for the harvest time. One drove the harvester. This circumstance enabled us to replenish our vacant purses, and by the next Sunday we were ready to settle for the hall, for the paper advertising, our hotel bill for two days, with a small balance over to help us on our way.

While following our peregrinations in that section of Iowa, Cerro Cordo County, and adjoining counties, we made the acquaintance of a Mr. Stevenson, who represented himself as profoundly interested in Joseph Smith and the New Dispensation of the Gospel, which under God he had founded. But he proved to be a member of what was called the Reorganized Church of Latter Day Saints, the leader of which was the eldest son of

Joseph Smith, the prophet. We frequently came across people of this organization. Mr. Stevenson was a prosperous retired farmer and had turned the management of his home and farm over to the care of a son, recently married, who with his new wife lived at the old homestead. Mr. Stevenson invited us, if we came into his neighborhood, to be sure and call upon him, and he would extend the courtesy of his home to us. It happened a few weeks later that we made our way to his house on a Sunday morning in a cold drizzling rain that had saturated us. The night previous to this we had slept upon the floor of the schoolhouse, where we had given out an appointment for preaching, but the people did not come on account of the rain. Mr. Stevenson agreeable with his promise received us cordially, but as much cannot be said for his family at this time.

A series of protracted meetings under the direction of a "United Brethren" persuasion was being held. A young minister recently from college had selected this district in which to try and found a church of that persuasion. Both the young minister and his rather pompously dressed wife were guests at the Stevenson home. Thus we were not a welcome addition to the home, and the minister's wife, when she discovered we were to be given lodgings, was especially annoyed. When she discovered that we were to be guests for at least a few days, she announced her intention to Mrs. Stevenson to withdraw from the home and go to other friends. Thus the minister and his wife and child went to the afternoon session of the protracted meeting and then went elsewhere for their night's lodging.

An incident occurred at the dinner table that day which led me to suspect that said incident was a factor in causing the removal of the minister and his wife. It happened during the conversation that took place at the close of the meal. The young United Brethren's minister was telling some adventure and conversation he had had with a contentious opposed minister. He remarked that said minister had quoted in support of his argument a passage from the twenty-second chapter of Revelation. "Of course," said this young minister, "as there are not twenty-two chapters in Revelation, there was no force to his argument. He completely confronted himself by a wrong citation."

I suppose that the quick glance I doubtless flung at the latter startled him. I happened to remember that there are twenty-two chapters in Revelation and that the citation was pertinent to the discussion which had been described. The minister became very uneasy. Excusing himself from the table, he left and stopped into a bedroom on the first floor, which he had occupied the evening before. Through the only half-closed door from the dining room to the bedroom, I could see the young minister turning over his Bible and presently, it was supposed, discovered the Book of Revelation had twenty-two chapters. Of course it had never occurred to me to expose the mistake of the young minister before his friends, but it evidently made the minister very uneasy. He was apparently very willing to acquiesce in his wife's demands that they would leave the Stevensons' home.

The drizzling rain was continuing, and as it was apple harvest season, we visited the barn in which scores and scores of barrels of apples had been made ready for the market and feasted on this healthful food. After the course of an hour or two which had been spent with Mr. Stevenson, I returned with him to the house. As the distance between barn and house was muddy, I paused at the door to scrape off the mud of my shoes, while Mr. Stevenson walked straight into the hall. Finding his wife in the living room, he said, "Hello mother, how are you?" She replied in no very gracious tone, "Well, I am at least as well off as you can be when I think of the kind of company you have brought to the home." This was a startling discovery—this manifestation of unwelcome to us. The first instinct which came to me was to step into the hallway also and to announce that since the presence of myself and companion was unwelcome to the lady of the house, we would withdraw and seek other lodgings. Then a second thought occurred. It was not quite becoming to be too deeply offended by this ungracious remark. I decided to swallow my pride and endure the latter's hospitality.

In the evening, we attended the so-called camp meeting of the United Brethren, for it had been arranged through Mr. Stevenson that our several appointments would be given out at that meeting. Moreover the meeting promised to be interesting. Since the camp meeting had been protracted through about ten days, what was referred to as the in-gathering of the converts to the young United Brethren minister afterwards would take place, and it would determine whether the new church in that neighborhood would be founded or not. So both of us were graciously ensconced in the congregation at an early hour, and every seat and window sill was occupied by an expectant group of "Christians." It was about the only protracted meeting that I had had an opportunity to visit in Iowa. Nearly all of the methods of excitation and hysterical excitement were used to bring converts to the mourners' benches and to establish the new congregation.

The mourners' benches enclosed a square, the floor of which was filled with sawdust from two to four inches deep, and here the excitement of conversion was to be carried on. The minister and those of other persuasions that were assisting him went among the congregation, fiercely exhorting the people to come to Jesus, and there was intense excitement created. Women with babes in their arms would pass them to others and then, letting down their hair and in some cases loosening their outward garments, would rave and scream and shout until they would fall in a fainting condition, screaming out their alliance to Jesus and the church. So it went on for hours, during which time young men and sometimes young women were slyly having the time of their lives in mockery, making uncompliment- ary remarks on the character of those who were showing forth the most blatant religious ecstacy. There was laughter and mockery in the rear of the hall, and it was extremely difficult to contemplate the same as a religious exercise.

But all things must come to an end, and so this revival came to an end. We were able to make our announcement of a series of meetings we would hold during the rest of the week. Meantime we were making our home and holding our meetings at the home of the Stevensons. "Sister Stevenson" was nursing her wrath against us, gathering her brow at times like a gathering storm. Yet she was a kindly old soul, and one morning, quite intentionally apparently, she asked me some questions to which I gave answer. Then most suddenly she broke down and cried and sobbed beside me. "Hello, mother," said the elder Stevenson. "What's the matter? Have the fountains broke up?" She made no answer to him but went on with her questions to me, and it resulted in hearty good-will talk between the twain until it was almost mid-day. The remark was made we had better remove from the table or we might be sitting there when dinner time arrived.

It was a beautiful day, the sun shone brilliantly, and preparations had been made for the planting of a new strawberry patch out beside an orchard. One of the hired men had plowed up the mellow soil. This was a piece of garden work that old Sister Stevenson was superintending, and as I had some experience in strawberry planting, I followed her out to the prepared ground, made some questions, and set the example of planting strawberry plants in the Utah way. She was proudly interested. The barriers were broken, friendship was established, and her solicitude for us became a great pleasantry in the Stevenson home.

CHAPTER 13.

The William B. Smith Incident—
Brother of the Prophet

I conceived the idea, knowing the sharp winter weather would soon be upon us, of opening a corridor of established friends between the point where we were now preaching and the Mississippi River. An interest in the meetings in the schoolhouse had waned, and Elder Jensen and I started on this peregrination to open stations that could be occupied by preaching appointments during the winter. We were called forth to find these hypothetical fields of labor.

We traveled directly eastward, which would lead us to a point on the Mississippi River some seventy or ninety miles distant at a place called Guttenberg. The place did not yield much encouragement for finding places of labor for the winter season, and so unfriendly was the population through which we traveled that we had to sleep out several nights. As we approached Elkader, Clayton County, we began to hear of the brother of the prophet Joseph Smith, known as William B. Smith, as living in the neighborhood. The initial was an addition to his name which he himself used when in the Union fray to designate him from the many William Smiths that were among the enlisted men.We passed a little south of Elkader and did not find him at that time but went on determined to finish the journey we had projected to the Mississippi.

About this time, Brother Hyrum Jensen's strength gave out, and some distance from Guttenberg he could travel no further. As the journey had been rough, attended with hunger and sleeping out of doors, he succumbed to an attack of malaria fever. As we were without any means whatever, I conceived the idea of going into Guttenberg alone, leaving Brother Hyrum in the shade of some clumps of bushes to await my return. I drudged on several miles to Guttenberg. I discovered it to be a town where English was not spoken. Feeling uneasy about Elder Jensen's condition, I offered to a jeweler an open-faced luminous dial watch, which I had purchased before leaving home for a mission. The jeweler did not purchase the watch but was persuaded to take it and a pledge for a loan, the loan amounting to between seven and ten dollars. The watch was particularly serviceable because of its luminous dial, which without any other light would disclose the time in the darkness. Of course, letting it go for so small a sum, I hoped to redeem it, but as the stay in Guttenberg was very limited, I never saw the watch again.

Having raised this small sum of money, I returned to where I had left Elder Jensen and helped him in his walk back to Guttenberg, the town nearest to us. I took my companion to a hotel and nursed him for two or three days with quinine and hot lemonades to fight off the malaria, which was successfully done. Then we decided to return to the residence of the Stephensons without apparently opening any place for our winter campaign.

On this return journey, passing by Elkader, we resolved to run down the rumors that we had heard of Joseph Smith's brother living in that vicinity and by an inquiry finally found his humble log and frame home in the hills two or three miles west of the town of Elkader. When first appearing at this home, William Smith's wife took us to be elders from Plano, the headquarters at that time of the so-called Reorganized Church of Jesus Christ. From that misconception we received a hearty welcome, but as soon as it was discovered that we were from Utah rather than from Plano, the atmosphere became frigid, especially on the part of Mrs. Smith. She was vehement in her expression of her opposition to us in very uncompliment-ary, not to say insulting, attacks upon our people in Utah. I resented her unkindness and explained that as we were passing through the vicinity, we had heard that Joseph Smith's brother was living in Elkader or close to it. Learning this fact, we, at some pains, inquired our way out to his home and had come to visit with him. I explained that I was not out in the vain hope to convert him to Mormonism, who had once been an apostle to the church of the Latter Day Saints. I was following no such forlorn hope but merely wanted to see him as a brother of the prophet and make some inquiries of him. I did not want to enter upon a religious controversy with him. If it was agreeable for us to remain for such a purpose, we would be made very happy, and if it was not entirely agreeable, we could withdraw.

This rather quieted things, and William Smith expressed a desire for such a visit. His wife subsided with the understanding that we would stay for the night for such a visit. It was Mrs. Smith, however, who dominated the household, and William, once the proud, rebellious, pugnacious, and dominant spirit both in his father's house and likewise in the church was now tame and submissive enough to his arrogant and dominating wife. It is not to gratify any personal resentment that these circumstances are men-tioned but to refer to another matter to which this condition is pertinent. To make a point, it must also be known that a daughter was at the home, a girl perhaps seventeen years of age. I noted that of several requests which the father made of her, she gave disrespectful and even impudent in her answer to him. The day of our arrival, a son had that morning run away, supposedly for Chicago. Another son, and I think he was the eldest, was lying sick, supposedly of malaria, in an adjoining room. William Smith asked his wife if we might be invited to administer to him. The request she spurned with all the contempt her nature was capable of, and so this son was not administered to.

They provided supper for us and after the table was cleared, William Smith with us sat about the table in an interesting and animated conversation. William Smith disclosed some photographs and manuscript papers, which were of great interest to us. At that time we were not very well informed as to the Nauvoo period history of the church, and William had his own way in the explanations that he gave of his difficulties in Nauvoo. Never before had we seen copies of the *Times and Seasons*, several of which William Smith had. William Smith at this time was very advanced in age. He was an unusually tall man and, though emaciated, disclosed a symmetrical and splendid skeleton of what must have been a man of about 215-30 pounds, erect, full of form, with aggressive appearance and boldness that would well nigh surpass understanding. Now, emaciated as he was, the head appeared unusually large. The features, however, were strong and fine. He was slow of speech, owing perhaps to being so subdued by the members of his household. The eyes were soft but deep blue, easily converted by the depth of them to almost dark eyes when animated or stirred with emotion. He expressed at this table conversation complete faith in the divine calling of his brother and the ultimate triumph of the work he had introduced in the world.

About midnight it was suggested we might wish to retire, and we were shown to a loft, a half story structure leading up to the sloping roof of the humble house. Brother William accompanied us up the open stairs and indicated a bed in the corner upon which we might sleep. Weary with the day's journey, we were glad of our opportunity to rest and went to bed without any inspection of the room. Sweet sleep wrapped us in a delightful unconsciousness, and it was a little late when we awoke. We were awakened then by the rising of William Smith from an opposite corner of the room where he had slept upon a palate improvised from some miscellaneous clothes. He had surrendered his own bed to us, and I felt like severely reproaching myself for having taken the man's bed. It was a sacrifice that I would not have accepted had I known that the humble circumstances of the family made such an arrangement supposedly imperative.

Meantime Mrs. Smith had prepared breakfast but was in no pleasant mood when her lodgers came down from the loft to partake of it. The conversation during breakfast time was extremely unpleasant on her part. Breakfast over, William Smith proposed to accompany us to Elkader, for it was clearly impossible for us to remain longer at the Smith home. In that walk from his home to Elkader, something like two miles, William disclosed his own pretensions to the right of leadership in the church. He conversed that he had aspired to be the successor of his brother and sought to uphold that claim by calling attention to what he thought were the facts about the brother of Jesus, James. He was a member of the Jewish first council which settled the question of circumcision of the Gentiles, etc. William said that James gave it as his sentence that "we trouble not them, which from among the Gentiles are turned unto God." William's line of reasoning was this: Since James, the brother of the Lord, gave the sentence or decision of that council he was president of the council and then was president also of the church in that dispensation. So should it have been in his case. At the martyrdom of the prophet, he as the one remaining brother in the Smith family should have been made the president. Of course with his announcement of this, I did not agree, nor did we feel ourselves called upon to enter into contention about it.

Arriving in Elkader, the three of us went to a drug store, the manager of which was a close friend of William Smith. Here he explained to us that since he could not hope to pleasantly entertain us at his home, he had resolved to send us to a friend of his living some distance from Elkader, whom he felt sure would receive us gladly and give us entertainment. Accordingly he wrote letters to his friend, a well-to-do farmer by the name of Robinson, whom he enjoined to receive us as he would himself and to see to it that no one insulted us recommended by him. It was a most feeling and pleading letter in maintenance of his chief proposition to the entertainment of Elder Jensen and me. This time we resolved to not only accept the letter but immediately make the journey to the Robinson home, William Smith accompanying us to the outskirts of the city to set us upon the right roadway.

This road at the edge of the town ascended a sharp incline up to the common level of the prairie country over which it led. As we reached that point, William Smith indicated his intention to return to Elkader and so extended his hands, grasping the hand of each of us, and then burst into a flood of tears accompanied by a clinging warm clasp of his hand. What was it that moved him to such emotions? Was it the recollection of his own youth when he too under the favor of God had been an itinerant missionary going from house to house to present the great message of the New Dispensation. The question could not be determined, nor all the dramatic experiences of William Smith in the church at Nauvoo, Kirtland, and in New York. A short distance up the hill, we stopped to look at the retreating form of the prophet's brother and found that he had turned too. Looking at us, he waved his hand in farewell to us. Midway up the hill, again we turned only to see the prophet's brother turn to look at us, and again a farewell wave of the hand—so again at the crest of the hill. The third time we looked and saw him turn again looking at us. A wave of the hand, and the contour of the hill had him for the last time from view. This was my contact with the nearest relative to the prophet Joseph Smith that I had ever made.

Joseph Smith was evidently not blind to the defects in this younger brother's character, for in a blessing pronounced upon his head, he tells wherein the weakness of his character should be manifested. This blessing was pronounced upon the head of William by Joseph Smith, Jr., the Prophet, on Dec. 18th, 1833. "Brother William is as the fierce lion, which divideth in the spoil because he is much strength, and in the pride of his heart he will neglect the more weightier matters until his soul is bowed down in sorrow; and then he shall return and call on the name of his God and shall find forgiveness and shall wax valiant in the cause of truth; and therefore he shall be saved unto the uttermost, and shall be endowed with power from on High." Then follows a long list of specifications of the power that should be manifested through him, which unhappily did not follow— doubtless because of William's return unto the Lord not rising to the heights necessary to attain unto the generous promise made by his prophet brother. That William was fierce and endowed with mighty strength, and in the pride of his heart he neglected the more weightier matters, was sufficiently demonstrated by his departure from the church and the iniquitous life which he led in Missouri, in the eastern states, and also at Nauvoo. It was abundantly demonstrated that his soul was bowed down in sorrow as I sufficiently witnessed by my visit to him in Elkader, where his family was in rebellion against him and where he was under the fierce rule of his wife and steeped in poverty.

Fortunately I can also bear witness of William's return to a defense of the truth in Elkader, where I met up with the evidence of such a return. At a drug store in Elkader where Elder Jensen and I called to inquire specifically as to the location of William Smith's home, the hotel proprietor or manager, when he learned the nature of our mission, stated that all through their country, people had become convinced through William Smith that his brother Joseph had as much right to be a prophet in these days as Ezekiel or Amos or any of the old prophets had in ancient times. This had been brought about by the following circumstances. A few years before, a man had come through Elkader lecturing on the American Mohammed or Joseph Smith, the Mormon prophet. These lectures were numerously attended, and a very ugly impression was created concerning the prophet and his alleged mission and religion. William Smith was among those who were present at these lectures and startled the audience with the announcement at the close of the lecture. He announced himself as the brother of Joseph Smith, and this lecturer had grossly misrepresented his claims, his conduct, and the effect of his life's work—and most of all his character. He volunteered, if he could obtain the use of the hall, to set forth the truth in relation to his brother, the Mormon prophet.

The hall was instantly pledged, and one of the merchants of the town also proposed that money be raised for the purchase of a suit of clothes for William Smith in which to appear before the public. It was immediately supplied, and William Smith, asking just a few days in which to dig up his documents in refutation for his lecture, to the amazement of the community delivered a very logical and effective reply to the lectures. He so vindicated the claims and the character of his brother that ever afterwards the people would say whenever the question of Joseph Smith came up, "He had just as good a right to be a prophet as any man mentioned in the Bible."

That was the sentiment of the people throughout that county. To quite an extent this verdict was maintained by actual contact with people who conversed with us upon that subject. Whether this can be accounted as the fulfillment of the prediction in blessing upon the head of his wayward brother William Smith, I represent is not for me to say. But certainly there was, subsequent to the blessings of 1833 by Joseph Smith upon his head, a neglect of weightier matters of the law of righteousness. This was followed by a period of deep humiliation in poverty and rebellion of those who should have been obedient to him. There was at least this much of a return to a defense of the truth as stated above.

But it may be that the end and blessing upon the posterity of William as stated in this blessing by the prophet Joseph in 1833 is not yet. The son of William, who lay ill in his father's house and whom his mother did not permit us to administer to for his health, many years afterwards found his way to Utah and joined the church. I had the satisfaction of meeting him at work on the public grounds of the church property in caring for gardens and lawns. It was represented to me that this descendant of William Smith had joined the church and was faithful therein as a member. Let it be hoped that through his posterity the blessings of William may be realized through his stake driven within the pale of the church.

We were heartily received by the friend to whom William Smith sent us, a Mr. Robinson, a member of the so-called "Josephite" church. We stayed in this neighborhood about two weeks at least and found opportunity for preaching in schoolhouses surrounding the district within where he lived. But no very promising hopes of a permanent field of labor could be entertained, and therefore we resolved to return to the neighborhood of the Stephenson's home. We remained on our second visit several weeks and preached in a number of schoolhouses in that section. Young Mr. Stephenson and his wife were so favorably impressed that some hopes arose that they would join the church. In this, however, they failed.

Meantime by correspondence from relatives at home, I was informed that a Mr. Thomas, who for some years had lived in Utah and worked in the mines of the territory and who had married a daughter of Mr. Dustin, my stepfather, lived somewhere in the part of Iowa where I was laboring. Inquiry was made concerning his place of residence and was finally discovered to be in Hardin County, near the town of Eldora. A visit to him was projected. He was found with his family in this place, but he was in very humble circumstances and scarce could give us an abiding place more than for a very few days. During this visit we found opportunity to speak in a schoolhouse in this neighborhood and through these meetings came in contact with a very wealthy farmer by the name of Allen Hughes. He invited us to make his house our home, which we did to quite an extent during the time we remained in Hardin County. Meeting places were multiplied for us until four schoolhouses enclosing a large square were obtained, and we preached in rotation in these schoolhouses for some length of time. Mr. Hughes became deeply interested in our message and professed much faith in many of the things we were proclaiming. He furnished an excellent young team and a carriage and placed it at our disposal that we might go from one to the other of the schoolhouses from his home and return the same evening.

Although it was now the month of November, Mr. Hughes had not yet completed his wheat threshing. It was the custom of the farmers of that portion of Iowa to harvest their wheatfields early in July, stack the wheat in their barnyards, and leave the threshing of it until the months of November and even December, after the Indian corn crops were gathered. This Mr. Hughes had done, and now the question of getting sufficient men to carry on the wheat thrashing was quite a problem for him. At some of the meetings attended by him, he sought to drum up hands for the thrashing but failed to get enough. Then I volunteered that Elder Jensen and I would be glad to render him assistance for a few days in thrashing his grain. This was a matter of wonder both to Mr. Hughes and the congregation present, who heard the tender of this kind of service. "What," said they, "preachers turned thrashers, it is inconceivable." The following morning, however, the thrashing machine having been set at Mr. Hughes's stacks, Elder Jensen and I walked out to where the hands were gathered. I said to Mr. Hughes, "If you have any old overalls about the place, you had better let us have them."

"Do you really mean that you intend to make good your offer of last night?" asked Mr. Hughes, and he was told we meant just that. If he had some overalls, they might help to preserve our clothing. Some overalls were found and donned. With this the question arose as to what part of the job we would do. Hyrum selected the hauling of the grain from the machine to the granary. I said I would work in the chaff and straw end of the machine or would mount the stake and pitch bundles to the feeder of the thrashing machine. The latter job accepted, I climbed the stack with two other men to do that part of the work. Preparing a table in the side of the stack, a circle of horses was started, and soon the familiar hum of the machine gave out a familiar sound to us, who had helped the home farmers many a time on the same station. The other two men began tearing away at the stack to supply me with bundles to pass on to the feeder of the machine. I had things stopped for a moment until I showed the two Iowa hands how to begin at the very top of the stack of bundles to be passed onto the feeder of the machine and take it down systematically, circle by circle. In this way the stack was taken down systematically, and the whole work proceeded orderly and without confusion.

Soon after the machine had started, I saw Mr. Hughes making a beeline for his house, but for what purpose I did not know. At dinner time, however, it was discovered that Mr. Hughes had ordered the roasting of an immense turkey gobbler that had been designed for Christmas feasting, but he resolved now to have the gobbler cooked for his men. After washing at the common pump tub, we all entered the house. I was seated at the head of the table, and presently this mammoth bird, nearly all that one man could carry, was brought in and set before me. I was invited to do all the carving. At this I held up my hand in protest. I had never carved a turkey in my life. "What," cried out Mr. Hughes, "a preacher that can take down a grain stack like he would do a problem in geometry and yet can't carve a turkey! Whoever heard of such a thing as that!" He insisted that I should, notwithstanding my inexperience, carve the turkey, which I did after a fashion, and such a fashion! At any rate each of the hands got his, and the portions were so generous that there was no second helping required from this turkey and another fowl that had been roasted with it.

As I looked upon the skeleton of the chief bird, I apostrophized, "This turkey has been highly honored. He has undoubtedly achieved all the glory of his mortal life by coming to this table all browned and glorious and then distributed to hungry men. So much the better than living to die of old age and perhaps decrepitude. He reached his fate at the very height of his glorious existence and how we appreciated him." At the close of this, there was a boisterous hand clapping which indicated acquiescence in the above sentiments. This fact of our assisting Mr. Hughes in the several days' thrashing became the talk of the neighborhood and did much to establish our welcome throughout this district. The meetings, thirty in all, were generally very well attended in rotation at the four schoolhouses which had been secured for this purpose.

In addition to the friends of Mr. Hughes and his family, there was a Captain Heath, who had served in the Union Army of the not far distant war between the states. A Mr. Severson, an infidel but a fine man nevertheless, was quite wonderfully interested in our message. These and several others were interested listeners and frequently went from one schoolhouse to another to hear the unfolding of the message brought to them. Mr. Thomas continued his interest also. The latter would often refer to the discourse he had heard Orson Pratt deliver in Salt Lake. One thing he used to say, which was always impressive, was that when listening to Orson Pratt preach, it made you think of a column of Roman soldiers marching by in stately regular fashion. Or it was more nearly like the unfolding of a scroll, which you followed chained to the reading of it as it was unfolded – its stately treatment of the facts of which you never tired. This was so nearly like my conception of the orderly discourses of Elder Pratt that it is recorded here.

While in this neighborhood another interesting circumstance developed, and that was the offer of the prominent families within the neighborhood to hire me as a minister for a year. They brought to me a written contract that pledged themselves to raise for me $1,600 for my services for that length of time. They were all of opinion that the sum might be enlarged, but this much the signers of the proposed contract announced to one of my audiences. But I announced in answer to it that I was not for hire. I had come into their neighborhood without purse or scrip to preach the gospel. They were welcome to my services, and I would remain and preach for them as long as they manifested interest in the things which made up my message. But I could not bind myself to stay a year nor a month, nor even a day. I was not for hire, and I would leave the neighborhood whenever the inspiration of the spirit of the Lord would suggest that I should go elsewhere to find people who would hear my truth. With many expressions of regret about it, this ended the incident.

I too continued to make and fill appointments in these four schoolhouses as often as six or seven times a week, but Elder Jensen seemed to lose interest in the meetings. In fact, at the close of the three-day thrashing help that we furnished Mr. Hughes, Elder Jensen received from that gentleman a proposition to continue to work for him from then to at least spring, taking charge of the stock feeding on the farm, etc., etc. Elder Jensen presented the proposition to me, who advised against his accepting the employment and for continuing in the work of the ministry. This, however, Elder Jensen claimed would be impossible for him to do, as he was then in need of clothing. He made a proposition to share the wages with me to assist me in the purchase of clothing. This I declined absolutely and said that I felt confident that the way would be opened to supply both of us with clothing and whatever else was necessary. But Elder Jensen still insisted upon continuing to work for Mr. Hughes, to which, at last, I gave reluctant consent. I had the satisfaction, however, of finding that my belief was verified in the matter of the Lord providing things necessary for our mission. Long before Elder Jensen's first monthly payment was made as wages, I had been given by the community sufficient means not only to supply myself with underclothing, which the sudden fall of temperature made imperative, but to supply Hyrum also with these necessary things. Indeed I never did receive any part of Elder Jensen's remuneration.

Meantime, through gifts from the people I was able to supply myself with necessary things, among others with an overcoat which was by this time very necessary. Mr. Hughes invited me to Eldora with a load of grain he was delivering at one of the elevators. Once in the city, he took me to a clothing store and urged me to select the above said overcoat. While one of the clerks was showing me through the stocks to find a suitable garment, Mr. Hughes had been in conversation with the proprietor of the establishment and told him of my helpfulness in the community—how I had assisted him in thrashing but claimed that I had never carved a turkey; also the incident of helping a man who had met with an accident. Also I had induced others to help with the gathering of his corn crop. Notwithstanding these labors, I had held public meetings every night. At this the proprietor called to the clerk waiting upon me and told him to be sure and select the finest overcoat that he had and that he intended to meet half the price of it. Mr. Severson had bought himself a fine pair of handmade boots to his measurements. He pretended, however, that they were not quite satisfactory to him but perhaps would fit me – all of which, of course, was only an excuse for presenting them to me. If my own feet had been measured for them, the feet could not have been more perfect, and the material was the best that could be had. So it went on, one thing after another that came to hand necessary to equip me reasonably well both for inner and outward garments.

Meantime I had received a communication from President John Taylor that I had been transferred from Iowa, where the severe coldness of the oncoming winter was seriously affecting my ailment of a head trouble from swollen membranes of the sinus cavity. It was thought better that I be sent to a milder climate. Having announced my intention to make this transfer, money was given to me sufficient to meet the railroad and other expenses in the journey. As Christmas approached I designed starting on the journey, but Mr. Hughes insisted that Christmas be spent with him. As Christmas approached three ladies, the wives of young men who had graduated from college with Mr. Hughes, made sudden appearance at his home, coming down from Chicago for the Christmas holidays. They arrived about three days before and with Mrs. and Mr. Hughes made a merry company. They were the wives of merchants in Chicago, for at the close of college the four young men, companions in graduation, divided off for their vocations, the three of them turning to merchandizing becoming wealthy. Mr. Hughes had turned his attention to a large farming project, while rearing his family on the Iowa farms which he owned. Now came this reunion.

Seeing that the Hughes home was likely to be crowded through the holidays, I prepared for leaving the home to go to Mr. Severson. He had long urged upon me to pay more frequent visits to his home, where he was as anxious to have me located as Mr. Hughes was at his home. Accordingly I began packing for this change. About noon following the morning his new guests from Chicago had arrived. Mr. Hughes came into the house and inquired about me and was told that I was making ready to move to Mr. Severson's. Mr. Hughes came to the bedroom that had been assigned to me in the home, and with mock severity he demanded to know what the occasion was of the packing. I explained that there had been such an increase of visitors at the Hughes home that I thought it only reasonable that I should vacate this beautiful bedroom and give place to the other guests. Mr. Hughes stepped to the bedside and taking the half filled valise dumped its continents on the bed and said, "Mr. Roberts, if the Queen of England should come to the Hughes residence, she would not be permitted to disturb your lodgings here. I want you to stay and visit with these ladies and teach them your faith."

This was final, though proper excuses were made to Mr. Severson. The matter of holding meetings every night in the four schoolhouses enclosing the square was continued with extended conversations and explanations to the three ladies from Chicago, who became intensely interested in the message I had to deliver.

CHAPTER 14.

Mission to the South – Southern Hospitality

Christmas passed, and now the journey for Tennessee must be undertaken. Letters both from Elder John Taylor and President John Morgan of the Southern States Mission urged my departure for the new field of labor. It was with some reluctance that this field of labor so wonderfully opened should be abandoned. There occurred to my mind probable future expansion of the work in the state of Iowa, with myself sent in the capacity of the president of the work in Ohio. But the requirements of rapidly failing health were imperative, and so as the Christmas holidays were over, preparation was made for the journey south. Tickets were secured over the railroad to St. Louis.

The winter was intensely cold, and the discomfort of a journey, even by train, was considerable, as pullman and dining room accommodations were scouted on account of their expense. The Mississippi River, as in 1846 which marked off the beginning of the exodus of the Saints from Nauvoo, Illinois, was frozen over completely. At St. Louis, and for one hundred miles below, it was running with floating fragments of ice and much snow. Trains were delayed and thrown out of schedule, and a day or two was lost in getting started from St. Louis. The weather was so severe at this point that, leaving the St. James Hotel to catch a streetcar for the depot to resume the journey, my ears were frozen white and stiff, both hands being engaged in carrying my valises, books, and clothing. From this little incident I suffered quite sharply for several days.

The route down was over the Iron Mountain Railroad, which ran parallel with the Mississippi River southward. That season there had been a large exodus of the Negro race from the South, and now under the pressure of the intensity of the cold weather, that migration was leading southward. At one point some distance from St. Louis at the close of the first day of delayed travel, the train was boarded by an immense number. In fact, all that could be crowded into the car of river men and Negroes took place. Up to that time the day coach had been occupied wholly by a young southern man from Kentucky on his way home and me. As soon as the car was crowded, this young man came back to my seat and proposed an alliance between us – offensive and defensive – against this onrush of rivermen and Negroes. He said with some excitement, "We must form such an alliance, or these men may cut our throats and throw us out of the train." He stated that he was armed and prepared to do his part in such an alliance to the limit. I had to tell him that I had no arms and never carried them, but I was glad to welcome the strength that would come from the alliance so proposed. We shook hands on the compact and determined to face whatever might happen.

The floating ice in the Mississippi continued on some distance further south. At a railway station on the Iron Mountain Railroad route over which I was making my journey, I had to cross the river to Hendersonville in Kentucky. It took several hours to make the crossing because of the floating ice which jammed up the ferry. Fortunately the young Kentuckian was taking the same route, so we left the Iron Mountain train together.

It was about midnight when we reached the other side, and the town, such as it was, was in complete darkness except for one glimmering light up the east bank of the river. To this we two chance companions made our way. It proved to be a lodging house not of the better class. By thumping on the door long enough, we succeeded in rousing a Negro boy who was asleep near a red hot stove in what was the office room of the lodging house. It was explained to the colored boy as soon as he was sufficiently awake that we wanted to obtain rooms, but he said they had no rooms; the house was crowded by transients. He finally succeeded, however, in waking up a man in an adjoining room, and we could hear him explaining to the man that there were two men in the office who wanted rooms. The lad was saying, "We done got no rooms 'cept one and there is a colored man sleeping in that one." At this I called out, "Don't disturb that man of color. We can get along by staying here in the office out of the bitter cold of the night." The man apparently subsided, and the boy came back saying, "You all can stay in the office." Pouring more coal into the stove, the boy returned to his sleeping carpet under the table, and we wore out the night on the chairs and the tables of the office.

The young Kentucky friend had relatives in Hendersonville, whom he went to call on when day broke. I went in search of some better lodgings and found it at the principle hotel of the town. By this time owing to the delays in the journey at St. Louis and other points, I was again penniless. But following an impulse that rushed upon me, I hunted up the proprietor of the hotel and explained to him the situation. I was on my way to Tullahoma via Nashville, and while I had my railway transportation, all money had been expended owing to said delays. I would take it as a kindness from the hotel proprietor if he would grant me lodging and food until I could make the necessary train connection for my destination. And here I met my first exhibition of polite hospitality in a southern state. The hotel proprietor bade me welcome to lodging and food until said railroad connections could be made. When breakfast was announced, I was honored by being placed next to the lady of the house, who acted as hostess for those who were staying at the hotel and with charming grace served the meal. I was asked as a special honor to say grace at the table, and this I did.

The next day I made my train connection and continued the journey through the state of Kentucky to Nashville, Tennessee, and then on to Tullahoma, where again I was to change trains to go to Manchester in Coffee County, Tennessee. Here I expected to meet Elder Joseph Ford from my own home town, Centerville, and Elder Carver, companion to Elder Ford. Elder Ford was released from his mission on my arrival.

It was a backwoods, primitive kind of train that ran from Tullahoma to Manchester. The roadbed was rough, the engine and cars primitive, and the journey of thirty miles from Tullahoma to Manchester was tiresome enough. The fuel used in firing the engine was cordwood, and keeping up steam on the wheezing engine seemed to be a difficult task. Manchester was not reached until about nine o'clock at night.

Elders Ford and Carver failed to show up, owing doubtless to the uncertainty of my arrival. Without money I did not have the heart to try to get lodgings in the strange town. Instead I made inquiry for the residence of Mr. Fagan, some six or eight miles distant, at which Elders Ford and Carver were supposed to be lodging. The directions I received towards his house were through a dense wooded country and along a ravine down which a mountain stream bored its way. The cold wave of the north had reached even this far south, though of course less severe. A mile or so down the gulch which I was following towards the Fagan residence, the road crossed the mountain stream. Ice from each bank nearly met in the middle of the stream, flowing dark and somewhat turbulent and how deep I did not know. Securing a heavy cane which I wrenched from a clump of bushes and holding my valise in one hand, I walked out on the ice, knowing of course that it would break presently. When it did it dropped me into the cold water waist deep. Feeling my way to the ice on the opposite bank, I broke it down until it was strong enough to hold my weight.

Thus I came out in crossing number one, and by this time chilled to the bone, I pursued my journey as rapidly as possible. Three times afterwards I crossed the stream and began to wonder when I would have to wade it lengthwise. But coming through the third time, I observed on the left of the stream a footpath that led slantingly along the face of the bluffs. Though this was on the wrong side of the stream on which the Fagan residence was supposed to be, I resolved to leave the road leading down the creek and see if the path would not lead me out of the gulch and out into the common level of the surrounding country. While climbing the pathway I heard the tinkling of a cowbell and concluded I must be near some residence. This proved true, for in a short distance I could see a house, where a firelight was coming through the chinks between the logs of which the house was built.

I passed the heifer tied to a sapling and went on to the house, which I finally reached and knocked on the door. This afterwards I learned was a very unusual proceeding in the south. It was the custom there and especially in the backwoods country to walk up to the gate of a house or ride as the caller might be doing and shout until someone appeared from the house. Then the person would say to the caller, "Get down and come in," if riding, or "Youns come in," if walking. So bidden, the caller would come to the house. But this knocking evidently was a mystery to the inmates of this log cabin, and there was a good deal of caution in opening the door a little way and looking out to see what the mystery might be. Through the partially open door, I saw a log fire blazing, a fire typical of the south, black hickory green logs with dry wood blazing before them which diffused a warm glowing light through the room. Spontaneously I said to the man still holding the door, "I am wet, tired, and hungry, and I would like the privilege of sitting by your fire until morning."

At this he bade me to come in. It was a welcome warmth that fire dispensed, and soon the log bench was placed near the corner of it for me. By this time several other inmates of the family appeared, two or three boys and a bright-eyed girl and an elderly lady, evidently the mother of the children and the wife of the passed middle-aged man who had opened the door. It was explained to this gentleman named Anderson that I had been trying to find my way to the Fagan residence but had become lost. My account of my adventures between Manchester and this point, especially in the matter of crossing the creek several times until I thought I would have to wade it endwise, amused the youngsters of the family. Meantime the lady of the house was preparing for me something to eat. This consisted of a corn pone baked before the fire and my eyes, and it was the first time I had connected with corn pone. This was made by pouring a little water out of a gourd into a cornmeal bag and raking the meal, without leaven of any kind, about until a sort of dough was made. This was patted and patted into a thin slice, spread out upon a board, and held up before the fire. The meal was not really cooked; the water was just evaporated from it and the cake thus formed slightly browned. This with a small gourd filled with buttermilk made the supper, and a good one it was to me.

Meantime, through several changes about the beds, a sleeping place was found for me, and as I retired to the bed surrounded by curtains put up to the four high posts of the bedstead, I sank luxuriously into a southern thick featherbed, which was the most comfortable sleeping quarters I had had for several days. It was rather late the next morning when I was awakened by the moving about of the family.

It was Sunday morning, and breakfast was ready. This consisted of some more corn pone, a dish in which a few pieces of bacon were floating about, and black coffee. The black coffee was set aside and replaced by buttermilk for me. The corn pone was much improved by the bacon, which seemed to have a pleasant and peculiar flavor because the hogs from which it was made had been fed upon the fallen nuts of the forest, which grew in great abundance. By the time breakfast was finished, three horses had been saddled and brought up to the door of the house, and two of the boys of Mr. Anderson were prepared to pass me over the river and to bring me in full view of the Fagan home.

This was a remarkable consideration to a Mormon elder by Mr. Anderson, who I afterwards learned was a violently disposed anti-Mormon and had declared that it would not be safe for a Mormon elder to present himself at his "clearin,"—his farm in the woods. Of course, I had already explained that I was a Mormon elder in search of other Mormon elders supposed to be at the Fagan residence. But notwithstanding this he had extended to me the night before the comforts of his fire and bed. He had mounted me on a horse and sent his two sons to be my guide. It was rather a fine example of southern hospitality, even to one esteemed as his enemy. When I related to Brother Fagan my stay at the Anderson home, he marveled that I had not met with refusal of hospitality and wondered that I had escaped violence. The old gentleman Anderson was quite a notable "fire-eater" in the neighborhood.

Elders Ford and Carver were not at the Fagan home, but I suspected that they were staying with another member of the church two or three miles distant by the name of Adams. As I remember it, this was the nearest clearing and home to Mr. Fagan's. The country was very sparsely settled, and it was a densely wooded region. Mules were saddled, and a ride taken to see if the elders were there. Unfortunately they were not. Both at the Adams and Fagan residences, I was urged, the day being Sunday, to hold religious service in the evening. This I refused to do until I had contacted the elders that were somewhere in that field of labor. However, neighbors calling in to the Fagan home were indulged in doctrinal conversation for an hour or two.

The next day Elders Carver and Ford walked into the home of Mr. Fagan, and the long desired union with these elders was made. Elder Carver was especially glad for my coming since that was the signal for a release to return home. He did not, however, immediately avail himself of that but did separate from Elder Ford and me to go into Hickman County into a neighborhood called Duck River. Here some wealthy members of the church lived and Elders Murdock and Riddle had their headquarters, for John R. Murdock was the president of the Tennessee conference. There Brother Carver remained for a few weeks and thence made his journey to the west.

CHAPTER 15.

Lebanon, Tennessee, Book of Mormon Debate

Elder Ford and I meantime visited all the members of the church and a number of friends in the Fagan-Adams neighborhood and then undertook a journey beyond the extreme limits of the Ford-Carver district of visitation. This was regarded as a new field of labor and altogether undeveloped. The principle friend to us in this neighborhood was one Irvin Saunders, a rather remarkable man of large influence. He possessed large acreage, chiefly valuable for its cedar timber growth which was being sawed up into cedar lumber by several mills in the county. Elder Ford and a group of elders had fallen in with Mr. Saunders when they were on their way to their fields of labor and he was returning from a big lumber deal in St. Louis. The elders confessed themselves Mormon elders en route to the South on missions, and Mr. Saunders, who had learned something about Mormons, gave them a hearty welcome into his company. An animated conversation continued through the whole first day's ride. On separating he gave them an urgent invitation to come into his neighborhood some thirty or forty miles from Nashville, and he promised them both entertainment and an opportunity to preach. Later two of the elders, Ford and Carver, accepted this invitation and partially opened the field of labor as aforesaid.

Mr. Saunders was a very popular man in Wilson County. When lean years in crops of corn and other grains were scarce, he had provided food for hundreds of people, sending out of Nashville and making large purchases of corn and pork. It was due to his munificence that the people of the county had been carried through and because of him saved from famine. He was, however, a man loose in his relations with women, and in addition to his own large family by legal marriage, he was the father of many children to whom he sustained an attitude of great kindness.

The first meeting was held in the vicinity of Baird Mills. Mr. Saunders's home was near in a neighborhood called Moccasin, not so much for the numerous snakes of the cedar covered areas as for the lawlessness and general character of the people. Mr. Saunders, though wealthy and engaged in large enterprises, could not read or write and in these respects was dependent upon the learning and skill of his employees. Perhaps because of that he was nearly always involved in large legal controversies over the possession of the large acreage he held. It was at his spacious but ill-furnished home that the first meetings of Elder Ford and me were held. Later a schoolhouse which Mr. Saunders had built in the woods some distance from his home became the principal place for holding the meetings. In addition a number of other homes were opened to them for the same purpose in remoter parts from this center.

It was an interesting field of labor that was developed here, and meetings were held almost every night in one place or another, where we were requested to hold forth. It was in the very early spring months through which this season lasted, cold enough for the big large fires to be laid in the immense fireplaces common to the region in these homes. The people would assemble and listen with intense interest to the story of the advent of the New Dispensation of the gospel. At first there was some resentment about the presentation of that dispensation through the narrative of facts connected with it. The people were much attached to the New Testament scriptures but not inclined to readily believe the Joseph Smith story of revelation from the Lord in this age. Gradually, however, the minds of the people were changed, and they began to believe in the possibility and fact of revelation in this age as in other ages. Quite an extensive faith was being promulgated in these things. The people would gather in front of the huge log fires in semi-circles, while we with our backs to the fires for the advantage of light in reading our scriptures would expound our message of which the people seemed never to tire. After the formal services were ended, they would remain and engage us in animated conversation.

Sometimes these conversations took on an amusing form. I recall the experience one evening of Elder Ford, who was a great favorite among the people. Because of the success of persuading people to accept the message, he was known as the "silent hunter." He was not so forceful in public speech, but he was effective in conversation, and the people greatly respected and loved him. On one occasion in conversation with a group, I overheard him say, "Well," adopting their vernacular, "what are uns going to do with this message weuns are telling you about? Are you going to accept it or pass it up? It will be pretty serious with you if you pass it up. Remember Elder Roberts read out of your Bible tonight: 'Christ once suffered for sins, the just for the unjust, being put to death in the flesh, but quickened by the spirit by which also he went and preached unto the spirits in prison which sometime were disobedient when once the long-suffering of God waited in the days of Noah while the ark was a preparing, wherein few, that is eight souls were saved by water.' Now they ignored Noah's message, and when they went to the spirit world, they were shut up in prison where they remained over two thousand years before they got another chance. That's pretty serious, and you folks will have to stay in prison that long or longer if you reject our message. That be a pretty long time to be in prison two thousand years and perhaps more. You'll get awfully tired." A solemn silence fell upon the group and the whole house full of people who stayed and heard this conversation.

On another such occasion I heard a very prominent woman in revival services known for extravagant hysteria say, "Mr. Ford, we all like you but say you can't preach." On still another occasion a woman of like type to this and noted for extravagance in shouting and otherwise carrying on at the mourners' bench stood with feet far apart immediately in front of Elder Ford and said, "Mr. Ford, you all don't believe in shouting." Brother Ford said, "Well, I can't see that it does any good." "What," said the latter, "if I couldn't shout, I'd just bust." Elder Ford with a flickering, vanishing smile and a twinkle in his bright eyes replied: "Well then for heaven sake shout." This lady afterwards became a member of the church and lost her inclination to either shout or bust.

It was a doctrine of very great interest as to the imposition of hands for the reception of the Holy Ghost. It may be said that the Disciples' or Campbellites' doctrine prevailed in this vicinity urging repentance and then baptism for the remission of sins, but there the ordinances of the Christianity they taught stopped. Most of them had not so much as "heard of the Holy Ghost." But when the Latter-day Saints elders taught in addition to water baptism the baptism of the spirit, it aroused quite a universal interest and likewise a very widespread dissent from the doctrine. So when this lady joined the church and received the imposition of hands for the Holy Spirit, a number of her former religious association called at her house and badgered her not a little about what had been the effect of having the hands of the elders laid upon her for the reception of the Holy Ghost. Presently she very gently and with fine wisdom answered, "Ladies I can tell you one evidence I have that being baptized of the Holy Ghost has been a reality with me. If when I was Baptist you ladies had come into my house and insulted me as you have done this morning, long ago I would have been in your hair in violent resistance of your insults, but now I have not felt the least disposition to do you a violence or to be angered by your contemptible treatment of me. I am sure that that could only come to me because of the presence in my soul of the Holy Ghost received in obedience to the Latter-day Saint gospel."

During this period the fame of these numerous meetings had reached Lebanon, the center of higher education in Tennessee. Here was stationed the rather famous law school of the state, and the Presbyterian Church South had an extensively attended college for educating the young men for the ministry in that church. On several occasions a number of gentlemen including one or two merchants, lawyers, and a number of professors came down to verify the character of the meetings that were being held and attended. A discussion of these meetings and of us was published in the local paper at Lebanon.

"We were introduced," said the account, "by Mr. Ben Baird and found the elders to be very quiet and dignified gentlemen ready to answer any questions relative to their religion. Their names are Brigham H. Roberts and Joseph Ford." Then follows a rather bungled statement of the doctrine we had set forth. "We made a slight attempt," said their account, "to turn the conversation on Bishop John D. Lee and the Mountain Meadows Massacre, but failed. . . . Brother Joseph took the floor and read from a small card the creed or articles of faith of the church and made a few remarks. Roberts did much better. He is about 28 years old [I was then twenty-three], light complexioned, had a good eye and face and is a natural orator. He spoke about an hour. He said the Bible and the New Testament so far as they were rightly translated is the word of God and the Book of Mormon was written for the nations of the American continent, etc., etc."

The outcome of this visit was that these gentlemen in behalf of a portion of the people of Wilson County, where we were laboring, demanded that their nine Christian ministers in the county should meet us Mormons in public debate. They ordered a schoolhouse to be the place of meeting, and then and there they should prove that we were not worthy of confidence. They published a notification for us that we must meet this group of ministers and defend ourselves and our faith or else prepare to leave the county, for this Christian people would not tolerate our presence under any other circumstances. The proposed debate was to begin on the 5th of February 1881.

Before the debate came off, however, we had secured the courthouse at Lebanon in which to deliver some discourses at the invitation of this group of gentlemen above mentioned. At the time appointed we in the evening entered the courtroom and found it crowded, including aisles and window sills. Those in the audience were chiefly law students and candidates for the Presbyterian ministry from the colleges established, as already noted, in this center of education. We were pleased with this opportunity of coming to an organized center of education, so that it would be understood that we were not laboring in the backwoods district alone. One singular thing about this congregation was that there was not a woman present in all the throng.

The historical development of the New Dispensation was dwelled upon in this first meeting, and in two following lectures the doctrinal phases of the New Dispensation were developed. By this time we had exhausted our spare funds and thought we would for that time have to discontinue the meetings further. However, a general protest was made from the body of the congregation, and I explained the reason for the present discontinuance, that being our funds were exhausted. The proprietor of the hotel where we had stayed several days arose and invited us to make the hotel our home as long as we should choose to stay. Other offers for assistance were made from the body of the congregation, whereupon I gave notice of a meeting the following night.

The community, it was said, had been greatly agitated over the question of the Mormon marriage system, including at that time the justification and practice of plural marriage. This was stated as the reason for the desire for further meetings, so I announced my intention to speak upon that subject the next night. When the night came every part of the building was crowded. There possibly were all of one thousand men assembled, for no women yet appeared upon the scene. The judge's desk was used for a pulpit, and a Catholic priest of the city pompously took a standing position and ostentatiously spread a notebook before him, evidently intending to follow me and especially to get my scriptural references on this subject. The theme was opened upon rather a broad basis, and marriage systems of various peoples dwelt upon, including the Hebrews and some of the early Christians. Gradually came the introduction of this new system of marriage for eternity, and all the implications of that idea were developed with an incidental treatment of the polygamy feature of it.

The Catholic priest had been careful to note the citations made by me, but once in a while he apparently would fail, whereupon I, turning to him and pushing my Bible reference immediately before him, would wait for him to write down the citation. This created no little amusement among the Protestant student body of the college of the Presbyterian Church South and also from quite a number of the law students from the college and the practicing lawyers of the town, for Lebanon was famous all over the south for its bar. As this went on for some time and derision grew more emphatic in the laughter and applause following my exhibition of my scripture and other authorities for the benefit of the note-taking Catholic priest, he suddenly folded his notes and took a less prominent place amid the laughter and jeers of the audience. It was evident to them that I was not shrinking from a full exhibition of my sources of information and also was quite willing that these should be specifically noted down. I took great pains to repeat the citation until my Catholic friend got them written down without error. At the close of the meeting which continued long over the two-hour period, the church students and lawyer students gathered around the judge's desk in great numbers, and the questions asked and the answers given continued until after eleven o'clock that evening. Many complimentary things were said of the treatment of the subject, and the divinity students expressed their surprise that so much could be found in the scriptures and in the nature of things for the Mormon system of marriage. Thereafter the way was cleared in Lebanon for respectful deference for us Mormon elders whenever we visited that place.

At last the time for public debate in the Moccasin district came, on the 5th of February, 1881. Of the nine ministers invited to the discussion, only one put in an appearance to accept the gauntlet of battle thrown down at their feet by the people of the district. The schoolhouse was crowded to capacity. Even in the window sills and aisles and on the outside, a still great throng crowded around the structure within hearing. The one minister who came to engage in the debate was a Mr. Alsup of the Campbellite or Christian faith. He was a noted preacher not only in Wilson county but throughout central Tennessee. He was about fifty-two or three years of age and noted as a debater. In fact, it was his boast that he had never engaged in debate but what he had driven his opponent from the platform. He was tall and gaunt in stature, bearded and aggressive.

He proposed that the debate be limited to a consideration of the Book of Mormon. Why, Elder Ford and I did not understand until he explained that he knew little or nothing in general about Mormonism, Mormon theology, or the organization and pretensions of the church, but he did claim to know all about the Book of Mormon. As a religious document, he said, it was of no more worth than last year's almanac. He proposed to establish the truth of this, and of course he held that if he proved the Book of Mormon a fraud and worthless, then the church founded upon it could not be a true church of Christ. Mormonism must either stand or fall with the Book of Mormon. Of course, this claim was conceded by us, and we expressed confidence in our ability to defend the divine authorities of the Book of Mormon and prove that it was of God. We only stipulated that when he had considered the Book of Mormon for sufficient length of time to establish what he said of it, we on our part would demand that his church in its organization and doctrines and authority be examined, and we would undertake to establish that its claim to being the Church of Christ was not true. To this Mr. Alsup consented.

It was arranged between Elder Ford and me that I should conduct the debate on our part with such assistance as Elder Ford could give by suggestion. Three chairmen were selected. The manner of the discussion was defined and the debate opened. Perhaps because of our lack of experience, we allowed Mr. Alsup to make the initial speech to disprove the claims of the Book of Mormon. This rather deprived us of the natural order of debate which would have given us the affirmative and the lead in the opening speech to set forth the truth of the Book of Mormon. The debate was to continue on the Book of Mormon for three days, five hours each day, the opening speeches being one hour in length and then one-half hour rebuttals. Before the debate closed, these were reduced to fifteen minutes in alternate speeches.

Mr. Alsup's opening was quite a skillfully arranged attack, and for us, two inexperienced elders in Book of Mormon matters, the speech was quite appalling, but gradually things righted themselves. Mr. Alsup had shot his far-reaching arrow at the first dispatch; and after that it was soon to be seen that he did not hold prestige with the great congregation very long. On the third day a very peculiar incident occurred. In the increasing rapidity of exchange of thought, Mr. Alsup made a claim as to a passage of scripture in the Book of Mormon, which I straightly contradicted as to its existence. The instant I made the contradiction, I remembered very vividly that the passage quoted by Mr. Alsup was in the Book of Mormon but was capable of a rational explanation. But I had contradicted its existence and charged Mr. Alsup with misrepresentation of what was written there. Incidentally there passed before my vision an incident in my boyhood when I was in Sunday school and this item came up in the class. The old gentleman who was teaching the class made the aforesaid reasonable explanation referred to. I was sorely perplexed for the moment. To concede then and there my mistake and withdraw it would lose my claims on what was gradually becoming the sympathetic attitude towards us in the debate. To let the passage stand against Mr. Alsup would be unfair to him. What to do I did not for the moment know.

A wealthy planter a short distance from the schoolhouse, whose house faced the Lebanon-Murphy's borough pike, had arranged for quite a large number of the prominent people attending the discussion, including each day us two Mormon elders, to be served a luncheon. It was agreed that at this function the debate should be silenced until the parties returned to the meeting place. At the close of the forenoon session of the debate on that third day, I spoke to my companion Elder Ford and asked him to excuse himself from attending the luncheon provided. I had not attended any of the luncheons because I was suffering very severely at the time from sinus trouble and used the lunch hour for relaxation and rest at a nearby friend's home. Elder Ford followed the suggestion, and together we went to a prayer meeting place that we had dedicated near this home where I rested, and to that place we repaired.

There I explained to Elder Ford my dilemma of contradicting the citation of Mr. Alsup to the Book of Mormon. Having made the explanation, I said to my companion that the only way that occurred to me that the situation could be handled would be to ask the Lord to take the whole matter from the minds of our opponents. Elder Ford expressed doubt as to whether that could be done or not, because he had heard when the contradiction was made the minister assisting Mr. Alsup (for on the appearance of Mr. Alsup to engage in the debate, the rest of the challenged ministers by the people all came in to render him such assistance as they could) note the contradiction and gloat over the blunder I had made. They had chuckled and were extremely joyous over the incident apparently, and the matter would doubtless be taken up by the opponents when the afternoon meeting began. It was in the closing address of the meeting that I made my mistake, and the opponents had up to that time had no opportunity to challenge my statement.

Given his observations Elder Ford thought that to ask that the subject matter be taken from the minds of their opponents was a little too much for Elder Ford to have much confidence in. I answered, "In spite of all that, Joseph, I want you to get down on your knees and ask that God shall take that matter from their minds and that we shall hear no more of it. If that is not done, we will be dishonored in the eyes of that great congregation, and our debate and the strength that it has built up will be destroyed." Elder Ford, to be one with me, his younger brother, knelt down and made a prayer, but it must be confessed that it did not ring much with faith. I was not satisfied, and so I prayed, and at the close of my fervent petition, for I felt the awkwardness of the situation, even Elder Ford seemed to get increased faith. I called upon him to pray again, which he did, and after a few minutes conversation and a glowing glow of faith, I prayed again, and the cloud seemed lifted. By now it was time for us to return to the debate.

Those who went to lunch at the wealthy man's home came back but apparently in no triumphant mood, notwithstanding the untoward advance that had come to their side of the discussion. Mr. Alsup was to make the opening address in the afternoon, and it was to be presumed that he would take up my blunder at once, but he did not refer to it at all. None of his associates promoted him to refer to it. It remained a blank, and that afternoon Mr. Alsup declared his intention of closing the debate with the afternoon session. I demurred, saying that I had not yet had the opportunity of examining Mr. Alsup's church, its doctrines, organization, and authority, and it was part of the agreement that this question should be taken up in this debate. Despite this, Mr. Alsup refused to go on with the discussion, and that afternoon the debate was closed.

What drove him to this conclusion was largely on several points. Complaint was made against the Book of Mormon because the people it represented and the prophets of God among them expressed knowledge of the gospel of the Christian faith previous to the birth of Christ. This attitude called forth the reply that not only was that true as to the Book of Mormon people but it was true also of the Hebrew people of the Old World. St. Paul had said that the scriptures before the gospel foresaw that God would justify the heathen through faith preached unto Abraham. He said, "In these shall all nations be blessed." This had reference, of course, to the seed of Abraham, that is the Christ, who brought to pass the salvation of men, so that knowledge of the gospel previous to the birth of Christ was known to the people of the Bible as well as the Book of Mormon.

The only answer that Mr. Alsup could make was that while there was a sort of a gospel taught to Abraham, yet it was not the saving gospel such as came to the world after the Christ. To this I made reply that there was but one gospel. That gospel was the one which brought salvation not only to those who believed after Christ came in the meridian of time in the flesh but also to all those from the beginning who believed the words of the holy prophets who spake as they were inspired by the gift of the Holy Ghost (see D&C 20:6). But Mr. Alsup's exposition of this passage would lead to the belief that a gospel was preached unto Abraham, which did not have the power of saving grace. This left the result that God taught the gospel unto Abraham with unknown results. The people gave an interpretation to that situation. Someone among them said that Alsup had left Abraham in hell, and I had dared him to get him out. This rose to a murmur among the congregation and made the position for Mr. Alsup unpleasant. At any rate he announced the debate closed—he would not go on with it—and left the Moccasin district for his home.

Within six weeks following this debate, we baptized enough people when added to the few who had already been baptized to make up a branch of over sixty in its membership. They continued to thrive for a number of years in that locality, and quite a number gathered to the LDS Colorado settlements, where they lived for some years, and many of them died in the faith.

There was one peculiarity that attached to the answering of the prayers of Elder Ford and me in relation to the taking out of the minds of my opponents my blunder. It was also taken out of my own mind, and neither then nor since then through all the years have I been able to recollect the particular passage, which I had so unfortunately contradicted the existence of. Neither can I remember the exposition of it as it had been given to me in Sunday school—it is a lost chord in that debate and also in the memory of the young elder who contradicted wrongfully its existence. Mr. Alsup after the close of the debate, and repeatedly afterwards, stated that he claimed no triumph in the discussion with "the young Mormon elder."

Years afterwards when on a special mission to some of the larger centers of population through the country, I stayed a few weeks in Cincinnati. On visiting the public library in that city, I remembered that this was a great center for the activities of Alexander Campbell and took advantage of my visit to that place to go through the collected works of that famous preacher. He was contemporary with Sidney Rigdon and Joseph Smith. I found in the *Millennial Harbinger* of 1831 the critique of Mr. Campbell on the Book of Mormon and there discovered all the points which had been introduced by Parson Alsup in the aforesaid debate. In answering Mr. Alsup I was really answering the criticism of Alexander Campbell on the Book of Mormon. I take the occasion to say I think it is the most powerful criticism of the Book of Mormon that has been written. This is why Parson Alsup was anxious to confine the debate above to a consideration of the Book of Mormon alone, because this pamphlet of Campbell's against the Book of Mormon supplied to him material which he thought invincible.

The critique of Campbell against the Book of Mormon I later copied in extenso in manuscript. It was especially bound and is one of the choicest manuscripts in my possession.

CHAPTER 16.

Meeting of President Morgan of the Southern States Mission

New interests were all the while coming in the development of the work in Tennessee. A Utah paper was received in which it was announced that very early from the date of it, Elder John Morgan, president of the Eastern States Mission, would go to Nashville to resume his labors in the south. Allowing a sufficient number of days for the journey of the president from Salt Lake City to Nashville, Elder Ford and I decided that we should go to Nashville and get in touch with our president. We accordingly tramped through the red clay of Murphysborough County and an adjoining county to Nashville and made inquiries at the post office for the whereabouts of Elder Morgan, only to find there a large accumulation of mail that President Morgan had not called for. Therefore he had not arrived in Nashville, and just when he would be there, of course, could not be ascertained. Finding ourselves in Nashville, we concluded to stay a few days, during which time it was hoped President Morgan would arrive, and we could be making ourselves acquainted with this largest and sometimes called "Queen City" of the South.

The question of where we would stay became something of a problem, and this had to be determined by Elder Ford, because he was generously meeting the expense of both of us since I was without funds. However I somewhat influenced the choice because I was averse to taking quarters at a rooming house and proposed a first class hotel. We finally settled upon the Hotel St. Nicholas, one of the most exclusive hotels of a semi-family character. We were not clothed for such associations as we would find there. The rain to which we had been exposed through some forty-five miles of tramping had made our shoes red and there had been bespattering of mud upon the clothing – my threadbare clothing in fact – which had been much exposed to outdoor adventures in Iowa. A visit to the barber shop for a shave and shoeshine and thorough scraping and brushing by the obsequious darkies improved our appearance a little, and so brushed up, we registered at the Hotel St. Nicholas with its wealthy fashionable people and some of the remnants of old families in the South.

I distinctly remember our entrance into the magnificent dining rooms, the interior of which was reflected in the splendid plate mirrors of earlier days of the rich south. Also the traditional dramatization of the dining room was observed by the immaculately clothed colored waiters who stood in their almost Apollo-like pose with their silver service trays held in place, which attitude was not changed until we were seated. We were the first to enter the room, and this released the pose of the waiters. Dinner, of course, was elegantly served with all the flavor of the old South and its high-sounding dishes new to us rough-clad elders from the West. After this a visit to one of the fashionable theaters ended the day except for the return to the wonderfully spacious bedroom which had been engaged by us. Such splendor as all this was an entirely new experience for the rural inhabitants of Davis County. When finally we decided to retire each to his bed, almost mountain high, we sank into the luxurious depth of a featherbed of the old south and rested and slept until late.

The next morning, however, we came to our sober senses out of all this luxury, and, of course, Elder Ford by the measurements of his funds announced that he could not continue at this high-pitched style of life very long. On my part, I could not easily accept the sacrifice Brother Ford would have to make for the hotel fare, and after consultation, we decided to find cheaper quarters and did at last bid farewell to this temporary and much admired touch of luxury in our grey missionary life.

Several days spent in Nashville in visiting its capital and other points of interest along the Columbia did not bring Elder Morgan into town, and hence it was concluded that we return to our friends in Wilson County and stay until Elder Morgan should come and announce his arrival to us. This happened several weeks later, as President Morgan announced his arrival in company with Alonzo Snow, a son of one of the twelve apostles, Lorenzo Snow. President Morgan wrote a special invitation to Elder Ford and me to join him in attendance upon what was known as the Duck River conference in the vicinity of Shady Grove. This was long-time a center of Mormon activities extending back to the days of David Patten, the martyr of Crooked River Battle, and Elder Wilford Woodruff in 1833-34, who afterwards became one of the twelve apostles and president of the church.

This invitation of President Morgan's to us to attend this conference was the occasion of a second journey of ours to the capital city of Tennessee. As we were on penance somewhat for our extravagance at the Hotel St. Nicholas, we tramped the forty-five miles from our quarters to Nashville through red mud and rain. I had been for a short time a student in the Morgan Business College, conducted for a time by Elder Morgan. But my studies had been so brief that no thorough-going acquaintance with Elder Morgan had been formed, and I was not registered in this remarkable president's remembrances. But his companion, Alonzo Snow, had been a schoolmate of mine while I was in attendance at the University of Deseret and unfortunately held in recollection the horrible suit of clothing in which I had attended the university and delivered the valedictory address.

On the evening of the arrival, a point had been designated where we would meet. Elder Morgan had amused himself in imagining what the possible appearance of me was and had drawn variable sketches of me as he waited for our arrival. He gave a rather favorable appearance of me, but Elder Snow said, "He won't look like that. You will find him different." And sure enough when he saw me with slouched hat, bespattered wet clothing, and red muddy shoes, the favorable picture Elder Morgan had drawn of me was dissipated on my arrival. But bless his heart he did not then or ever seemingly take note of the appearance of us elders with whom he labored, and with extended hands and a bright emotionally looking face, he drew me into an embrace that sealed a friendship between us forever.

The next day the journey was made from Nashville to Columbia by train, thence by livery teams from fifteen to eighteen miles to Shady Grove district, where we were made welcome at the home of Uncle Robert Church. He was a well-beloved member of the church and baptized when a lad by the prophet Joseph Smith in the Mississippi River. His father had taken himself and his two sons, this Robert Church and Emmos Church, his brother, to see the prophet, and this had resulted in all three of them being baptized by him as aforesaid in the Mississippi River.

Elders from other sections of the South were gathered here. A priesthood meeting was held in the forenoon of a Saturday, in which they variously gave report of their labors. I included in my report my wanderings in the state of Iowa and some of the adventures through which I passed in preaching the gospel. All seemed to be intensely enjoyed by my new found president and fellow laborers. This was the first conference I had attended since leaving my home in April of 1880, and I was as hungry for companionship as the other elders seemed to be rejoiced at it. Rather pessimistic representations were made by me of conditions in Wilson County, and I told of an effort that Elder Ford and I had made to withdraw from the field in order to find a people more ready to accept our message. President Morgan cancelled all that by saying that what was needed in this field of labor was not for the elders to withdraw, but we needed more help to carry on to the successful conclusion, which he felt would attend our labors. He, therefore, appointed the aforesaid Alonzo Snow and Elder James Hammond from Logan, who afterwards became the first secretary of state of Utah. After Elder Morgan had delivered a very earnest and deeply interesting public discourse, the Duck River Conference disbanded, and the elders returned to the several fields of labor as designated by him. Elder Ford and I returned to Wilson County accompanied by Elders Snow and Hammond.

Here we must refer to some dearly beloved spiritual experiences that attended upon our return. In this Moccasin center of Wilson County had lived a southern planter by the name of Huddleston of very great influence and possessing large plantations, abundantly supplied with slave labor. The elder Huddleston, now dead some years, had been one of the kindest masters to the slave laborers and wealthy and prosperous withall until the war released his slave people and led him in his old age to divide his large plantation to his sons and other relatives. Among these sons was one known as Perk Huddleston, generally known throughout the neighborhood as Uncle Perk. He had little taste for raising cotton or corn, but because of a nature given to his easy and luxury-loving complex, he followed the rather fashionable vocation in that region of raising specially trained game chickens, which he himself had developed. The Huddleston breed was very widely known. He had an extensive establishment in raising this breed of chickens and shipping them throughout the United States for fighting cock game battles and also for breeding purposes. The usual set in which they were sold for breeding purposes would be two hens and a young cock–for fighting purposes only. The cocks were shipped, and there was wide demand for them. They were especially game and in popular demand, so that he had converted his share of the elder Huddleston's plantation into this industry and prospered in it. The fowl were usually sold for $25 per set, and where the eggs were ordered, they cost $6.00 a dozen. The fighting cocks were sold readily at very high prices according to the degree of training which he himself had supervised.

It was rather strange to think that a condition of absolute friendship would arise between this gentleman and us in the Moccasin vicinity. But he became intensely interested in the message of the New Dispensation, as all his following did in the neighborhood. Several members of his family became baptized converts, among them a very beautiful young woman, his daughter, now married and possibly thirty-two to thirty-three years old. She had married a young confederate soldier, who had served with some distinction in the war and was now attending–being patronized by his father-in-law–the Nashville Medical Institution, one of the foremost medical schools of the South. His wife, Mrs. Vaughan, had become intensely interested in Mormonism, and it was rumored among friends that it was her intention to join the church. The visit to the Duck River conference of Elder Ford and me had interrupted her interest.

The Huddleston planation consisted of a broad lawn with here and there hickory trees scattered over its mound-like shape. One central building served as the home, offices, and rooms of Mr. Huddleston, while those who assisted him in his vocation of special fowl raising lived in single-roomed cabins, scattered through this young grove. One of these cabins was set apart as our quarters when we visited Mr. Huddleston and was kept exclusively for our convenience. Dr. and Mrs. Vaughan occupied another of these larger cabins. Formerly they had been the quarters of the family negroes, belonging to the estate. Just before leaving the conference, I had this dream. I came through what was called the "woodslot," a tract of land adjacent to the Huddleston home, extending several hundred yards out to the Lebanon-Murphysborough pike.

In the dream I found myself coming over the winding path from the turnpike road towards the residence. There were four in our company of elders approaching the homestead, and as we came to the gateway of the woodslot, entering into the before described mound, two of our number passed by, and one came through the gate with me to the Huddleston home. It seemed we had been away for some time and received a very hearty welcome to the quarters where we had before stayed. Shortly after the dinner was announced, being served out of doors on the lawn. I noted the absence of Mrs. Vaughn but said nothing of the absence. Presently, however, observing that I had finished my dinner before the rest of the table had done so, I good naturedly said I would excuse them for not getting through as soon as I had and arose and walked out under the young tree on the lawn. Presently in my dream I saw Mrs. Vaughan standing in the doorway of one of these cabins on the lawn, and as I drew nearer, I noticed she was crying. She made an effort to stop the tears and extended her hand to me, as I drew close, saying, "I am so glad that you have returned. I was afraid you would never come back, and I want you to baptize me." This was a matter of surprise, because directly we had heard nothing of her joining the church and with this the dream closed. But on returning from the conference at Duck River, there was a wonderful definite fulfillment of all these terms.

We four elders, Ford, me, and our new companions, Snow and Hammond, were on our way from Nashville when we came along the Murphysborough pike to the path that led into the Huddleston woodslot. We walked on until we arrived at the gate leading into the Huddleston home, and here Elder Hammond stepped in with me, while Elders Ford and Snow went to visit another friend, living something like a mile further on, by the name of Bruggt. Elder Hammond and I were very heartily received that day at the Huddleston home; dinner was spread on a table out under the trees.

Passing one of the cabins, I saw Mrs. Vaughan framed in the doorway with one arm extended to one of the door posts, and she was making an effort to stop her weeping. As I approached she said exactly the same words that I dreamed, "I'm so glad. I was afraid you would never return, and I want you to baptize me." But she added, and this was not in the dream, "Richard" – that was her husband the doctor, now student, but called doctor by courtesy – "is opposed to my being baptized and is making things disagreeable for me in connection with this matter. What is to be done?" I inquired if the doctor was in their quarters, to which she gave an affirmative answer. "Well," said I, "let us go and see him and perhaps we can arrive at an understanding." Doctor Vaughan was found and the matter explained to him, and I discovered that the doctor had taken umbridge in what he supposed was the prospect of his wife being baptized against his wishes. Whereupon I explained, "Doctor Vaughan, your wife will not be baptized until you willingly give your consent, and if that doesn't happen while I am here, then I shall leave careful instructions that no one will baptize her until she has your full consent to be made a member of the church."

The doctor expressed great pleasure, and in a few days came to us and expressed his entire willingness for her baptism to take place. This was fixed to occur on the next Sabbath day, and other women who had long been under conviction heard of the event and arranged also to become members of the church. At one side of the Huddleston home lawn and yard was a beautiful clear spring of water, perhaps twenty feet across it both ways. It was deep in the center and of sufficient depth near the margin for the ordinance of baptism. Here gathered a very large company of friends and converts, and nine were baptized that day. From time to time the glorious old spring was used for this sacred purpose, extending through some months of time, and among the happiest converts of all was Mrs. Vaughan, who seemed somehow to drink in by nature the spirit of the New Dispensation. Later her husband also joined the church, and they made a journey to Salt Lake and received the sacred mysteries of the temple ordinances, much to their satisfaction, and afterwards returned to Doctor Vaughan's practice in the Moccasin district of Wilson County, Tennessee.

Necessarily we must pass some very interesting experiences that followed these events in the summer of 1881. Among these, however, I feel impelled to report was an effort on the part of Elder Alonzo Snow and me to extend our Wilson County field of labor into the adjoining county of Rutherford, extending up into the hill country on the east side of that county east of Murphysborough. Elder Snow and I moved leisurely through the country, engaging in conversation with the mountain folk as we met up with them. About noon we came to a small town that could boast of a town pump in the little square around which schoolhouse and business concerns centered, and here we stopped for a drink and sat on the well curb for a time, which was on the hillside. We could look across the little square through the open door of a mercantile store, where a man in his shirt sleeves was sitting upon a keg conversing with some other person out of range with our vision. After a few minutes of witnessing the animation of this person in conversation, I suggested that we go down to the store, observing that perhaps we could have a conversation. Accordingly we went in, and the gentleman in spotless white clothing rose and arranged seats for us and continued his conversation with a gentleman, who was stretched out upon the counter with a bolt of cloth for a pillow.

It was soon apparent that the conversation was a religious one. Shortly after our entrance the man stretched out on the counter said, "Huddleston how do you account for that passage of scripture in St. John X:16 which says: 'And other sheep I have which are not of this fold; them also I must bring, and there shall be one fold and one shepherd.' " The quotation startled me because it was a passage that had been prominent in my discussion of the Book of Mormon with Parson Alsup a few weeks before down at the Moccasin district in Wilson County, Tennessee. The gentleman referred to as Mr. Huddleston replied that undoubtedly the other sheep had reference to the Gentiles, to whom the gospel was afterwards preached after first being presented to the House of Israel. At this point I entered the conversation by saying, "I would be inclined to think, sir, that your exposition is sound if it were not for the fact that the Saviour on another occasion said: 'I am not sent but unto the lost sheep of the House of Israel' (St. Matt. XV:24). And therefore when the Christ saith: 'Other sheep I have which are not of this fold,' it must have reference to some branch of the House of Israel." "Well, I never heard that suggested before," remarked the gentleman, evidently owner of the mercantile establishment. "It is new to me."

The argument was carried further, and I took occasion to say that the prophecy was not fulfilled until the Savior personally visited the House of Israel in America, where a witness for God as revealed through Jesus Christ had been raised up. This led on and on in conversation and argument until at last the gentleman, Mr. Huddleston, halted in the midst of an earnest discussion, his hands raised in the air, to ask who we were. It was explained to him that we were from Utah and were Mormons, fulfilling a mission in the state of Tennessee by preaching a restored gospel to the earth. The man stretched out on the counter then bounded up and slapped his hands on his knees, exclaiming, "I knew it, I knew it, the minute they came through the door."

It seems that this gentleman was a cousin to Parson Alsup, with whom we had held the debate in Wilson County sometime before on the Book of Mormon, and had been informed of the prominence given to this passage of the other sheep, which I had emphasized in the debate. Having the suspicion that we when we entered the door were the Mormon missionaries, he had propounded this question to Mr. Huddleston. Mr. Huddleston, the merchant, was the cousin of our friend down in the Moccasin district. As soon as the conversation had reached the point described, the dinner bell at Mr. Huddleston's rang out, and he invited us to take dinner with him and finally to stay all night. His family was quite remarkable and worthy of him. His wife was a fine matronly lady typical of the better womanhood of the South. A beautiful daughter was also there to grace the home and also a son, who had come home from the law college in Lebanon as full of mischief as ever a young man was in the world. We made our stay under pressing invitation of Mr. Huddleston, who kindly arranged for two public meetings, the Sunday following.

Meantime the Liverpool edition of Elder Orson Pratt's works was given him to read, and he followed the various articles of that book on "the Kingdom of God," "Remarkable Visions," "Discussion of John Taylor in France," etc., etc. Whenever possible he seemed happy to engage us in conversation upon our mission. One evening in the presence of all the members of his family noted above and some neighbors, Mrs. Huddleston inquired about Mormon hymnology and if we had any songs that were peculiar to our people. Elder Snow promptly responded, "O yes, we have songs." Then turning to me, he said, "Brother Roberts, let's sing for them 'O Ye Mountain High.' " That was a cause of anxiety because I knew that Brother Snow had some peculiar notion of singing bass to that song, from which he could not have been persuaded. This bass consisted of dropping two notes from the melody of the song and then singing the air straight through, thinking that that was singing bass. But the situation had to be met, and so Elder Snow and I sang "O Ye Mountains High" and got through with it, Elder Snow singing bass. At the end of this Mrs. Huddleston said, "Mr. Snow, what is that you were singing? Do you think it was bass?" Elder Snow replied, "O yes, that's bass." At which Mrs. Huddleston said, "It is the strangest bass I ever heard." Then turning to her student son she said, "Henry, you sing bass to that song with Mr. Roberts that Mr. Snow may see what we think is bass." The tune of "O Ye Mountains High," of course, being an old English air, "Lilly Dale," young Huddleston knew it and sang the bass to my lead. Two verses were sung, at the conclusion of which Mrs. Huddleston broke in to say, "There Mr. Snow, that's our bass to that air." Whereupon, of course, Elder Snow had nothing to say, as it must have been that he himself detected the harmony, and ever afterwards he was practicing to get that new idea of "bass" to "O Ye Mountains High." All of this was a great pleasure to me.

Mr. Huddleston's friendship proved to be of the permanent sort, and this little mountain village of East Rutherford County turned out to be a field of extensive preaching for us, and quite an interest was developed, but no baptisms were recorded as fruits of the strenuous labor performed. Mr. Huddleston himself was a devout member of the Disciples of Campbellite Church, and while he became deeply interested in so-called Mormonism, he never manifested any intention of joining the church.

One Sunday morning on leaving the Huddleston home for an appointment at a considerable distance, there was brought from her special cabin the oldest member of the plantation. This was a colored woman, known definitely to be 104 years of age, and she had expressed a desire both to see us Mormon ministers and relate to us her own religious experiences, which had converted her for membership in the Catholic Church. She had asked permission of the family to meet us, and since all her desires were cheerfully granted, arrangements were made for the visit. Her own experiences were very colorful, but too much involved in detail for recital here.

At conclusion we bid the woman and the family goodby for that day and started down the path to the gate. On reaching the gate we heard that rascal Harry Huddleston calling after us, "Say, I have just told Granny that you all believe that colored folks are brothers to the devil, and she wants to know about that." To this I replied, "I reckon we are all brothers to the devil. He was a very prominent and bright spirit personage in the spirit world and was known as the 'Lightbearer,' who was in rebellion against God. But all the spirits were brothers to him at that existence, so tell granny it's no disgrace for anybody to be considered brother to the devil. Cheer up her heart with our message Harry, and don't let her be offended by what you have told her." With this we continued our journeys for our appointment.

After several weeks of preaching in this locality, we returned to the Moccasin district in Wilson County, where I received word from President Morgan of my appointment as president of the Tennessee conference, which at that time included the whole of the state of Tennessee. I prepared for a visit to all the groups of elders located in the state. I was loaned the use of a somewhat noted horse owned by Sister Laura Church, wife of Uncle Robert Church, a dun colored horse named Traveler after the famous warhorse of General Robert E. Lee. Several elders had used him, and he had "suffered for the gospel's sake." He had had both ears cropped and his tail bobbed by rough action of a mob down in Georgia when he was ridden by Elder Parley P. Pratt, the "Son of Promise," the far-famed missionary in the church. The horse was a pacer in gait and a very easy rider. He carried me on my first and second tour of the Tennessee conference, then first created. We became fast companions, mutually and dearly beloved. The companionship of horse and man continued until March 1883, when Elder Richard C. Camp succeeded me as president of the conference. I returned from this first mission sometime in May.

CHAPTER 17.

The Tennessee Massacre

President Morgan represented to the people of my home town my faith and devotion in the work and suggested the raising of means for properly returning me home, a request heartily responded to by my friends of Centerville. My first work on arriving home was a sheep-shearing job for the Ford brothers, carried on where their flocks were assembled for early summer shearing near the Marsh Basin in Idaho. Changing from preaching to sheep shearing was a radical change in work. In the fall of that year, I returned to school teaching. This was done in the town of Bountiful, Davis County, where part of my boyhood days had been spent. It was before the time of the organization of county high schools, but the trustees of the district assembled in the central schoolhouse the advanced students of grade schools, so in a way it became the forerunner of the subsequent high schools.

During the winter President John Morgan came to visit me, a returned traveling elder in Tennessee. He spoke of my confining my labors within four walls and intimated that he thought the sphere too limited, and thus he conceded in an indirect way what was really afterwards materialized–a suggestion that I return to the mission field. Elder Morgan had presided in the Southern States Mission about thirteen years and really was preparing to retire from that service and had already suggested my name as his successor. In the spring of 1884 this plan was consummated by my being appointed to succeed my late president. Owing doubtless to my extreme youth for such a responsibility, it was understood that I would labor under the direction of President Morgan and therefore was set apart only as the assistant president of the mission with instructions to report to and receive directions from President Morgan. But I was expected to occupy the position of field man in the aforesaid eleven states and would be presiding elder over eleven states of the south with more than one hundred traveling elders and a large number of members of the church, with the responsibility of conducting the occasional emigration of the Saints of that region to San Luis Valley in Colorado.

I arrived in the mission in the month of March 1884, being accompanied into the field by twenty-four new elders from Utah. Among the first activities after arriving in Chattanooga as the acting president of the mission, I paid a visit to Shady Grove District, which had been so central to my activities when president of the Tennessee conference. I crossed Duck River on a flatboat and climbed the steep bluff cutting across the lawn to the spacious log plantation home of Uncle Robert Church. The inmates of the home hailed me from the flatboat and were standing on the crown of the lawn bluff of the river with outstretched hands to welcome me, and an informal social greeting took place on the lawn. As we stood overlooking the river with our backs to the house, I felt the persistent pushing and pushing of someone to the rear of me. Turning, there was old Traveler who had come across the lawn to join the group in the greeting. It was an affectionate embrace around his neck that he received from me, as all the journeys and adventures thronged my memory. Old Traveler was an institution in the Southern States Mission and claimed his place.

Returning to Chattanooga I began my tour of the states comprising the mission by visiting the conferences in Georgia, Mississippi, Alabama, and Tennessee. By this time midsummer had arrived, and I was prepared to visit the next conference in Tennessee which had been appointed in what was known as Kane Creek District in Lewis County. In the early summer I had appointed Elder John H. Gibbs and William H. Jones to a special mission to visit prominent cities and capitals of counties in east and middle Tennessee.

Here let it be explained that Tennessee like Caesar's Gaul was divided into three parts by the Tennessee River. The Tennessee rises in the Cumberland mountains in the eastern part of Kentucky and flows thence southwesterly past Knoxville through the entire state of Tennessee, sweeping through the north end of Alabama and then almost directly northward into the Ohio, which at Cairo flows into the Mississippi. This course of the river cuts off the eastern part of Tennessee into east Tennessee. The southwestern movement of the river past Knoxville into Alabama and then northward makes the section of the state between the north-flowing Tennessee and the southwest-flowing portion known as middle Tennessee. Between the northern course of the river and the Mississippi is the section of west Tennessee. It is one of the noblest states of the south and one of the most historic states of the entire union.

In the course of their directed mission through prominent cities and capitals of counties in the state, Elder Gibbs and Jones were to distribute large quantities of congressional speeches made in the senate of the United States, chiefly by southern senators on the Rights of Religious Liberty. This was a commentary upon the constitutional legislation in congress against the marriage system of the Latter-day Saints. These men ably defended the rights of Utah territory in the exercise of the freedom of religion, and incidentally they bore splendid testimonies to the character of the "Mormon" people in Utah. These senators, chiefly from the South, were notably Senator Morgan of Alabama, Senator Call of Florida, Senator De Lamar of Mississippi, Senator Pendleton of Ohio, and Senator West of Missouri. These with others had nobly defended the rights of the people of

Utah on the floor of the senate. The delegate from Utah, John T. Caine, had these speeches printed and sent large quantities of them to the headquarters of the mission at Chattanooga. With these speeches Elders Gibbs and Jones were supplied and requested to distribute them among prominent people in the parts of the states they visited.

They had completed their special mission and had gone to the branch of the church on Kane Creek to await the forthcoming conference. When I arrived in Chattanooga, I found Elder Jonathan G. Kimball in a precarious state of health. Jaundice and malaria has fastened upon him, and it was quite evident that he needed a respite from the strenuous work of correspondence, etc., at the mission headquarters. Thus I, instead of going to join the elders at Kane Creek with a passing visit to Shady Grove, concluded that Elder Kimball must have a vacation and directed him to go to the home of the Church family on Duck River, there to recuperate for a few weeks. I then undertook the secretarial work at Chattanooga. So time drifted on to the important date of August 20, 1884, reaching a climax in the south of what has become known in our church annals as the Tennessee massacre.

For a number of years there had been brewing in the South a very bitter spirit against Mormon missionary work. There had been pending before Congress numerous propositions of national legislation against the people of Utah, based largely upon their marriage system. Some bills had become law, and the Supreme Court had passed upon the constitutionality. All this gave rise to mobocracy in many instances, resulting in some whippings and driving elders from their fields of labor. In the state of Georgia some two years previously Joseph Standing and Rudger Clawson were taken by a mob and Joseph Standing brutally killed, while Rudger Clawson narrowly escaped with his life. This fatal action had prompted attempts in other localities having the same objectives.

The Sunday previous to August the 10th some baptisms had taken place in Kane Creek District under the direction of Elder John H. Gibbs. This was the baptism of two young ladies, whose parents had consented to their joining the church, and a great throng had assembled at the river's edge to witness the ceremony, Elder Gibbs performing the ordinance. As the candidates for baptism were led into the water and turning to look at the crowd before performing the ordinance, Elder Gibbs observed that many heads were covered. Noting this, he called their attention to the sacredness of the ordinance to be performed and plainly suggested that it would be becoming for all heads to be bared on such an occasion. All heads were uncovered, and he proceeded to the baptism of the young ladies.

Meantime the opposition was strenuously at work. There had been received from anti-Mormon sources in Utah a copy of an alleged address by one Bishop West at a small town in Juab County, Utah, which was represented as hostile and defiant of the United States government. It supposedly called for the vengeance of God to fall upon it and its representatives in Utah holding a federal office and altogether was violently sensational and altogether untrue, a faked canard, for it proved that there was no Bishop West and no such speech ever delivered. However, it was held as the truth by the anti-Mormon press in Utah and was widely scattered throughout the United States, but more especially in the South. The county papers in Lewis County reproduced it, and it started a wave of baseless opposition to the work of the elders. It was numerously circulated in the Kane Creek district and began the savage wounding of one. The circumstances in outline are as follows:

A meeting had been appointed by Elder Gibbs and his associate elders, five or six in number, at the home of Condor, whose home was on the bluff above the little stream of Kane Creek that winds through the valley of that name. It was a beautifully bright day in August and the brethren seated in the main living room of the Condor home had been singing hymns, one of which was:

> When shall we all meet again,
> When shall we our rest obtain
> When our pilgrimage be o'er
> Parting sighs be known no more.

And so followed several stanzas. The singing closed at about ten o'clock, the time at which the meeting was to be called. Elder Gibbs reached across the table for his Bible, saying as he did so, "That hymn suggests a text." He began looking through the Bible for it. At that instant there was a rush across the narrow roadway from the elevated banks of Kane Creek opposite the house of masked men in Ku Klux Klan garb. This was a white sheet drawn together in a peeked hood, the sheet covering the entire body; in the hood were cut eye holes and space for breathing. It appears that the mob of some fifteen or eighteen persons had been concealed in the underbrush of the woods which lined Kane Creek at that point, and they apparently had timed their assault about the time the meeting was to begin.

The first man who rushed over the threshold of the Condor home turned to the elders seated at the table and shot down Elder Gibbs, and apparently he was instantly killed. The person who seemed to be the leader of the mob crossed the room to the fireplace, over which a Kentucky hunting rifle quite common in that hunting section of the South hung upon deer antlers. The people who had gathered to attend the meeting had not yet assembled in their capacity as a congregation but were out in the Condor orchard, where they were pleasantly visiting with each other and partaking of the ripening fruit at the invitation of the Condors. Others were out in the front of the house. The elderly Brother Condor was passing between the roadway and the doorstep at the front of the house and was leaning over the gate. As soon as the masked mobbers rushed from the underbrush to come through the gate to the house, he shouted at the top of his voice to the two sons of the family back in the orchard to come to the rescue of the elders. These two boys were both the sons of Sister Condor, one of them (Hudson, the older) was the son of a former husband, the other the son of Mr. Condor. A night or two before this event occurred, Sister Condor had dreamed of such an attack and Saturday afternoon had related the dream to the family. She had directed the two young men to be prepared to defend the elders if possible. Accordingly they had loaded their guns. One was the aforesaid hunting rifle above the fireplace. The leader of the mob had gone direct to secure it before either of the young Condors could obtain it. Hudson's gun was up in the left of the dwelling room, and when they heard the shouting of their father that the mob was upon them, they rushed to the rear door of the house. Hudson, the older son, climbed the open stairway into the loft to get his gun, and the younger Condor tried to secure the gun hung over the fireplace, but he met face to face the leader of the mob with the gun already in his hands. Instantly the lad seized it. He was not yet twenty and began a struggle for its possession. Apparently he must have been getting the better of the struggle, which the mob leader recognized, and he drew from his waistband a pistol and shot the lad dead.

Meantime Hudson, having secured his gun from the loft, came down the open stairway with it in hand just as the mob leader had shot his brother. He then apparently rushed to leave the house by the front doorway, whereupon Hudson drew his gun in place and shot him, and he fell dead in the doorway. At this the cry was raised outside, "Hinson has been killed," and the mob lingering around the house immediately rushed through the doors and drove their guns through the windows and began shooting indiscriminately. One of these shots was aimed at Elder Thompson, who was making his way to the rear door. Elder Berry was standing in the middle of the floor amidst this melee. A gun from behind him was thrust in, but with both hands he pushed it aside so that the shot entered the logs at the side of the door. Elder Thompson made his escape through the door and out into the wood-covered hills behind the house. In the promiscuous shooting into the house that followed the killing of Hinson, Brother Berry was shot down. Hudson was killed as he came down the open stairway right after he had shot Hinson, and old Sister Condor was savagely wounded in the hips.

Four of the elders, namely William S. Berry, Elder Thompson, John H. Gibbs, and William H. Jones, had spent the night at the home of Mr. Tom Garrett some two miles above Kane Creek from the Condor residence. Early on that fated Sabbath morning, Elders Gibbs, Berry, and Thompson walked down the little valley to the Condor residence, while Elder Jones remained at the Garrett home to finish reading a copy of the *Deseret News*, which during the week had arrived in the mail. Thus he did not make his way towards the Condor residence until an hour or two after the other brethren had gone. Just below the bluff on which the Condor residence stood, Kane

Creek was crossed, a stream that usually was clear and between three and four feet deep at the crossing. The elders had gone through the trees and underbrush lining the creek about 100 yards, and there a Brother Michael Garn had cut down, leaving a high stump, a large cottonwood tree and felled it across the creek about one-half way up the bluff to the Condor residence. He had then trimmed it and flattened it as a foot bridge across the creek to the Condor side of the stream. This log bridge was considered quite wonderful by the people, and its constant use had made a pathway through the underbrush and the trees along the creek. Coming to where this path reached the road, Elder Jones started towards the log foot bridge. About half way down he was suddenly rushed upon by the Ku Klux mob who had been concealed along the footpath by the river and in a close adjoining cornfield running down close to the pathway on the right. They commanded his silence as to any outcry for help that would reveal their presence, and they demanded of him to know where the elders were and if they too were coming down from the Garrett home.

All of this leads to the conclusion that this mob had early in the morning concealed themselves along the pathway and doubtless intended killing the elders as they moved in single file between the road crossing of Kane Creek and the log foot bridge. But finding Elder Jones coming alone, they captured him and through him tried to locate his brethren, surmising rather than being told that the other three elders had passed down the pathway and over to the Condor residence before they had concealed themselves along the pathway. They relegated Jones to be guarded by one of their numbers with orders to shoot him if he intended to escape.

They made their way to the Condor side of Kane Creek and attacked the home as already described. When the shooting began Jones's guard became very excited, and the screaming of women and children, as well as the shooting of the men, filled him with alarm, for he exclaimed "My God, they are shooting the women and children." Whereupon Jones began to plead for his guard to allow him to escape. To this the guard consented and followed him through the aforesaid cornfield across the clearing to the woods beyond. Jones was afraid to run lest his guard would shoot him down under the plea that he was making an effort to escape, but once in the woods Jones received instructions from the guard how to proceed to get out of the neighborhood and then himself turned back to join his companions about the Condor residence. Thus the Kane Creek massacre became history.

While these transactions were going on in Kane Creek, I was at the mission headquarters in Chattanooga, attending to my secretarial duties, answering mail, etc., etc. On Sunday night I worked rather late on an article that I was preparing for the *Juvenile Instructor*, telling a mission story of a mother's influence, which happened a few weeks before in northern Alabama. The article finished and made ready for mailing, I prepared for retiring and extinguished the lamp. To my astonishment there was no diminution of light in the room. Every object was vividly seen as before the lamp was extinguished. This, of course, was something of a mystery to me, and instead of immediately retiring, I walked about the room trying to account for the strange phenomenon. I thought perhaps it was an unusual afterglow of the lamplight, and with the thought of correcting my sight I threw myself upon the bed with my face in the pillow, hoping in this way to exclude the light until my eyes became properly adjusted. After a time on raising my head, I still found the light undiminished and lay wondering at it for some hours, nearly through the night in fact. With the breaking of the day, I fell into a restless sleep, and when I awoke the sunshine was brightly slanting in the room from the east.

The mission headquarters was made up of an office room and sleeping apartments, and we had been taking our meals at the Florentine Hotel in the heart of Chattanooga. I arose and dressed preparatory to going to breakfast. As I entered the foyer of the hotel, I found the inmates regarding me unusually, but none spoke. When the morning paper was brought to me, I was astonished to see in flaring headlines an account of Mormon elders being massacred on Kane Creek in Lewis County. The thing was too horrible to believe as true, and I, neglecting breakfast, returned to headquarters that I might ask in prayer if these terrible things had occurred. While on my knees in the office of the mission engaged in prayer, the voice which had so frequently spoken to me in times of crisis told me to return to the hotel and I would receive a message on the subject.

Accordingly I immediately went back to the hotel and found awaiting me a telegram from Jonathan Golden Kimball, the secretary resting up at the church's home near Shady Grove. The telegram confirmed in general the newspaper account of the killing of the elders and the Condor boys on Kane Creek. I at once wired Elder Kimball as soon as possible to gather the elders who had escaped at the town of Columbia, to locate them there, where I thought they would be at least temporarily safe, and to keep me informed of his movements. Meantime I would reach Columbia myself as soon as possible. This done the thought occurred to me to secure the bodies and send them to their friends in Utah. But there was no money at the headquarters, and it would take some time to obtain it from Salt Lake. I wired for funds necessary to this project, about $1,000.

Meantime it was impossible for me to remain inactive while these means were arriving. Accordingly I went to Mr. Bernard Moses and his brothers and presented the case to them and stated my own anxiety to be on the way to secure the bodies and send them home. I needed steel caskets in which the bodies could be hermetically sealed, as the railroad would accept no other. Mr. Moses kindly consented to leave security at the undertakers for the caskets and in addition withdrew several hundred dollars from his own bank account and loaned it without security or even a note certifying such a loan. The caskets were sent to a friend, Mr. Sam

Hoover, a member of the church, living part way between Shady Grove and the point on Kane Creek where the tragedy had occurred.

My first move was to start for Columbia by way of Nashville. I went to the latter place, the capital of the state, hoping to see the governor and secure assistance through him for going under guard to Kane Creek to secure the bodies. Governor Bates was absent from the city. In fact, he was conducting his campaign for reelection in an adjoining county to Lewis County. I then called upon the lieutenant governor, but he was unable to make any move in the direction of giving assistance because the governor was still in the state, and he could not act unless the governor was absent from the state. I then asked if the lieutenant governor would give me a letter to the state sheriff of Lewis County saying at least that it would not be contrary to the law for him to render me such assistance as he could and to go with me to Kane Creek as a protection against the mob forces. The mob when they heard of these several moves on my part to get legal assistance in securing the bodies expressed their determination to so guard the roads entering the county from the north and the east that the bodies could not be obtained. I personally knew the sheriff of Lewis County, a Mr. Carrol, at whose home I had several times stayed over night, and the sheriff was very favorable to the Mormon elders and inclined to receive their message.

Finding that this letter was likely to be all the assistance I could obtain, I started for Columbia over the railroad and arrived about midnight. My first anxiety was to locate Elder Kimball and such elders as he had brought into the city. This took some time. At last, however, I found them in a fourth-rate rooming house in the south edge of the city and learned from the proprietor of the establishment that they were much alarmed on account of threats of a mob coming to drag them for their rooms to do them violence. I immediately had the elders transferred to the principal hotel of the town, where I myself had registered, and while the elders, including Elder Kimball, slept, I wrote the authorities in Utah a statement of what had happened.

When morning came I began making preparations for the journey to Kane Creek, the first fifteen or twenty miles of which would have to be covered by a livery and buggy as there was no other way of reaching Shady Grove enroute to the fateful Kane Creek. I secured a livery outfit from one of the chief livery stables of Columbia, owned by a Mr. Dobson, whom I had before patronized in making journeys about the country in company with President Morgan. A single horse and buggy was secured. While the horse was being harnessed and attached to the buggy, a company of rough looking men gathered near the entrance of the livery stable and seated on the grass began an animated conversation in which the word Mormon was frequently used. I drew as near to this group as I could without seeming to do so, if possible to catch the drift of the rather excited conversation.

While in this position I felt the sharp cut of a whip across my arm and turned towards the door of the livery stable in time to catch a glimpse of Mr. Dobson dodging into the door of the office of the livery stable with whip in hand and beckoning me to come in to him. This was done, and Mr. Dobson apprised me of the fact that this group of men seated outside the stables were the men who had been trying for a day or two to arouse a mob in Columbia to drive from the city the several elders who had arrived there under the direction of Elder Kimball. Mr. Dobson was much moved emotionally and taking me by the shoulders gently shook me saying, "Notwithstanding your pretense to send other parties after those bodies, I know it is your intention to go yourself, and now Mr. Roberts let me tell you. You are a young man. You have only one life, and if you go into that Kane Creek section of Lewis County, you will be killed. Dave Hinson the leader of the mob down there had a large number of friends and a political pull that will make things go hard for you if his following are once aware that you are in their midst. So now let me beg of you not to go." At this caution, however, I laughed and assured Mr. Dobson that I would take care of myself and avoid all the danger I could.

By this time the horse and buggy were ready, and Elder Kimball and I climbed into it and drove off for the first stage of our journey to the Shady Grove district. By this time it was afternoon, and it required all the time until nearly dusk to reach the Church residence on Duck River. Here we raised the necessary two teams in order to make the journey with the caskets. It was not an easy matter to secure teams and wagons at that time in this part of Tennessee, for wagons were little used except the running gears of them in hauling timber, and travel was made chiefly on horseback. However, during the night the teams were assembled, and a friend, not a member of the church, a Mr. Harlow, volunteered to drive one wagon on the expedition with one of the members.

It was true what Mr. Dobson had said about my intention to go myself after the bodies. While making the journey from Nashville down to Columbia, sitting alone on the train, I heard the familiar voice whisper to me quite clearly, "You will go to secure those bodies and all will be well with you, but you must go." From that time, of course, I had no other intention than to go myself on this expedition, but whereas I got one pair to drive one of the wagons, I thought I would like a companion to be with me on my wagon.

Along about midnight it occurred to me to ask a young fellow not a member of the church but very friendly to me, Rufus Coleman, about eighteen years of age. On inquiry, however, I learned that he was a number of miles distant at a road camp making a turn pike and impossible to communicate with at once as the expedition was to start in the morning. A Sister Phoebe Church, daughter of Emmos Church, whose homestead adjoined that of his brother Robert Church, was mounted and sent to the road camp to bring Rufus back to the Robert Church residence where the journey was being planned.

Sometime before daylight, while making all the arrangements, Brother Kimball was much concerned as to who would be the man to go with the second team. I revealed to him that I was to go with the second wagon. Brother Kimball thinking that he was the one nominated said: "All right, President Roberts, if you think I should go I am willing." "No, No," I said, "it is not you, but I myself am going." Brother Kimball raised a lusty protest, saying that I was so well known in the Kane Creek district of the country that my being there would raise the mob and they would kill me. However, I assured him that that would not be the case and that it was the proper thing for me to go. But Elder Kimball continued to protest. Then I said to him, "I know, and if you are in doubt about it, go and ask our Father." Up to this point I had said nothing to him about my whispered voice on the train. I observed that Brother Kimball made several trips out into the corn field, coming up close to Brother Robert Church's house, and I knew that Elder Kimball went there to pray, but apparently he received no impression confirming the wisdom or rightfulness of me to go on this journey.

Meantime Sister Phoebe Church had returned with Rufus Coleman, who came up into the loft chamber where I had donned an old suit of clothing, a hat and rough cowhide boots belonging to one of Robert Church's hired help. I was now trying to hide the indoor complexion of my face and hands from the soot and grease accumulated on the walls, for the loft room had been used as a smokehouse by the family. As Rufus came into the chamber, I said to him, "Rufy, I am going down to Kane Creek with two teams to secure the bodies of the elders who have been murdered. Brothers Church and Harlow have consented to take one wagon. Will you go with me and drive the other wagon?" He stood apparently relaxed before me with his hands in his pockets, but as the request was made he straightened up and said in a delightful southern drawl, "Why yes, Mr. Roberts. I'll go anywhere with you, sir." The simple answer shook me with emotion at this symbol of trust and fidelity.

With this, the teams having been hitched to the wagon and the separation with Elder Kimball given, lunch was provided by Sister Laura Church. Rufy and the other two brethren started with their teams, purposely going a little out of the way to drive through Shady Grove that it might be seen that I was not in the company. I, in company with Robert Church, cut through the cornfield of the church plantation, intending to intersect the teams several miles beyond Shady Grow, where they were headed to pick up the steel caskets at the home of Samuel Hoover. The teams were intersected some half mile from Hoover's residence, and I joined Rufus and drove to the Hoover home, where happily I learned the caskets had been delivered safely. They were loaded into the wagons brought from the starting point of the expedition.

I moved freely about the Hoover home, meeting the inmates thereof and some neighbors from surrounding homes who had gathered in their curiosity about the activities going on. It created assurance in my mind that my disguise was sufficient, as none of these people with whom I had mingled in former years recognized me. The caskets secured, the journey was continued. Learning at the Hoover home that the roads leading into Kane Creek country from the east were being watched by members of the mob who had done the killing, a swing to the south was made, and the mob-guarded roads both on the north and on the east were avoided. The wagon expedition arrived at the home of Mr. Garrett, a friend of the elders, who lived near the Condors.

There had been two elders laboring in Hickman County, directly north adjoining Lewis County. Their names were Willie Robinson and W. B. Robinson. The wildest rumors had permeated the district where they were laboring, and how many had been killed and whether any of the elders had escaped or not was unknown to them. Nor could they find any reliable account of the wild rumors that were passed from mouth to mouth in that sparsely settled country. This determined Elder Robinson to make a journey into Lewis County to Kane Creek itself to ascertain what there was to the wild rumors. Elder Robinson at this point did a very remarkable thing. Of course it was generally known that these Mormon elders wore their endowment garments received in the temple ceremonies. It is quite generally regarded as a protection, morally, spiritually, and even physically. But unfortunately if Elder Robinson should fall into the hands of enemies, it would be a betrayal of him as to his being a Mormon elder. He therefore retired to a densely wooded section of the country and, stripping off these garments, rolled them up and climbed a tree and tied them securely.

This time he started out alone and went directly into the enemies' country, Lewis County. He had resolved upon the plan of representing himself as something of a special cotton picker hunting a job. This was in order to satisfy those who might intercept his journey and ask awkward questions. Truly enough he met with such an experience. There was a narrow-gauged road extending from Hickman County into Lewis County. This he used as his line of travel, thinking that he would likely not meet so many on this journey. But approaching the neighborhood of Kane Creek where the elders were reported to be killed, the railroad passes over a bit of trestle work over a very deep and quite large ravine, and near the middle of this trestle work he observed three men approaching from the other side, guns in hand. There was nothing left to do than to go right on.

These men proved to be members of the mountain guard watching for me. On meeting Elder Robinson they questioned him as to where he came from and what his purpose was, and when he told them that he was looking for a job cotton picking they laughed saying, "A damn fine cotton picker you would be. Look at your hands." And, of course, as Elder Robinson had not engaged in physical labor, his hands were white and soft, not at all characteristic of cotton pickers. He then told them of having been sick for sometime, and that accounted for his pallor in his face and hands and that he was just now beginning to get about and was now strong enough to begin cotton picking. Hence he was in search of that job. They invited him to sit down while they thought things over. No sooner did he do that when one of the three grabbed his shirt by the collar and tore it so as to expose his body, but they found no garments incriminating him as to his Mormonism and finally allowed him to pass.

He did not arrive at Condor residence till about midnight. Knowing that the Condors would doubtless be on guard against surprises especially from the threatening mobocrats, he remained concealed in the underbrush and threw gravel at the door and windows. Presently the door was cautiously opened, and he called softly to Brother Condor who was opening the door, telling him who he was and the inquiries he wanted to make about the report of the killing of the elders. At this the door was thrown open, and he was made welcome into the stricken home and the true account given to him. He stayed with them about two hours, during which time they provided food for him.

Then remembering his experience on the railroad trestle and what would likely follow if he went that way again, he decided to take an easterly route and then circle northward until he should reach his point of starting on the journey. Going eastward he met another group of the mob watching the entrance into Kane Creek district from the east, and again he was challenged. Again his shirt was torn open in search for the identification which his garments would give, but, of course, no garments being found his captors consented to let him pass. By this time he met with instructions sent out from Nashville to elders in this central part of Tennessee for them to repair to Nashville and obtain lodgings, where they could be more likely to find safety than remaining in the country. The heroism of Elder Robinson required no commentary. His action in going into the danger zone will be sufficient to all that.

Mr. Garrett for some years had been a great friend of the elders. His daughter, a school teacher, was already a member of the church, and Mr. Garrett was kindly disposed towards that organization. I handed to him a letter signed "President B. H. Roberts" and ostensibly given to me, a strange rough-looking man, who had been employed by the president to come and get the bodies in his behalf. The letter asked Mr. Garrett to render this stranger all the assistance he could in taking the bodies from the graves and preparing them for shipment over the railroad. Mr. Garrett attentively read the letter and not recognizing me, who through a number of years occasionally had been his guest, said he would render the stranger all the help he could and asked what he could do.

I suggested that we walk on ahead of the teams down the road until we came to the Condor residence. As we walked along ahead of the teams Mr. Garrett replied to the questions that were asked as to the manner of the killing at the Condors' residence on the previous Sunday and about the location of the graves and other things connected with my mission. Where the road dips down into the Kane Creek crossing, after entering upon this path through the woods lining Kane Creek, I dropped the use of the southern accent, which I had assumed thus far in the conversation. The log foot bridge was reached, and as the underbrush and trees were dense at this point, I ventured to say to Mr. Garrett, since changing my accent had not revealed my identity, "Mr. Garrett, you don't know me?" With that Mr. Garrett started and looked at me more narrowly and then raising his hands he said, "My God, are you here?" And this in his excitement he repeated twice more. Then, of course, there was joy between us two friends, and Mr. Garrett was noticeably more eager to render the assistance he had promised to give.

We crossed the log foot bridge and moved along the steep path to the roadway running by the gate of the Condors. Mr. Garrett led the way to a point beside the road, where under the directions of the county coroner the elders had been buried. Already several wagon tracks had passed over the graves, and were they not to be moved the resting place of the elders would doubtless have been obliterated by the road travel. The two Condor brothers had been buried back of the Condor residence in the orchard on the plantation.

By this time quite a number of people had arrived upon the scene, men and women and some children. Among others had come members of the mob, whom Mr. Garrett whispered to me were know to have participated in the killing only a few days previously. They came armed and were on the alert for my reported coming. Nine of them assembled in all and stood in a group about twenty yards from where the work of exhuming the body was going on. Opening the graves was completed, and the task of drawing the coffins out of the graves was next. This was not an easy accomplishment, for, of course, the members of the mob would render no assistance, and the church members who were assembled there were reluctant apparently to give much assistance. But finally at my demand and after sharp reproves had been given to their backwardness, finally the ropes were passed under the ends of the coffins, and they were drawn up and each placed beside the open grave.

With an ax the plain board coffin lids and sides were pried open, and the bodies lifted into the caskets. I had supplied myself at the church home with two clean white sheets, and these were now spread over the bodies and carefully tucked under the shoulders and hips and feet and head so that they had the appearance of being completely swathed in the pure white sheets. The bodies having been in the warm earth for several days had become much swollen, and the face of Elder Gibbs had pressed up against the cover of the coffin in a manner to a little disfigure the face by the pressure. The necessary putty or oil paste was spread over the lower flange of the caskets, the covers were adjusted with bolts running through the upper and lower flanges, and the small bolts about one to every two inches were screwed down so that no fumes could escape. While performing the rather tedious task of screwing on the lids of the caskets, Mr. Garrett followed with a burning rag in which tobacco was wrapped and kept it burning under my nostrils to disguise the odor arising from the dead bodies. However, I was well nigh overcome with the fumes rising from the dead. A bucket of water had been brought up from the creek and set between the caskets, and as I felt myself being overcome, I so fell as to drive my head into the bucket of water, which saved me from what might have been a faint. Revived I continued the task.

Meantime the mob was receiving additions by new arrivals and there was some manifestation of uneasiness among them and the people. The task of screwing down the lids on the caskets was completed as the sun went down. The caskets were loaded into the wagons, and start was made for the residence of Mr. Garrett.

During the time of fastening down the casket cover, I explained to Mr. Garrett that it would be necessary to obtain the certificate from a physician that the men had not died of disease. Perhaps accomplishing this would necessitate a visit of someone of official standing to Hohenwald, the capital of Lewis County, some twenty miles distant. Mr. Garrett expressed a willingness to go himself. As the company of rescuers and the wagons arrived at his gate and were preparing to drive into the barn, who should come along but the very physician who had given the certificate of burial at the coroner's inquest and who only had to dismount and go into the house of Mr. Garrett and sign the certificate which had been previously secured.

All things considered it was rather a bold move, this going to the graves, exhuming the bodies, and taking them away. It was done without any official action or permit at all, and I at the time and since marveled that there was no legal objection urged against my summary proceedings. However, it is doubtful if the county or state officials would have given any such permit, so to go and get the bodies was doubtless the only way in which it would be done, and the doctor's certificate was made all the more necessary for the express and railroad companies to receive the bodies.

The wagons containing the coffins were driven into Mr. Garrett's barn and the barn door securely fastened against intrusion. The little company gathered into the home of Mr. Garrett, where supper had been provided. Of course there was more or less suppressed excitement, as it was not known but that at any moment the mob might arouse their courage to the point of making an attack upon the Garrett home. However, Mr. Garrett under the stress of the excitement could contain himself no longer, and as the company was seated around the table, to the astonishment of all, he said,

"Elder Roberts, will you say grace?" Whereupon before the grace could be said, his daughter, clapping her hands and jumping about, said, "I knew it, I knew it from the time he came to our gate. I knew it was Elder Roberts." But she had said nothing to her mother about the identification and only spoke when her father had so unexpectedly spoken his name and revealed that the rough ill-clad person was the president of the mission.

Grace said, supper was enjoyed, and shortly afterwards Mr. Garrett placed a living room stand in front of the stairway leading to the sleeping room above. On it he laid two heavy dragoon pistols and placed a rifle leaning against the wall within easy reach of the stand on which the pistols were placed. He then said, "Elder Roberts, you look worn out. Now go up to the loft, and we will stand guard down here, and there is no company of men in this neck of the woods that will get by me in this stairway." The invitation was welcomed, for I had had no sleep during the three previous nights and days and was, as Mr. Garrett stated, worn out.

I slept soundly. Only a small incident happened during the night. Mr. Garrett had the bars leading to his barnyard doors down, and a single horseman led his horse around the barn and inspected the front doors, which he found locked, and therefore he failed to open the doors. After spending some five or ten minutes in this inspection, he mounted his horse and rode away. Mr. Garrett had watched him, gun in hand, from the window and intended to resist any violent effort.

In the morning, Mr. Garrett notified me of the incident, whereupon I joined the man who had been keeping guard with Mr. Garrett during the night and prepared for starting the day's journey. The teams were grained, early breakfast was had, and as the day dawned the wagons were in front of Mr. Garrett's gate ready to start for a station on the railroad some twenty or twenty-five miles distant. This was supposed to be the station of Carpenter on the Louisville and the Nashville Railroad. But checking up later, it was discovered that I had given out three probable destinations where I would take the train, and this without designing it so. One was Naper and the other Carpenter and another Sandyhook station, and finally the one I arrived at was none of the three, but Mount Pleasant in the county adjoining Lewis on the east.

Leaving the Garrett residence a rough road led up a steep ravine out to the flat woods of the district, and I surmised that if an attack was made upon my expedition, it would likely be while going up this deep cut ravine to the flat woods. So after turning from the Kane Creek road up this wood road to the flats beyond, I cautioned Rufus whatever happened to pay strict attention to keeping his team in the road. The same caution was given to the other two men driving the other wagon, as the road was rough and any departure from it might lead to disaster for the caskets encased in the outer boxes.

When I took my leave of Mr. Bernard Moses of Chattanooga, the latter persuaded me to take a gun with me which he provided and really insisted upon my taking it, saying, "You are going among a lot of heathens down there. No telling what might happen. You had better take my gun." He had thrust it in the inside pocket of my coat, and hence when the journey began up this heavily wooded ravine, I took the gun in my hand and threw my coat over it. The other members of the party were not armed, as I had dissuaded them from arming lest they might begin in excitement to start shooting before a crisis might come. I told Rufus that if we were attacked that I would take care of the mob, while Rufus was to look solely after the team. The flat woods reached, the wood road disappeared, and for miles and miles we wandered about in the flats unable to determine the direction we were following. As nearly as we could judge, we moved in the direction, as we supposed, of Carpenter station. But it had to be confessed that we were wholly lost.

Toward four in the afternoon, however, we emerged from the flats into another rather well defined wood road turning sharply to the east and passing a solitary uninhabited log cabin. We followed this road for several miles. Meantime two or three men on horseback rode up and examined the caskets, on the outside boxes of which was written the name of the occupant. In the wagon in which I rode was contained the body of Elder John H. Gibbs, and his name was written on the outside of the box. Having read these names, the horsemen seemed satisfied and, without passing a word, turned back and rode rapidly away. A fourth horseman overtook the wagons, and he asked what station we were headed for and was told the Carpenter station. The horseman said that we had long since passed east of Carpenter, and the best thing to do to reach Carpenter station would be to turn back on the road, and we would doubtless come to the station before dark. This suggestion, however, was silently refuted, and we announced that we would follow the course eastward until we came to some station upon the railroad.

Shortly after this incident the road, which was stony and stumpy and hence rough, circled ahead of a ravine down which a small stream of water trickled. Some distance below, a rough-looking character was squatted beside a tiny stream throwing up the water with his hand into his mouth, and I noted that he was about as mean-looking a person as I had ever seen. At the head of the ravine, however, where the road became a dugway, I stopped the teams and went down to speak to this man, inquired the distance to the nearest station eastward, and passed the time of day. I tried to be a little agreeable but without success, for the man was not only vicious-looking and vicious of speech, but he urged me as the other horsemen had done some distance back that I turn about and go to Carpenter's station. This station was nearer than any other point of the railroad, where I could intercept the train for Nashville. The more the man argued for this course, however, the more determined I became to continue eastward. Asking the nature of the road, the man told me that it was very rough and that I would scarcely make any station before nightfall. When I made my decision to go on eastward, the man with smothered cursing dipped down the ravine. Just why, I did not know.

Within a mile or so, the wood road ended, and we came upon a well built turnpike, running somewhat parallel with the railroad, and within two or three miles from the man who had urged me to turn back, we came to Mount Pleasant. There an express company took charge of the bodies and would ship the bodies to Nashville by way of Columbia. The teams were turned over to the drivers, and lodging was secured at the hotel. When I asked a number of colored men at the station to assist in the unloading of the caskets and putting them in care of the express company, the negroes refused to move and demanded what there would be in it for them. Whereupon I said that I did not ask for service which I would not pay for. There was a rush both of white men and colored men to render the assistance called for, and each received a tip which more than compensated him for the assistance rendered. A comfortable night was spent at the hotel, and early the next morning I boarded the train on which the caskets were loaded, and the journey to Nashville was completed by ten o'clock. So that made the journey in less time than I had calculated it would take me to secure the bodies and reach the railroad and so to Nashville.

Elder Kimball was to have returned from Shady Grove by way of Nashville to Chattanooga, obtain the money that had been telegraphed for from Salt Lake City, pay the indebtedness to Mr. Moses for the money he had loaned me, and return with the balance to Nashville. From there the bodies would be shipped to Salt Lake City in care of some elder. On my part I was to secure the bodies and get them back to Nashville, probably by the evening of Monday. But I had managed to reach Nashville at ten o'clock in the morning and put the caskets in charge of the railroad express company to be shipped on a late train that night for the west. Elder Kimball did not return to Nashville until between nine and ten o'clock that Monday evening.

There was nothing for me to do but await the arrival of Elder Kimball from Chattanooga, and being without suitable clothing into which to change, I was compelled to wear the rough-looking garb I had worn during my journey for the bodies. This was not quite suitable apparel in which to meet newspaper reporters, mayors, and governors that I had contacted a few days before my adventure. My appearance doubtless drew upon me the attention of the police about the station, and I soon discovered that I was being followed by them. Of course, I was anxious to know what was being said about the recent massacre in the newspapers, and therefore I went to the newspaper stand and inquired when trains from St. Louis, Louisville, and Cincinnati arrived in the central depot of Nashville. Soon I observed that the two policemen evidently following me up made a halt at the news stand and engaged in conversation with the news agent. I surmised that the newsman had been told to ask why it was that this rough-looking man was so eager to have the papers from the cities above named.

On my next passing the news stand and inquiring for papers, the news man asked me what I was keeping track of by buying up all the papers that came in with the trains. It so happened that one of the papers that came in from Louisville contained an account of some man who had visited and had entered the hole at the North Pole and had performed something like a three-year journey on the interior of the earth. There he found a salubrious climate and a fertile country within the earth, which received its light chiefly through the North Pole opening. After three years of wandering this man had seen what he at first took for a star way off in the distance, and as he made his journey southward, the star seemed to grow brighter. He was climbing an ascent from the interior of the earth and found the star to be the mouth of a cave opening up way down in Texas and thus came out of the earth's interior to the surface of the earth again.

So when asked what was interesting me in the papers, I told the newsman in a stupid way by asking him if he had read the account of the man who went into the interior of the earth at the north pole and had emerged from a cave in Texas. The newsman roared with amusement at this silly circumstance and expressed his unbelief in the correctness of it. But I said that I was mighty interested in that thing, and I wanted to see if the other papers besides the one from Louisville had anything more to say about it. Then retiring to the open-ended station I watched for the coming of the police to the news stand to get what had passed between the newsdealer and me, and as they were told the story, they doubled up with laughter and concluded that it was some fool following up this raw incident of alleged adventure.

Relieved from the spying tactics of the policemen and realizing that Elder Kimball could not return from Chattanooga until night and desiring to avoid meeting the reporters and city and state officials that I had contacted a few days before, I wandered out to the outskirts of Nashville and walked about on the heights overlooking the river. While doing so I chanced to pass a colored man's tin type photograph gallery and thought perhaps it might be a family interest if I could show them the outfit in which I made the trip. Accordingly I walked inside and seeing that the photographer was looking out of the window preoccupied, I took a seat on an imitation stump in front of a screen of an outdoor scene and waited until the photographer should turn and discover me, which presently he did, and he gave a jump at being in the presence of so hard a looking character. He asked if I wanted my photograph taken and was answered in the affirmative. After shifting about for a few minutes, he rather timidly suggested that there was a wash room in which I could make myself ready for the picture if I chose to, but he was answered that it was not desirable for me to do so. I wanted my picture as I sat there and told him to get his machine ready and shoot. This the photographer did. This photograph without my wish was reproduced widely and published in Utah.

At nine o'clock Elder Kimball came up from Chattanooga, and I met him in the Union Depot of Nashville. Although Elder Kimball had been present when I started my journey in the disguise I assumed, nevertheless he was startled when confronted by his erstwhile companion. Elder Kimball had to report that no money had yet arrived from Salt Lake, and he had been under the necessity of further testing the kindness of Mr. Moses, who had advanced him several hundred dollars more to carry out the plans of sending home the bodies of the dead elders. Elder Kimball had brought the ordinary suit of clothing, which I had been wearing, and I immediately repaired to the hotel, where I could change my clothing.

I hurried to do this in order that I might meet representatives of the press and correct the accumulated misrepresentations that had taken place during my absence from Nashville. I especially wanted to contradict the reported statements of Governor Bates, who had represented that the elders had been killed because of alleged improper relations in the families of the people where they had labored. This gave me an opportunity not only to correct these misstatements but to tell of my adventure in securing the bodies of my brethren. These statements were published at the time in the Nashville papers. Also I decided that I myself would not return with the bodies to Utah but would place them in the care of Elder Willie E. Robinson, who had been the first to visit the Condor residence on Kane Creek and found out the extent of the massacre. The bodies were started westward by train, which left Nashville at midnight for St. Louis and the west.

In due time Elder Robinson arrived in Salt Lake with the bodies, and relatives from the south where Elder Berry lived and from Cache Valley where Elder Gibbs had lived took charge of the bodies, and memorial services were held by the mourning people. General services were held at the same time in Salt Lake City, and the martyrs were eulogized by prominent church officials residing in Salt Lake City. Other leading brethren had also gone to the respective homes of these families to manifest their respect for these brethren. The services were impressive, and the eulogy praised highly the fidelity of these recent martyrs to the cause of the New Dispensation. Steps were also taken to raise the necessary funds for aiding the members of the church in the Kane Creek district to migrate to the settlements of the Saints in Utah and Colorado. This resulted in most of them accepting the aid to their migration.

Mr. Garrett and his family, who had so prominently aided me in this undertaking of moving the elders' bodies to Utah, also found it necessary to move because of threats of violence made against him and destruction of his property. He settled in Bond County, Illinois, where it was necessary to forward to him some assistance in surviving his forced departure from Kane Creek to a place of security. The Condor family received assistance from the church, and while they removed from the scene of their sorrow, they nevertheless elected to remain in Tennessee and lived for a number of years in the western part of that state on the Buffalo, a tributary to the Tennessee River.

CHAPTER 18

The Aftermath of the Tennessee Massacre — Emigration of the Southern Saints to Utah

I had chosen to remain in the mission rather than myself accompanying the bodies of the martyrs to their homes in Utah, since I deemed my presence necessary to meet the violence that was still rife in the South, more especially in Tennessee, Georgia, and Mississippi. Elders in charge of those states were in various localities taken from their lodgings at night, tied up to trees, and cruelly beaten with hickory rods. In one case they were beaten with heavy halter straps by mobs who seemed to take courage from the mob violence that had operated at Kane Creek. In Georgia also an elder by the name of Alexander was captured by a mob down in the woods, tied to a tree, and shot at by the mob, one bullet piercing the straw hat he wore. Happily he escaped with his life. He came to the Chattanooga headquarters and was sent home in the care of Elder Samuel Parrish of Centerville. The experience of Elder Alexander had so shattered his nerves that it was felt necessary to return him to his home.

Everywhere throughout the summer the threats of mob violence prevailed until under advice the work was slowed down and only kept up in sections where it was felt that the safety of the elders would be preserved. Near Baird Mills, Elder James A. Eldredge and companion were served notice that they must leave the neighborhood or they would meet with the same fate as had fallen to the elders on Kane Creek. This the elders reported to me, who was well acquainted with conditions in Wilson County, it being my field of labor on my former mission. Knowing the threatened action as perhaps being taken by some irresponsible parties, I wrote Elder Eldredge not to be driven from the field but to take precaution of staying only with the staunchest friends. He was to arm himself with a shotgun and in the event of a mob coming again avoid putting himself in their power by going out to them. He should give them full warning that he would defend himself and, if this was disregarded by the mob, should turn the shotgun loose in their very faces and have it understood that the Mormon ministers did not propose to yield without resistance to mob violence.

This advice I related in a letter to President John Morgan with whom I was sharing the responsibility of presidency in the mission. President Morgan cautioned me not to be impulsive in resistance to mob violence, for there was divided opinion among the leading brethren as to whether the work in the South should be continued or not. Many felt that the elders should be entirely released from the Southern States. Since Elder Morgan and I had been insistent upon the continuation of the labors of the elders in the South, if any more martyrdoms occurred we might be held responsible for the fate of the brethren. This illicited a reply from me, in which I reported that every elder in the South was exposed to extreme danger and each carried his life in his hands. If there was any weakening on the part of the authorities of the church, I thought this fact should be reported to them. I knew that my own life was in danger, and I asked none to become responsible for it if it were lost. But I was unwilling to assume responsibility for any other elders' lives being attached to me and requested that this report be made to President John Taylor. This was done and President Taylor sent word officially back to the mission that while due care was to be used as far as possible to protect the lives of the elders from mobs, there was to be no abandonment of the missionary labors. However, the injunction of Christ was to be observed that if they persecute you in one city flee unto another. With this word received from the president of the church, the embargo of activity on the part of the elders was lifted, and the earnest prosecution of the work of propaganda was renewed.

Thus passed the summer of 1884. The latter part of September I received suggestion by letter from President Taylor that I had better take a brief vacation from the strenuous position I had occupied in the Southern States Mission and meet with President Joseph F. Smith of the First Presidency, Erastus Snow of the Twelve Apostles, and President John Morgan. All of these brethren would be in attendance at a stake conference at Manasseh in San Luis Valley in the latter part of that month, and they intended to project a series of meetings in the settlements surrounding Manasseh. Accordingly I made the journey and met with the above-named brethren at Sanford, one of the settlements of the San Luis Stake, and with these brethren spent several weeks in holding the proposed series of meetings.

It fell to my good fortune to be assigned to the company of Elder Erastus Snow in making these journeys, so that I had the example of this apostle under observation during that time and was much instructed from said observation. Erastus Snow was an ideal apostle in spirit and work. The most of his time during the later years of his life was spent with the people in the outlying settlements, and being a pioneer of wide experience, he was able to give practical counsel on affairs of the settlements he visited. He had the time and patience to listen to the trials and problems of the common people and gave such individual advice that it was uplifting and encouraging. He was a moving center of light and truth and counsel.

Elder Snow was accompanied by his wife Elizabeth, his second wife as I remember it, at least a plural wife, now well beyond the heyday of youth and even middle life. However, the gallant attitude towards her by Erastus Snow was such that would equal any possible attention and solicitude for her comfort and welfare in the journeys made wherever they were lodged. It must have been a period of exultation and satisfaction to Sister Snow to receive the satisfaction of such a man. This deportment on the part of Elder Snow exercised towards a woman approaching the period of scar and yellow leaf of life must have made his attentions of more than double value. His deportment had quite a remarkable influence upon me.

I had seriously contemplated myself entering into this law of plural marriage. In fact, when I left for this second mission, there was one cause of anxiety in my mind. I had had a premonition that I would be called upon to lay down my life while on my mission, and before leaving home I made such definite arrangements as I could as to providing a home of my own to be inherited by my family. To this end I had done what I could in forwarding the erection of a house as a dwelling place for my family and to this end secured the release of the mortgage upon the two city lots in Centerville that I had taken in settlement of my accumulations while an apprentice to Mr. Baird in the blacksmith trade. I hid in my own heart the secret impression I had received in relation to my life being sacrificed while on the mission, but I did all in my power to make provisions for my family.

Contemplating this probability of martyrdom, the thought which oppressed me was that so far as I could recall I had obeyed the whole law of God except that which required the full entrance into the marriage system of the church—marriage for time and all eternity and including plural marriage. This latter I had not obeyed. In prayer I had several times expressed to God my desire to be able to say when I appeared at the throne of the Almighty that I had obeyed every law revealed, and if my life was preserved, I would obey this law relating to plural marriage. The summer adventure had passed, and now that I was urged by the leading brethren whom I had met to extend my journey for a short visit home, I was confronted with the problem of making good on my expressed intention to obey the whole law of God if my life was preserved. Hence the beautiful spirit exhibited by Elder Snow of the Council of the Twelve towards his wife Elizabeth had a tremendous significance. In my contemplations I knew enough of the world to appreciate the passage from Burns:

> The sacred low o' well placed love
> Luxuriantly indulge it,
> But never tempt the illicit rove,
> Though nothing would divulge it!
> I waive the quantum o' the sin
> The hazard o' concealing,
> But Och: it hardens a' within,
> And petrifies the feeling.

This had not been the effect of the plural marriage relation upon the life of Erastus Snow. His association in that plural marriage had left him in an exalted state of mind, kindness, a beautiful appreciation of a wife, calling forth the tenderest emotions and care for the other at every turn. Nothing within him had been brutalized or perverted. Gentleness, kindness, and love unfeigned had possessed him. The corruption of promiscuity had not entered into his life or nature. His love was purified and exalted, and if the plural wife associations under such sentiments and principles in which he had practiced it was a symbol of the effect of such associations upon men, the principle of plural marriage stood vindicated, and one need not be in doubt on that score – on the score of the effect upon the nature of upright men. I felt that I had witnessed an example of the fruits of this system in the case of Elder Snow and his wife Elizabeth, and the convictions deepened in me as a result of this observation upon them. These convictions led me firmly to resolve to honor this principle of religious faith if opportunity arose to that end.

This was a matter, on my returning home two or three weeks later, which I laid before my wife Louisa, and she consented thereto. Under this arrangement I asked in marriage Miss Celia Dibble, granddaughter of Elder Philo Dibble who had been so savagely wounded in the mob violence in Jackson County, Missouri, when the saints were seeking to reestablish the city of God in that county. Ultimately that relationship was entered into with this upright and good woman, who brought to me the birth of eight healthy children.

After finishing the tour of the San Luis settlements, I continued my journey westward and spent a few weeks with my family and friends in Utah. It was a time of refreshing and renewal of pleasant associations, and in midwinter I returned to my field of labor to continue my presidency of the Southern States Mission.

The immediate business to be attended to was the renewal of emigration contracts in behalf of the Saints from the South to the Colorado and Utah settlements. Hostilities had not altogether subsided, and the emigration from the South gave indications of being more numerous than ever in consequence of the continuation of opposition. Some threats were repeated on the streets of Chattanooga, and as Elder Kimball and I made the journey back and forth to the Florentine Hotel for our meals, we frequently heard threatening remarks on the street and in the doorways of saloons and office buildings.

Early in the spring it became necessary for me to meet at Cincinnati the representative of the Santa Fe Railroad, Mr. Lippincott, to whom had been assigned authority to make the contracts for the other railways used in the western journey. As the threats were still rife in Chattanooga, we had at our headquarters taken precaution to make resistance to violence should any attack be made upon our quarters. When I had to go on this journey to

Cincinnati, I suggested to Brother Kimball that he keep the door barricaded and keep at hand means of resistance including the gun Mr. Moses insisted upon me taking to the Kane Creek district. In Chattanooga this gun rested under my pillow as a means of resisting threatened violence. Having made these precautions for Elder Kimball's self preservation, I departed upon my mission of signing new contracts for emigration.

The experience of Elder Kimball makes a point of interest. He was plumb fidgety about resisting a mob. He was still emaciated from his recent illness and strenuous work in the office. On the second or third day after my departure for Cincinnati, he was looking in the mirror above the dresser in the office, and looking at himself so thin and frail, he said, "Well, by heck, if anybody can come here and look at me and then make an attack upon me, I'll let him do it." So that night he took away the barricade of the door, and taking Mr. Moses's pistol he put it in the bottom of a trunk and piled all the books that I was keeping in that trunk on top of it. He then lay himself down to sweet and peaceful sleep and so continued each night until I returned.

Then came the preparation for the migration of the spring companies. This was arranged for in March and April. The first companies would include migration of the Saints from Kane Creek, for which the church had advanced $1,500 to remove those who were in danger zones. The first company was a large one, consisting of several hundred from all parts of the South. Some of them came with insufficient means for the railroad fares and for food en route. Some came with children, which under the contract ought to pay full fare, others half fare, and some misrepresentations were made of these facts. Some arriving in Chattanooga without means flatly threw themselves upon me, who was supposed to be able to engineer their way through to the West. So I called upon Mr. Lippincott asking him to give instructions to the conductors of the various roads over which the journey would be made that they must not look into the age of the children too closely. As a result many were passed through without the payment of fares. Some of the families that arrived in Chattanooga had never seen a railroad train before they boarded the one which brought them to Chattanooga where the organization of companies took place. They were literally afraid of the cars.

The waters were high that season. The Columbia, the Tennessee, and the Ohio overflowed and the similar tributaries of these large streams also. In approaching Cincinnati and Nashville, the passengers had to be taken from the trains and loaded onto freight cars and towed by small steamers for long distances. The trains were run upon tracks that were covered by water for scores of miles, and sometimes the fires of the engines were put out. These floods multiplied the difficulties of the journey as far as St. Louis. At St. Louis there was quite an army of railroad emigrant passenger agents, and when the Mormon train of eight or ten cars had arrived, there was a general rush of these agents, apparently anxious to vindicate the necessity of their claims upon their jobs, to direct the Mormon emigrants to the waiting room of the station. Mr. Lippincott, who was on the train, shouted to them in a voice to be heard throughout the great station and ordered the agents to let these Mormon emigrants alone. He stated that they were in the charge of a young man, who knew more about shepherding emigrants than they would ever know. They should stand by and see how he managed it.

Instructions had been given to each car before the train arrived in St. Louis. Each man was to take his family or group out of the car, divide them in the center, and move to each end, where they would descend to the platform and then move up on the side of the car to the middle. The men and larger boys were then to re-enter the car and gather up the hand baggage and see that everything was gotten out and located with each family to which it belonged. After this a line of march was formed to go to the waiting room of the station, where they would have to spend several hours before the journey could be continued. Such delays and hindrances had arisen by reason of the high water that season, and some of the companies had failed to arrive from parts of Alabama and Tennessee to the gathering place at Cairo on the Ohio River. After the passengers had been assembled at the sides of their respective cars and the hand baggage brought to the respective families, I took a lad by the hand and headed a march through the lane of the throng that crowded the depot to the waiting room.

I requested Elder Kimball to come up in the rear of the column of emigrants. This experience was demoralizing to Elder Kimball's nerves, for he could hear the comments made by the crowd as the companies passed. One of the things the crowd amused themselves by doing was to pick out the better looking members of the company among the girls that most likely would be seized by the fellow leading the throng. Finally all were seated and instructed, and guards were stationed to keep the emigrants free from impudent scoundrels who might attempt to harass them with questions and improper remarks. Brother Kimball was sweating when these arrangements had been completed. As a number of companies were yet to depart at Cairo, it was proposed that Elder Kimball continue the journey westward with these companies, while I would return to Cairo to bring on the companies who had missed their connection with this main body of emigrants. Whereupon Elder Kimball, approaching me, said, "For the Lord's sake, Roberts, don't send me off with this crowd alone." Then he related some of the remarks he had listened to as the companies marched through the depot shed to the waiting room. But there was nothing else to do unless he would go back to Cairo for the remnants of the companies and then bring them all the way through to the Colorado settlements. It was finally decided that he would go on with this main company while I would return to Cairo.

The district was still flooded with the overflow of the Ohio. Meeting the station agent, I found him chattering with the ague and remarked, "This must be a very unhealthful district with these annual overflows of the river." "O," said the station agent, "it comes along regularly in the spring, but it has one advantage when you are sick here. You know what's the matter with you and reach for the quinine and whiskey." His lips were blue and his body drawn up into almost helplessness. By early morning of the next day, the delayed emigrants began to arrive, and their railroad fares were purchased for the west. I continued the whole journey with them to the Colorado settlements of San Luis Stake and supervised their location into various settlements there.

During the summer and fall of this year 1885, other companies were gathered out of the South and conducted to the Colorado settlements. By this time a number of Josephite missionaries from the so-called Reorganized Church of Jesus Christ of Latter Day Saints began operations in the Colorado settlements, trying to discourage the newly arrived emigrants of the South. These efforts were opposed by me in public discourses and through the Denver, Colorado, papers.

CHAPTER 19.

Mission to England

Through the remainder of the summer and fall, conferences were held in all the eleven states of the Southern States Mission, and there was great work in gathering of members into the church. Winter came and passed and again arrangements were made for other emigration companies to go to the west. The first company went in March, and in making preparations to accompany this first migration, I bound up all my books and clothing to take with me. Why I should do so was a mystery somewhat, both to myself and Elder Kimball, but I had received one of those impressions I occasionally received, and it was my impression that I would not return to the South, and so it happened. For upon arriving in Salt Lake with the intention of visiting my family, I found that Elder John Morgan was under fire because of having entered into the order of plural marriage, and United States deputy marshals were dogging his footsteps. For this reason and in conversation, he suggested to me that he would return to the South in my place to look after the other migrations from the South and visit the conferences for a month or two. By then he supposed that the present impetus to enforce the anti-polygamy laws would have spent its force. We did not dream of its continuing as long as it did for a number of years.

By this time my financial condition had been growing steadily worse towards non-existence, so I suggested that I be allowed to seek occupation for several months to provide for my family. To this President Morgan agreed and departed for the South, and I found employment with the old *Salt Lake Herald* as the associate editor thereof, with Mr. Byron Groo as editor-in-chief, Horace Whitney as business manager, and Heber J. Grant as owner of the paper. This, of course, turned out to be quite congenial, as writing in editorial style was agreeable to the methods of thought which I had acquired.

It lasted, however, only until the fall of that year, 1886. By then the federal office holders in Utah had succeeded in unearthing the fact of my own violation of the anti-polygamy law, and warrants were issued for my arrest and served in the editorial office of the *Herald* by Arthur Pratt, the territorial marshal. I was taken before Judge McKay, U.S. territorial commissioner, and put under bonds of $1,000 to appear the next morning in the federal court to answer to the charge. Junius F. Wells and Charles R. Burton became sureties for me upon the bond. The arrest took place about six o'clock in the evening, and a consultation was had with the bondsmen and several of the apostles, among whom was Heber J. Grant and John Henry Smith. It was pointed out that if I should be subjected to an investigation, the case would in all probability develop into a charge of polygamy, for which the sentence would be five years and a fine of 500 dollars. It was therefore suggested by Elder Junius Wells that his father was still in charge of the European mission and had been for the past two years and that I might be of great assistance to him if I was sent to England on a mission to take editorial charge of the historical *Millennial Star*. To this all agreed, including Mr. Burton, the other bondsman, and so by nine o'clock I was behind one of the livery teams of Heber J. Grant and started for Peterson, a railway station on the Union Pacific, where I was to take the train for Evanston and thence on to New York and England.

About the time that the commissioners court was convened and the case of Roberts vs. the U.S. was being called, I was boarding the train at Peterson. I had merely called at my home in Centerville, thrust into a valise some clean clothing, and made the night drive to Peterson, where I arrived in time for a ten o'clock eastward bound train. I took the precaution to wear a second best suit of clothing and a slouched hat, and I took second-class passage in the smoking car for Evanston. It had been arranged that tickets on through to New York would be sent to the railroad agency in Evanston by friends in Salt Lake. I was unobserved in boarding the train at Peterson by anyone who knew me. When approaching the ticket window at Evanston, however, I observed two men, evidently on the lookout for possible escaping technical violators of the Utah law, and as I approached the window, the inward voice that so frequently guided me said, "Don't inquire for transportation. Buy second class ticket to Denver." This I did, so that if the two men I suspected as watchers at the ticket office were looking for me, they got no clue from my purchasing a second-class ticket to Denver. As the train, on the next afternoon, drew into the Denver station, an officer accompanied by the conductor came through the car announcing a telegram for James Reed, the name that had been agreed upon with my friends I would travel under until arriving in England. As soon as the telegram was announced, the voice said again, "Don't take it up. It is a trap." And so my fictitious name was not revealed, nor the telegram taken up.

In Denver I changed my course to Kansas City and there arranged with railroad officials of the Santa Fe for special passage to New York, where in a day or two I took passage for Liverpool. On board there were quite a number of young Englishmen from western Canada, where as younger sons of titled English families they had been homesteading or preempting lands from the Canadian government and were now on their way to visit their families in England. There were ten or twelve of them, and a care-free crowd they were and full of Christmas spirit, which was approaching.

With this company I freely mingled, and it was soon proposed that a

British mock parliament should be organized for our amusement and the entertainment of the rest of the passengers, who enjoyed it to its capacity. At that time Gladstone's home rule bill for Ireland was before the House of Commons, and most of these young men were conservatives and opposed to the Gladstone measure. During my recent editorial work, I had taken the Irish home rule bill into favor and had written much upon this subject and was familiar with the details of the measure and of its probable effect upon Ireland and the British commonwealth. So pronounced were my views on this subject in the informal discussion that went on that I was dubbed the Parnell of the mock parliament and headed those like-minded in the discussion which followed. Early in the parliament I made a speech that occupied the evening and so thoroughly maintained the justice of the Irish cause that it installed me as a noted character and general favorite on the whole shipload of people. I formed some very cordial friendships by the time the ship arrived in Liverpool. The morning of the landing, with the parliament's cry of "gangway for Parnell," a lane through the crowd of passengers was formed to the gangway, and I was escorted to the Liverpool docks by a cheering crowd of my associates of the now defunct parliament.

I was given a hearty welcome to the British missionary force, where I labored for about two years, chiefly at the *Latter-day Saints' Millennial Star* office. On first arriving I met a very trying situation. Elder George Teasdale of the Council of the Twelve Apostles of the church had been sent to relieve as president of the mission Daniel H. Wells, who after the conclusion of President Brigham Young's administration had been made a counselor to the Twelve Apostles. He was not satisfied with the form of his release and refused to accept it, so that he continued as de facto president of the mission, while George Teasdale, superior in office rank, was kept from assuming direct responsibility for the presidency over the mission. This situation continued through the first four months after my arrival. Brother Wells also continued editor-in-chief of the *Millennial Star*. When Elder Teasdale would write editorials, they were referred to the assistant editor, me, for acceptance and more frequently for rewriting, for Brother Teasdale's genius did not run along the line for composing acceptable editorial matter for the *Star*. And this created a rather delicate situation, which resulted in Elder Teasdale frequently withdrawing the editorials which he had prepared. Finally, however, a satisfactory release arrived for President Wells, and he embarked for home.

During the first year of editorial writing, I formulated quite an extended treatment of the gospel, and later these editorials became the foundation of the first book I published for the church. In the autumn of 1888, they were included in a brief course for the M.I.A., but more of that by and by.

The two years of 1887 and 1888 were characterized by much opposition throughout the British Mission because of the activities of the apostate William Jarman, who toured England in his series of anti-Mormon lectures and made a liberal distribution of anti-Mormon literature. In many cases the elders laboring in the various conferences felt themselves unequal to the task of successfully meeting this opposition of Jarman. From a number of conferences, they wrote President Teasdale to know if I could be sent to assist, and the proposition was put up to me. I expressed a perfect willingness to undertake the work of responding to the onslaught of the apostate, but if I did, I desired to have a free hand and devise my own methods. Hitherto this man Jarman had been permitted to lead mobs against the headquarters of the elders in the respective conference districts, to break down the doors, to scuttle the rooms, and to strew the contents of valises up and down the streets. My view was that the opposition should be taken to him and his debates instead of allowing the conference meetings of the Saints to be disturbed. Accordingly this plan was followed out–first in Burmondsy, a division of the city of London.

Mr. Jarman's lecture was attended in a large public hall, where some two thousand persons were in attendance. His lecture was divided into two parts. In the first he appeared in what he alleged to be the robes used in connection with the sacred mysteries of Mormon temple rituals. In the second he was clothed in an ordinary citizen's suit. During Jarman's retirement behind the curtains to make the change, his assistants flooded through the congregation a large quantity of leaflets, which made the most outrageous charges against the Mormon system of marriage and people and challenged any elders that might be present to meet him in public discussion.

Near the close of the second part of his lecture, I arose, informed the audience of my presence, who I was and my willingness to meet Mr. Jarman in public discussion. This action seemed to diminish Jarman's previously ardent wish for opposition from Mormon elders. It finally dwindled to his saying that if I would come to his platform the next evening, he would grant me fifteen minutes to make answer to his outrageous misrepresentations. "And is your boastful challenge for Mormon elders to debate with you reduced to this poor pittance of time and opportunity?" I asked. "Yes," was the reply, "that is all the time I can grant you." "All right then, while you have two hours in which to vilify my people, I will accept the terms and will be here tomorrow night."

Then pandemonium broke loose in the hall. The leaflets so profusely distributed in the congregation were chewed into paper wads and flung into my face as well as the faces of the two brethren who had accompanied me, Nephi Schofield and Father Ballard. The Jarman hall was on the second floor of a large building, and a flight of steps descended and a doorway opened into the streets. Below here as far as could be seen, the street was filled with an excited mob. A cab stood at the curbstone evidently awaiting the coming of Mr. Jarman. To this cab I forced my way through the dense crowd, which was throwing paper wads and spitting on me. Reaching the door, I suddenly flung it open and reached the inside. Nephi Schofield was following close behind, and the mob was literally tearing the clothes from him in their efforts from keeping him from entering the cab. I seized his coat collar and, pressing my feet against the sides of the cab, pulled with all my strength and brought him inside with such force that both of us nearly went through the other side door of the cab. The cab man, seeing the excitement, had rolled his cab windows and fastened them, and before he could climb into his seat and get started, men and women and gathered at the windows and expectorated their rheum on us helpless elders inside. At last, however, the cabby mounted on his seat, cracked his whip, and the horse forced its way through the crowd, which made a vain attempt to push the cab over.

The next day President Ballard of the London conference, father of Elder Melvin Ballard, now of the Council of the Twelve, visited the police authorities of the department of Burmondsy and solicited police protection. Elder Ballard was asked why it was, if his friends knew that there would be danger of riot, they would go to Mr. Jarman's hall. In response Father Ballard, as he was called by the missionaries, explained that that would be in accordance with his views, but the younger men insisted upon accepting challenges of Mr. Jarman and carrying the war into his meetings rather than permitting them to come to the LDS meetings and to break them up with his mob friends. The police officers, however, explained to Father Ballard that they had no legal right to enter Mr. Jarman's hall, even to keep the peace, unless the request would come from him, who had rented the hall.

When the time came, however, for us to make a defense of our people in Jarman's meeting, there appeared in the doorway of the lecture hall a force of sixteen policemen, in formation before the entrance to keep the crowds back. This they did effectively, and we entered the hall to find it jammed to the windows and doors. Mr. Jarman was busy on the platform among his score or more of lieutenants. A moment later I mounted the six or eight steps leading up to this platform and took a seat on the left hand of the stage. Mr. Jarman had evidently changed his mind about only allowing me fifteen minutes in which to make answer to his anti-Mormon accusations and had catered to that spirit of fair play for which English audiences are known to be partial. He asked his congregation if there was any one who would volunteer to take charge of the meeting and to keep order and to time the alternating speeches of the debaters. Instantly a typical workman of the better class arose in the congregation and stated that he would undertake to preside. This was Mr. John Cripps, a locomotive engineer who had relatives in Utah, the Haywards.

The discussion opened with Mr. Jarman, who had one hour in which to make an opening statement and set forth the charges to be maintained. He first opened by denouncing me as a "Mormon Thug," who had been sent over by the church to take his life. He was determined to haunt me out of

England. Mr. Cripps called the blatant raver to order and stated that the audience had not met for the purpose of hearing me abused. If I was the kind of man Mr. Jarman had pictured me, then Jarman had no right as a gentleman to meet me on the platform. His acceptance of me as an opponent in debate took it for granted that I was worthy of entertaining as a gentleman, though an opponent. Mr. Cripps would hear no more of abuse. At this the audience broke out into cheers, all of which disconcerted the anti-Mormon.

When he found himself confined to statements of facts against the Mormon church, his power was greatly reduced. He dealt with the story of his alleged escape from the hands of murderous blood atoners, who followed him into the mountains where he was compelled to remain concealed amidst the deep snows. According to him, the snow fell to the depth of thirteen feet in one night, and he was left shivering among the pine branches amid the lions and tigers in the Rocky Mountains. Finally he escaped, was received and entertained and given a hearing by Dr. T. Dewitt Talmadge in Brooklyn, and aided in his escape to England. This with a lot of other personal and general balderdash he averred had happened to him. Supposedly I had come to England to complete the vengeance upon him that had been thwarted by his flight, etc., etc. At one time he approached me seated at one end of the platform and, raising his heavy beard with his hand and baring his throat, drew his thumb across it. He asked me if it was not true that I would like to cut his throat. Again he was called to order by the chairman.

At last the opening speech closed, and I had my opportunity to reply, which was done by calling attention to the fact that the territory of Utah was an integral part of the United States of America and that federal leaders not local officers administered the law in Utah. Under the claims of the Congress, she exercised legislative jurisdiction within the territories. Was it at all likely that such murderous conditions as had been described could subsist in the highly civilized country of the United States? Thus the absolute impossibility of such condition of society was disclosed. The story of thirteen feet of snow falling in one night and this preposterous man hiding in the pine trees from the lions and tigers of the Rocky Mountains was the height of absurdities. Such animals were indigenous to tropical countries, not to the heart of the cold regions of the Rocky Mountains. Such absurdities broke down all claims to belief with serious minded people who had some regard to consistency and truth.

By the time I had concluded my reply to Mr. Jarman, the bubble was broken, and he never could afterwards make an appeal that aroused the intensity of the congregation. In his closing speech, for there were several alternate speeches of fifteen minutes each, he broke down in tears and accused me of forcing him into a debate, when he was broken in health and his strength was exhausted. Even that appeal, however, had no effect upon the audience who began his repudiation. In going to the steps that led from the stage to the stairway leading down to the door, I had to pass the table, which held the books and paraphernalia of Mr. Jarman. With an under-breath curse, he told me he would yet drive me from England, whereupon I stopped by the table surrounded by the lieutenants of the renowned apostate. I seemed hemmed in, but I took occasion to tell Mr. Jarman that he wasn't able to drive geese out of England and that for myself I would not leave my native land until he had. Also I took occasion to warn the thirty or forty lieutenants that had crowded around me at the table that they were following a very desperate leader in joining this Mormon apostate and that they were liable to get themselves into trouble. They had better desist from giving assistance and support to the contemptible procedures.

At this moment a clear strong voice rang out, saying, "Come this way, Mr. Roberts." Looking to where the voice came from, a young lieutenant policeman standing at the foot of the steps from the platform had flung back the cloak which had concealed his uniform. He was there to give me safe conduct from the hall. The crowd still remaining on the main floor of the hall opened a passage way voluntarily, and with my arm linked into that of the young lieutenant, I walked without any attempt to interrupt me to the stairway leading to the pavement below. There again a cordon of police was drawn up to hold back the crowd, which extended to right and left as far as could be seen. I and my one or two companions were placed in the charge of a group of police officers, who escorted us as far as the south end of London Bridge, from whence we could easily reach our place of lodging. This meeting broke up the Jarman efforts in London.

After that similar meetings were held in other parts of England and Wales, including Cardiff, Wales, and also Swansea in north Wales. Meetings were also held in Sheffield Park and in the Salvation Army barracks at Hoylland Common, a coal mining district near Sheffield Park. At this latter place, the Jarman craze seemed to rise to its height. The first meeting in Sheffield had been held in the Sheffield Park, where a crowd of nearly five thousand turned out to listen. After the close of the exciting meeting, a mob organized evidently with the intention of rushing upon me to get me under their feet—the method of mob rush in England. I had withdrawn from the platform in the park erected for the speakers and was standing in a road that had been cut through a hillock in the park, the sides of the cut rising some five or six feet high. While standing there in conversation with several friends, the organized mob came down upon me with great speed. A big two-fisted Yorkshire policeman standing by took me by the crotch and the neck, pitched me up the hillock, and scrambled up after me just as the crowd dashed through the cut. As I came scrambling up the sides of the cut, the policeman exclaimed, "Thou'll get thy nut cracked if thou don't mind." The mob rushed on through the cut-way.

At the meeting held that afternoon and evening in the Salvation Army barracks, a number of the mob came with short bars of iron hid in the sleeves of their coats and evidently intended to maim us with them at the close of the meeting. The meeting was a very exciting one. Jarman's ravings seemed to prevail with the ignorant coal miners in that region, but at the close of the meeting, the company of six or eight policemen came into the hall and opened a pathway through the aforesaid crowd and conducted us in safety to our lodgings. The meeting at this place was followed by a great calm, and the little branch was left undisturbed. In the fall most of the Saints migrated to Utah, where years afterwards I, now grown older, met a number of them at different times who were always apparently pleased to relate the experience in and about Hoylland Common.

The experience in the Jarman controversy was of intense interest at Swansea in Wales. Here Mr. Jarman had appeared several times, and the elders and Saints, having heard of my previous meetings with him, were anxious of having me come to Swansea. Accordingly I went. Mr. Jarman was delivering a series of sensational anti-Mormon lectures, and I as usual was at this meeting and announced my acceptance of Mr. Jarman's challenge printed in the leaflets scattered through the audience.

The people, however, had begun to doubt of Mr. Jarman's sincerity, and the editor of the *Swansea Times* began to call in question many of his extravagant statements. In a book published by Mr. Jarman, *Hell on Earth,* for sale at his meetings, he mentioned the fact that he had at one time been confined in the insane asylum at Exeter, and the editor of the *Times* suggested to me to send a telegram to the superintendent of that institution to get the details of Jarman's sojourn in the Exeter asylum. An answer was received stating the time Mr. Jarman had been confined there (about two weeks) and describing his escape from the asylum. He had cut a hole in the ceiling of his room and another hole through the roof of the building. He had climbed to the comb of the roof and moved down by means of the roof piping to the ground and thus made his escape. But no one seemed to be interested enough in his escape from the asylum to seek his capture and return to the institution. Hence he had been at large, lecturing in various parts of Great Britain.

The above-mentioned telegram was received a short time before the evening meeting began, and I took it with me to read to the large audience who would attend the debate, which was presided over by a committee of four–Mr. D. Clement, the mayor of the city, and the gentlemen associated with him, Messrs. Livingston, Darrett, and Craig. The meeting was so boisterous that the chairman, Mr. Clement, after his protest against disorder and boisterous conduct, left the building in disgust. But the meeting continued under the direction of the other gentlemen making up the committee. Finally the second member withdrew, Mr. Livingston, and then the third, Mr. Craig. This left Mr. Barrett, who was a Marine captain and president of the Sailor's Home at Swansea, in charge.

Towards the close of the meeting, I undertook to read the statement of Jarman's escape from the asylum as received that evening from the superintendent, but the crowd refused to listen, seeking to drown my voice at the pronouncement of each word of the dispatch. However, I continued reading it word by word, followed by jeering and cat-calls and other manifestations of displeasure. It took some time to thus read the telegram, and meantime Jarman's following had grown hoarse. Then stepping to the front of the platform, I raised my voice to the fullest volume and read the telegram consecutively and completed it until I was heard above the hoarse protests of the crowd.

No sooner was I through, however, than a rush was made to the platform by the audience. Fortunately the platform was rather high, and they could not scramble onto it very easily, only as they helped each other up. Meantime Captain Barrett had stepped to the rear of the stage where there was a door that opened to a flight of steps leading down into the basement. This he threw open and, grabbing me notwithstanding my protest, hustled and pushed me through the door, closed and barred the door, and led me down the stairway to the last step. Here Mr. Barrett attempted to impart some masonic message or token, which I of course did not understand, not being a Mason. After finally trying to exchange some kind of tokens, the captain exclaimed, "What, aren't you a mason?" I answered that I was not, and the captain said, "Well, I certainly thought you were, and it was because I thought so that I came to your assistance and led you down to this basement from the mob."

We remained seated upon the steps for some half hour until we thought the mob had departed and then left by a door leading out to the street. As soon as we reached the street, however, we were greeted by wild yells of the crowd who had merely gone into the street and kept silent, awaiting the emergence of the captain and me from the basement. Meantime the police had sent a small force into the street to give us protection when I should once more appear before the crowd. The police formed a little escort, and Captain Barrett continued to accompany me, linking arms with me and taking whenever possible the side on which the mob was most in force. Arriving at the house in which Elder Williams, the president of the Swansea Conference, lived, the policemen made a dash for the gate and took charge of it, opening it to admit the entrance of me but closing it immediately to exclude the mob.

By this time they were surging up and down the street in front of the building, where Sister Williams was lying with a newborn babe. At the side of the path leading up to the door was a cairn of stones and sea shells. This I mounted and called the mob to attention and repeated the circumstance that the wife of Elder Williams was in the upper room, from the windows of which streamed a light, with a newborn babe. If this crowd of ultra Christians had any respect for young and tender motherhood, they would silence their shouting and booing and retire, leaving the inmates of the home in peace. "You people," said I, "allow the Mormons to be represented as ruffians and murders. Yet I can truthfully dare you to produce any record of a scene and mob disturbance like this ever having happened in Utah. So now here's your chance to set those supposed boisterous and evil people, the Mormons, an example of Christian conduct by going to your homes. Goodnight." Strange to say the mob was quieted and left the vicinity, but when they reached the center of the town, they were divided for and against the Mormons and had a terrific street fight, the evidence of which appeared the next day as working men went to and from their jobs. These disturbances were called in the papers of the city the "Jarman-Anti-Mormon Riots."

Shortly after I left England, Jarman was hailed before the courts, complaints entered against him, and he was enjoined by order of the courts to observe peace towards the Mormons. Accounts of these disturbances will be found in volume fifty of the *Latter-day Saints' Millennial Star* for 1888. There were subsequent disturbances after this, but they amounted to little or nothing, and a few years afterwards the madman died.

The editorial work on the *Millennial Star* during the two years I was in charge of it also yielded some permanent values to my work. My first book, *The Gospel,* was included in the Mutual Improvement Association reading course and was first published by that association as chiefly a collection of a series of editorials on the gospel. Up through 1927, seven editions of this book with some enlargements were published. It was used in M.I.A. classes, quorums of the priesthood classes, and for the instruction of missionaries. Also there was laid during my two years missionary experiences in editorial work the foundation of the three-volume *New Witnesses for God,* much of the matter of which appeared in the *Star* editorials. The Liverpool office during the years I was there at 42 Islington was about five minutes walk from the very celebrated Liverpool Picton Library, in the same group of buildings with the great Walker Art Gallery. These were centers at which I spent my leisure time, making an immense collection of notes about evidences of American antiquities and archaeological works which provided external evidences for the Book of Mormon.

Also I was granted the privilege of visiting many sections of the British Isles as the representative for the Liverpool office. This included visits to Ireland, Wales, and various parts of England, also Scotland, especially the land of Robert Burns, who might be said to be my favorite poet. Byron land also, at Huncknall and Newsted Abbey, including parts of Sherwood Forest, scene of the exploits of Robin Hood and his band. This with the Scotch lakes of Loch Lomond and Katrine and Troachacs were scenes of romance and poetry, together with the cities of Edinburgh, Glasgow, Dunbarton, and the region of the Clyde river. These places were of immense interest to me. Douglas Castle, the lakes of Killarney, Cork Harbor and Blarney Castle, and the more somber but nevertheless grand and picturesque midland counties of England; the river Trent and Shakespeare's burial place and Leicester Castle. All these scenes and many, many more were visited by me during my two years sojourn in my native land, including trips up the Marsey which shortly after my departure from England was extended by great ship canals up to Manchester. It was something of a tradition in the Liverpool office that it made little difference where I was sent to a conference, I generally came by way of London, Birmingham, Dunham, and Edinburgh. These trips were educational and fed my fanciful romantic nature.

In September 1888, returning from one of these peregrinations, I found a cable message from President Wilford Woodruff advising me that I was released to return to Utah. Just why the release, I could not quite understand, but it became a settled conviction with me that doubtless the early and unexpected call to return home had something to do with the settlement of the $1,000 bond note that was to hold me to appear in court on the charge of unlawful cohabitation. In any event I prepared to leave the British Isles in response to the release. The account of my journey across the Atlantic and the continent to Utah we shall pass.

CHAPTER 20.

Back in Utah – Imprisonment

During the fall of 1888 and the winter of 1889, I took over the editorship from the underground of the Young Men's Mutual Improvement Association organ, then under the title of the *Contributor*, and in fact wrote nearly all of the monthly magazine as editorials and special articles contributed under the noms de plume of Horatio and Cratiano. Also it was at the October conference of 1888 that I was chosen and sustained by the general conference as a member of the First Council of the Seventy.

This organization has to do chiefly with the missionary work of the church. The Seventies are a group of men organized into quorums of seventy members in each quorum and presided over locally by seven presidents chosen from among the number of the quorum. They are presided over in a general way by the First Council. The seven presidents of the First Council of Seventy have a double office. First they preside directly over the First Quorum of Seventy, but the seven presidents and the First Quorum of Seventy is also the third general presiding council of the church, the other two being the Council of the First Presidency and then the Quorum of the Twelve Apostles. The first seven presidents also preside indirectly over all the Seventy in the church, of which in 1933, there are 234 such quorums. The special calling of the seventy is to be witnesses of the Lord Jesus Christ in all the world, acting under the direction of the Quorum of the Twelve with whom the First Quorum of the Seventy and its presidency is equal in authority. It is also equal in authority and power to the First Presidency.

The first quorum is a general quorum of the church unlike quorums in wards or stakes. Its responsibility is to assist the Twelve Apostles in preaching the gospel in all the world to every nation, kindred, tongue, and people. To be one of the seven holding the keys and right of presidency over this organization has always been held to be an important station in the church organization in the New Dispensation. It was considered that my experience in missionary work in Iowa, in the South, and in the British Mission tended to qualify me for such a high station. No compensation, however, was provided for by the church for such an ecclesiastical position, and I with my fellow presidents was required to and did serve in this capacity for a number of years without compensation. Indeed, the Mormon ministry does not really offer a vocation to those who engage in her ministry.

In the month of April 1889, the time arrived when the opportunity came to surrender to the federal authorities for violations of the polygamous living act for which I was under indictment. I, therefore, made arrangements under the terms fixed by Judge Young, which were that there would be no attempt made to collect the bond and that severe sentence would not be urged by the prosecuting attorney. I learned that my mother's anxiety about surrendering myself to the authorities had occasioned her mental distress. Therefore on my way from Centerville to Salt Lake to make my surrender, I called at the home of my mother and pacified her that this was an opportunity to get the penalty, whatever it might be, behind me.

In court Mr. Peters rather evaded a frank fulfillment of his agreement, and in making the statement to the court of my surrender, he took pains to point out that my offense in contracting a plural marriage was defined by the law, and I had, as he termed it, pretentiously defended my action under the plea of exercising what to me was a religious privilege. The Constitution barred the government from prohibiting the free exercise of religion. But the same argument was used to justify the continuation of the relationship which began with the plural marriage. The result of it was that the judge passed sentence for a term of five months and $400 as a fine. Judge Ogden Hyles spoke in an undertone to the court saying, "This man need not go to prison at all, if he will only promise to obey the law for the future." To this I remarked *soto voce*, "Judge, you know that would be a promise impossible for me to make."

There were still points in the definition of the law before the Supreme Court of the United States that had not been definitely settled. Hence to be true to my conviction and the contention then going on, as to the rightfulness of the position of the church, I was under the stress of moral obligation to uphold the position of the church, which I did.

That afternoon I was taken to the Utah State Penitentiary, arriving in the evening just as the prisoners on the three terraces of the cellhouse were standing in front of their doors prepared to leap back when the turnkey should throw the level which fastened all the cells at once. There was something of a good-natured rivalry between the prisoners and the turnkey in relation to closing the cells. The prisoners were anxious to stay on the outside of the cells to the very last fragment of the moment, and the turnkey resorted to trickery to throw the levers so as to shut them outside the cells. If this happened the prisoners would receive the infliction of further punishment by assigning them to the sweat boxes where they would be confined for so many hours or days on bread and water and in a dark and constricted cell.

As soon as the entrance was made into the cellhouse where cells would be designated, all the prisoners soon caught on to the fact that a new prisoner had arrived and the clamorous cry of "Fresh fish, fresh fish" was raised. All were anxious to know what he was, a "tough" or a "cohab." The "toughs" were those who were imprisoned for violence of the law in murder or robbery and other forms of burglary and misdemeanors of legally recognized crimes. The Mormon prisoners ensconced for violation of the special congressional laws about plural marriage, or unlawful cohabitation, in its various forms were called "cohabs."

There was a few minutes delay in the assignment of me to a cell in the prison, especially in the cohab departments since it was crowded and the prison officials made distinction between these groups of prisoners. The cohabs occupied for the most part the upper terrace, while the toughs were located on the terraces of the cell below. It was in the prisoners' library, opening to the cellhouse, where the consultation was had as to locating me. Presently, from the bottom terrace, a tough climbed up the bars and inquired of me whether I was a "tough" or a "cohab." When informed by the turnkey that I was a "cohab," the tough manifested real and almost tearful regrets that he was not a tough. "Mister," said he, "you ought to have cut someone's throat or robbed a bank or something so as to be among the toughs. We'd like you in our crowd." By this time I had been assigned a cell, and the tough had to scramble down mighty fast to reach his cell as the lever was drawn and fastened in the bottom terrace for the night.

Next morning before breakfast was served, the prison bars were opened and the prisoners granted the freedom of the enclosed court. An acquaintance from Provo who had been in prison for some time, a Brother Jones, linked his arm in mine and invited me to take a walk. I remember that we started eastward, and Jones explained that we could go as far as we pleased eastward but on the west of the deadline. If it was crossed, the prisoner was likely to be shot by the guards.

In the walk eastward, which I intended to be a morning constitutional, I walked rapidly until I brought Jones bang up against the wall with a thud, much to the surprise of the latter. Jones asked what was meant by contact with the wall. "O," said I, "you said we could go as far as we wanted to eastward, and I wanted to go eastward far beyond the wall." Then Jones explained that the east wall, being in view of the guns on the west of the wall, the prisoners could go to the wall without limitation. However, on the west, a dead line was drawn about two roads from the west wall in order to keep the prisoners always in full view of the wall guards, constantly alert for prison breaks. So the next was a turn and walk to the dead line and back to the east wall, which marked off the limitations for walking within the prison court.

Prison life was monotonous enough. The occasional incoming of "fresh fish" broke it a little. Eastern and local visitors to the prison, occasional release of the inmates, and learning personal traits and the lives of the prisoners were about the only diversions from the monotony. There was some interest, however, in contacting the great variety of criminals in the prison, the flotsam and jetsam of society, the failures. Here would be seen the natural born criminals, the unmoral, sometimes immoral, the brutalized or, what would be better to say, the evil-minded, who had not progressed downward but from the beginning and by the nature of them were brutal in instinct and obsession. Here too were college graduates, men who had known refinement and the uplift of aspirations to the highest ideals but had failed, their natures perverted. The cohabs, of course, did not fall under these characterizations, since we were men not of the criminal class but sacrificing ourselves for the right of our spiritual ideals. So far as morals and living in conformity to righteous principles, we were really exceptional men.

I found myself popular among the "toughs." I had the patience and broadness to listen to the stories of the worst prisoners, and they often confided to me the adventures which brought them to their present place of conflict with society and the laws. The worst criminals confided in me, not because I sympathized with their lawlessness and warfare upon society but because I had a habit, while their crimes were hateful to me, of considering the criminal apart from the crime and holding out hopeful possibilities for them. Likewise I had the opportunity of ministering to a few of their outward comforts. Some outside friends sent me boxes of cigars. These I distributed among the toughs quite generally, because my fellow cohabs did not use tobacco. Also delicacies of food, wholesome butter, boxes of oranges, and preserved fruits, were sent to me to add to the hard fare of monotonous prison foods, and these things I shared liberally with my fellow prisoners, both toughs and cohabs. All this tended to give me "standing" among my fellow prisoners.

The privilege had been granted to ministers of the Salt Lake churches to visit the prison and hold religious services, which the prisoners were required, irrespective of the sect represented, to attend. Sometimes these ministers failed to keep their appointments. Whereupon in such cases the warden of the prison, knowing my calling in the ministry, invited me to fill their places with this exception: that the prisoners were not compelled to attend the services when I, a fellow prisoner, held forth, as it was against prison rules for one prisoner to fill the position of preacher to the others. Still the attendance upon the services under my ministration was usually as well attended as when the services were conducted by outside preachers.

Frequently visitors from other states stopping over Sunday in Salt Lake City made it a point to visit the state prison, where they understood a large number of Mormons were incarcerated, in order to gratify their curiosity at seeing Mormons in prison. Sometimes these visitors came upon the scene of several hundred convicts in attendance upon religious service, many of whom were Mormons, and another Mormon, in prison garb, expounding and teaching the elements of the Christian faith and life. Of course, these visitors were doubtless scandalized at such a scene, but so far as I knew, it did not take on formal protest or objection.

In addition to these occasional opportunities for holding religious service, there was organized in the prison a Sunday school, which all the cohabs and some few of the toughs attended. Under the auspices of this Sunday school, glee clubs and quartets were organized and conducted chiefly by Mr. Lee. I was a member of one of these quartets but never took part in public other than before the prisoners. "It stands to reason," I was wont to say, "that Mr. Lee must have been an excellent trainer of quartets if he could get anything out of the voice and performance of B. H. Roberts."

I continued to befriend the toughs, who were all the while getting into trouble and sent to the sweatbox cell for punishment. The regulations denied them other food than bread and water, and they were allowed no cigarettes–something dear to the heart of the tough prisoners. Their companions in affliction sometimes brought food delicacies and substantials in the way of meat and potatoes to me to deliver to them and the much desired cigarettes. This I did by casually passing the sweatbox and, when the coast was clear, slipping under the only opening in the door to the sweatbox cells the delicacies of food and cigarettes and sometimes cigars.

Two months before the time came for the expiration of the term for which I was incarcerated, the barber who shaved me–by the way a man who was in for murder–refused to clip my hair or shave off the mustache. They had all taken it for granted that I would not be required to serve the extra month to cancel my fine of $400, since they all thought that my position in the church would lead to the church or some of my friends with means paying the fine in full rather than humiliating me by taking the pauper's oath–admitting I did not have the means with which to pay the fine. But this did not occur. I was compelled to take the oath and serve the extra time, and the prison turnkey gave direction to the barber that he must clip my hair and clean shave me. The barber refused to carry out this instruction, though he was threatened with punishment if he would not do it. One morning, some three weeks before I would be released, the barber performed the clipping and shaving ceremony at my request, as I did not wish to see him get into trouble with the prison officers. Hence I came out of the prison with the regulation clip and shave.

Especially in the last few weeks did the toughs of the prison open their hearts and confide their real names, for many were under aliases and their kindred outside. Some of these relatives were prominent in official life in Washington and also England. I refrain from particularizing lest some of those good people should find that some of their relatives scattered about the world were incarcerated for burglaries and other crimes in the Utah penitentiary. A number of these wrote letters to their friends, omitting the names in the letters but confiding them to me to be inserted before I mailed the letters from outside the prison walls. Also these relatives and friends were directed to write their answers in care of me in Salt Lake City. On receiving the replies, I copied the letters, omitting the names of friends and relatives, and thus aided those unfortunate men in communicating with their loved ones and often respected relatives without disclosing their prison location or identity to the officers of the prison.

When I was released from prison, I carried with me nearly a score of such letters. Had I been searched and the letters found upon me, I would have been returned to prison for months for violating prison rules. It may be considered by some an unwarranted thing to do, but it is something that I always prided myself upon. Though technically in violation of prison rules, nevertheless it was an act of humanity and good fellowship with the unfortunate, and anyhow it coincided with the disposition which was always constitutional with my case—to aid the under-dog in strife or those under the wheels of society's juggernaut.

While in prison the prison officers seemed at various times desirous of lightening the burden of my imprisonment, and it was suggested that I might be labeled a trustee and undertake the charge of herding turnkeys on the prison farm adjacent. This, however, I declined with scarcely concealed scorn and told the officers that I was a prisoner of honor and would fulfill my term as prescribed without favors.

Again on the 4th of July there was a celebration to be given to the federal officers of the territory, the dining room of the prison being commandeered as the place of banquet and subsequent celebration of the national holiday. Liquors and wines were to form part of the festivities, and the prison officers proposed to me that I take charge of this part of the banquet and be responsible for the proper distribution of the same. I need not appear in the banquet bill among those whom I might esteem my enemies, but they were afraid to entrust the handling of the liquor and wines to the tough element of the prisoners. This supposed position of trust and honor I declined with some expression of feeling. I would rather be a waiter to all the toughs in prison than to assume any part of the responsibility of serving these federal officers, judges, attorneys, with whom I had been locked in severe conflict in the issues arising in Utah. I would consider it an honor to wait on the toughs rather than to wait on this federal officialism of Utah.

Needless to say the request was withdrawn and though variously modified to meet my objections, I would have none of it at all. Finally a committee of toughs had to be substituted, and they passed bottles of the vintage in plenty to their fellow toughs inside of the prison. A tough who had been waiter by vocation was among the number selected to wait upon these federal officers in their celebration. But he had no clothing save his prison garb and came to me asking me if I had a dress suit and dress shirt that he might use for the occasion. Of course, I had no dress suit, but I did happen to have a rather fine dress shirt, which I brought with me in my clothing to meet possible emergencies. This I consented to let the tough have – not, however, as a loan. I made him a present of it that he might not be embarrassed to have the "thing" returned to me after having served such a purpose. So the tough got his shirt and I preserved my idea of appropriateness – I did not even retain ownership of a shirt that had been used in waiting upon the federal crowd.

With the autumn came the time for deliverance from the prison. I was duly admonished and advised to abide by the law in the future. The new warden from Ohio who had been installed as the successor of Mr. Arthur Pratt expressed hope that I would not be seen again within prison walls, a subject in which I heartily concurred. However, I did not expect that my escape from such contingence would depend upon my abandoning the plural family I had established. It is scarcely necessary to say that it would not be secured by such abandonment. On the contrary, I resolved that there should be no sacrifice or abandonment but contrived to establish my family where technically I would not be infringing upon the law.

Hence I arranged for the said family to be installed in the settlement of Colorado at Mannasseh in the San Luis Valley. This was done, and I through the several years paid such attentions to my family as could be effected and at the same time attend to my ministry in the church. I engaged in such labors as would provide for my rapidly increasing family, with a view to getting settled in the pursuit of some vocation or other. I submitted my embarrassing financial situation to the authorities of the church and asked their advice in relation to it, since I was receiving at this time no salary for the work required of me in my position as one of the first seven presidents of the Seventy. It was clear that something would have to be done to meet my financial condition.

I was advised that a man was certainly under obligations to provide for himself and his family and ought to make it his first duty to do so, since he who would not provide for his own would be worse than an infidel. The quotation is from the well known words of the Savior. Hence I began looking about for something to do, and it appeared strange to me that in the ministry of the church of the Christ it had been said: "Seek ye first the kingdom of heaven and all these things" – the material things of life – "should be added unto them." The strange thing about the counsel that had been given me was to seek employment in some secular project.

I was almost immediately called to join in a committee composed of John W. Taylor, of the Council of the Twelve Apostles, and Frank Y. Taylor, both sons of President John Taylor, in raising what was known as "The Defense Fund." This consisted of a long series of meetings held in various parts, in fact in nearly all parts of Utah, appealing for regular contributions to make up a defense fund. This fund would aid those who were hailed before the courts and had no means of providing for a defense before said courts unless it was supplied by the generosity of those who were not likely to be so hailed before the courts. The meetings were held, and the contributions subscribed with the result that a steady income of $165,000 per year was secured.

Perhaps my own experience – the humiliation I felt in being compelled to serve an extra month of imprisonment to satisfy the fine which had been imposed upon me – made me a more earnest advocate of this fund than I otherwise would have been. It left my own case the more pitiable by providing means in this line for others. It will be seen how awkward and humiliating this little event became when I was arraigned in the House of Representatives in the United States Congress and the fact brought forth that I had been compelled to take the pauper's oath and serve an extra month in the Utah prison. After the event had happened, there were a number of friends who expressed astonishment that I had not appealed to them for help. But they might have saved their wonder, because I, from my nature, could not have been expected to appeal for help in such a matter. For lack of other openings in the way of employment, I resorted to church literature.

CHAPTER 21.

The Constitutional Convention

In the fall of 1888, a territorial election took place, the election of a congressman and legislator. As I had for some time manifested a profound interest in political questions, limited as they were, I was solicited to participate in the conversion of the state to the People's Party, really the "Church Party." In this capacity I made a visit to all the principle counties and cities of the territory, supporting in my canvass John T. Caine as delegate on the Democratic ticket in the counties and territory. Two years later I repeated the canvass of the territory with Joseph L. Rawlins, an eminent lawyer of the territory. Both Mr. Caine and Mr. Rawlins were successful in these selections, and my reputation as political advocate received immense impetus. Without my being conscious of it, I was rising as one of the political factors to be accounted for in the future. The further development of my political activities continued through the remaining years of territorial existence, and I supported Mr. Rawlins again in 1892.

During this time some interesting developments took place. Mr. Frank J. Cannon, Mr. Rawlins's opponent, was making strong appeal to the Mormon population by intimating that the Mormon leaders had always been Republicans and favorable to protective tariffs. A pamphlet was turned out, which became somewhat notorious in Utah politics, called *Nuggets of Truth*. Copious quotations were made from miscellaneous church works, discourses, etc., etc., to give support to this idea. It was a direct appeal to religious authority and prejudices and was affecting the Mormon electorate. But notwithstanding all this effort, Mr. Cannon was defeated and Mr. Rawlins sent back to Washington as the territorial delegate. During his term of office, he introduced and got passed an enabling act authorizing Utah to form a state government which would be admitted into the National Union on equal footing with the other states. Mr. Rawlins was again the Democratic nominee in 1894, and politics were white heat in Utah—with a considerable dash of religious bigotry and intolerance injected into it by the continuance of the effort on the part of the Republicans to prove that Joseph Smith, Brigham Young, and other teachers were Republicans in sentiment and principle.

In September 1890 the celebrated Woodruff Manifesto was issued, declaring future plural marriages to be discontinued here by the church. Both the people of Utah and the politicians at Washington began to agitate in behalf of the division of the people into the national parties, Republican and Democratic, and an impetus was given to the hope of statehood for Utah. In the canvass of 1894, it was urged that no great amount of credit was to be accorded to the Democrats for bringing about the enabling act that prepared the way for statehood for Utah. Mr. Rawlins and I were in the south of the territory when this agitation was going on in Salt Lake City. On returning from the south, before separating from Mr. Rawlins, I asked him if he did not have some telegrams and letters of congratulation from the church authorities on the passage of the enabling act. Mr Rawlins replied that he did have such communications, almost fulsome in their tone, for an unexpected success. These he delivered to me, and in the speech made in Salt Lake City, those telegrams and letters were read which showed that a full credit by the higher authorities of the Mormon church had been accorded to Mr. Rawlins and profound thanks and commendation accorded him for his interest and success. So spontaneous was the reaction of the great congregation assembled in the sort of town hall known as the Richards Street Hall that prominent members mentioned in the correspondence and telegrams left the hall in haste as if ejected from it. But notwithstanding all the achievement of Mr. Rawlins, much influence had been generated in favor of the Republican party. Enough of the Mormon population joined with the Gentiles, who were leaving the old Liberal or American Party organization, to pile up a sufficient Republican majority to carry the election.

With the election of delegates to the constitutional convention, the question as to what part ecclesiastical officers of the Mormon church would take became an acute question. It was understood that something of an order had been issued discouraging our seeking election to these offices. Such were the complications which the matter seemed to involve that there was a trend of opinion that we should remain out of it.

During this time in the casual meetings between Elder Moses Thatcher and me, the matter was discussed by us and resulted in this: The difficulties seemed to be so great that Elder Thatcher said, "Roberts, let's you and I stay out of it and avoid complications." With this understanding I filled a church appointment to attend a conference in Wyoming and was absent during the election of the members to the convention. On returning, to my surprise, I was informed that I had been elected a delegate from Davis County. Having had the understanding that prominent church officers would not stand for election to the convention, I called at the office of the presidency of the church to ascertain if any change had been made concerning the under-standing before I left for Wyoming. I learned from this consultation that the previous conclusions had been modified to permit prominent brethren of the church to be elected. It was claimed that persevering in the policy of eliminating us from the convention would deprive the state of some of the best service that could be given in the convention. Also I understood that this conclusion concerned not only the membership in the convention but also political offices generally in the forthcoming state. With this understanding I accepted the election as a member of the convention and prepared for its duties.

The membership of the convention was to consist of 107 delegates apportioned among the various counties according to their population. Salt Lake County had 29 and Grand and Iron counties but one each. The act of congress further provided that the delegates thus elected should meet in convention in Salt Lake City on the first Monday in March 1895, which fell upon the fourth day of the month. Each declared on behalf of the people that they adopted the Constitution of the United States and that the said convention shall be "hereby authorized to conform a constitution for said proposed state." Accordingly the convention assembled on the 4th day of March 1895 in the City and County Building in the largest room on the third floor of that rather noble structure and continued in session until the 8th day of May of the same year, a period of sixty-six days. The political complexion of this assembly was 59 Republicans and 48 Democrats. The majority party, of course, prepared to and did finally organize the convention.

There was some delay by reason of the fact that in the third election district of Salt Lake City, there was a contest over the delegates. John Henry Smith of the Council of Twelve Apostles had been elected from that district, and as the Republican caucus had determined upon presenting Mr. Smith's name as candidate for president of the convention, they suspended definite action in permanently organizing the convention until the contests were settled. This delay led to a temporary organization in which Mr. James N. Kimball of Weber County was elected president pro tem, Mr. Heber Wells was unanimously elected temporary secretary, and Mr. J. F. Chidester of Garfield County was unanimously chosen as temporary sergeant of arms. Meantime the contest over the election of delegates of the third ward was settled, and Mr. John Henry Smith was seated and on the third day elected permanent president of the convention. The Republicans in the convention were censured for the delays in accomplishing the permanent organization. Thence followed the order day by day, of course, until the constitution was completed.

In these proceedings I took a prominent and earnest part, joining in the discussion of the leading questions brought up in the convention. Among these was the question of equal suffrage for men and women in the state to be. It was I who called up the possibility of the constitution being defeated at Washington if the suffrage clause was inserted in the constitution. It had been noted that President Cleveland was opposed to woman suffrage, and in the event of seeking a reason for rejecting the constitution of Utah, this course might give the occasion for effective opposition. Nor was it necessary to be involved in such an action, since suffrage could be granted to the women of Utah by later legislative enactment without having it inserted in the constitution. Therefore I urged, as a matter of expedience for safety to the constitution, it would be well to leave this matter to future legislation.

My proposition, however, was derided, and some of my friends who knew of my habit of meeting subjects directly and without compromise derided my presenting this question on the ground of expedience. The question was asked: "Did I not adopt this settlement by expedience because I was disinclined to discuss the question upon its merits?" At this challenge I changed my position and told those who mocked me in the convention that I had hoped my suggestion might be accepted by the convention without entering into a lengthy debate on the question of suffrage upon its merits. But since my opponents would have it, the discussion began which occupied so important a place and so long a season in the convention.

The trouble really arose over the idea that the question of woman suffrage had been canvassed in Utah many years before and that the women of the state were exceedingly anxious for this so-called "reform" in the electorate of the state. In early territorial days it had been urged by the minority Gentile population in Utah that if the women were given the franchise they would overturn Mormon rule in the territory and unseat their opposed tyrannical Mormon state officials. This view was urged at the seat of the nation's government. Whereupon Brigham Young without hesitancy accepted the challenge and urged a conferring of the effective franchise upon the women of Utah, and this act was made effective by Congress. Then contrary to all the claims of the Gentile population of Utah, they discovered, when it was too late, that they had doubled the Mormon vote. The people elected officers from the membership of the dominant church in Utah. Then there was a clamor for the disfranchisement of the Utah women. That action was taken by Congress and was supposed to have greatly humiliated and displeased the women population of the territory.

Hence when the people divided upon national party lines, both political parties, Democrats and Republicans alike, had each sought to outdo the other in their pledges to give by constitutional provision the franchise to women. The matter had not been discussed to any extent at all in the canvass for election of delegates to the convention. Therefore I felt myself authorized to call attention to the inexpediency of the parties carrying out these pledges if even in a slight degree it might endanger the approval of the state constitution at Washington.

The debate was of course decidedly one-sided; both parties were united in the proposition made. Each was anxious to appeal to the women electorate of the state-to-be for partisan advantages. Through the discussion, whatever changes of individual conviction took place, the pledges of the respective parties were adhered to. I made three sustained speeches. The first was on the expedience of keeping suffrage out of the constitution in the interest of eliminating objectives that might be raised to it at Washington.

The second was in response to the taunts that I was trying to settle a great question on the score of expedience – with the intimation that I was not equal to the task of considering the question on its merits.

This challenge I accepted and made the merits or rather demerits of suffrage the subject of my second speech. I answered those who set forth their reasons for favoring woman's suffrage on the ground of justice and equality, etc., etc. The second debate was brought down to the close of the week, and during the intermission before the assembly on Monday, opportunity was afforded to a number of gentlemen to come back on Monday with new and additional speeches. This brought quite a new flock of opponents into the field.

Meantime there had arisen the understanding that I would be permitted to close the debate. There were several efforts made to prevent this agreement. The time of the debate had been cut down by limiting speeches to ten or fifteen minutes, but enough on the floor of the convention gave up their time to me that I was able to announce and did announce to the convention that I had time for a two-and-a-half-hour speech if I should want to use so much. A like duration of time was given to me for a third speech.

Considerable amusement was aroused during the third speech, much of which was devoted to the more recent remarks of my opponents. I explained to the convention that there were a few personal matters that I felt it necessary to refer to before proceeding directly to the subject of debate. One was reference to the demand that had been made by Mr. John G. M. Barnes, chairman of the Davis County Democratic convention, from which I had been elected as delegate. Mr. Barnes had rather peremptorily demanded that I change my course in the matter of woman suffrage or resign. This I had, of course, declined to do and explained that the subject of woman suffrage was not mentioned in the Democratic platform for Davis County nor at any time discussed, either in that county or elsewhere. Therefore I had refused to regard it as binding upon me to support suffrage in the convention. With this explanation made and proved, I then continued addressing the chairman:

"Of course, sir, if you look at a range of mountains, there are here and there lofty peaks that rise above their fellows, and upon these peaks the eye naturally rests. So in this discussion, rising upon the common levels, there are a few gentlemen who have spoken to whom I shall consider it my duty to pay particular attention. I refer to this matter, so that if I do not mention each one who has entered the arena against me, he will not feel slighted (laughter). Perhaps if I discuss some of the remarks made by those more prominent speakers upon the subject, I shall be able to satisfy you.

"Among these particular ones to whom I ought to pay attention is my personal friend, a gentleman for whom I have the highest regard, from Weber County, Mr. David Evans; a man I take it, sir, who thought he answered my argument by telling me that I was mistaken and that my fears were ill founded apart from making these statements with more or less flourish and eloquence. The gentleman concluded by saying that if he was conscientiously opposed to woman suffrage, that no party platform would stand in his way of opposition: if he believed that suffrage would degrade woman, no party platform would prevent him from opposing it. So I take it that in the opinion of that gentleman since I am of the opinion that it (suffrage) would be injurious to the state and degrading to woman, I am absolved (by him). One thing else, the gentleman asked in fervent rhetoric that he would like to know what possible harm could come from his mother accompanying him to the polls. Well, sir, as I am of the opinion that his mother must be a most estimable lady, I think no real harm could come from her accompanying him to the polls, and I am rather inclined to think it would be a good thing for her to do so (laughter); and not only accompany the gentleman to the polls, but I doubt not it would be a most excellent thing for him, if she were constantly present with him to guide his footsteps through the meandering pathway of life (laughter and applause).

"Another of these mountain peaks in debate to which I ought to refer is a gentleman (Mr. Heber M. Wells, who later became the first governor of the state of Utah) who spoke to us yesterday 'out of his place,' as he himself put it (Mr. Wells had purchased himself a seat on the sill of a high window of the convention hall, giving his seat at his desk in the hall to some lady friends, hence "out of his place," but nevertheless "in the ring"). That gentleman detained the convention for a considerable length of time in a set speech which both amused and instructed members. I doubt not that there was much force in it. Finally though he told the convention that he had an 'aunt,' who, if she could have the privilege of the floor and the freedom of debate, would be able to make such a speech on this subject that the committee of the whole would immediately take to flight and pull the whole in after it. Now, sir, I doubt not that that possibly would be the result—that we all would be converted if the lady instead of the gentleman had had the privilege of the floor and the freedom of the debate. But there was one thing that appeared very curious to me, and that is, that the eloquent lady had not more effectually converted her worthy nephew to her views, for as I remember it, the whole tenor of his discussion was that he believes in woman suffrage. Why, sir, I could almost strike hands with him and vote as far as he is willing to vote for suffrage of woman.

"Now we come to the proudest peak of them all (laughter). This has reference to Mr. Orson F. Whitney, who had been set apart by the suffragettes to make the principle argument to the speeches of Mr. Roberts. He was supposed to be the 'curled darling' of the debate (laughter). You seem to know whom I mean before I enter into a criticism of what that gentleman had to say upon this subject (suffrage). I ought to pause upon the threshold of the undertaking and ask myself what I am, what here has been selected to represent me, but most important of all I ought to discover whether I am fish, flesh, or fowl and locate myself in the animal kingdom as well as to seek out what my place among the heroes of history might be. The assault of the gentleman, for it could be nothing else, was deliberately planned in the silence of private study. The arrows were sharpened and I must needs think, sir, dipped in the gall of the gentleman's own bitterness. He denies me the honor of being Horatius at the bridge beating back the Tuscan enemies of Rome. He would not permit me in his comparisons to be represented by Leonidas at the cause of Thermopoly. He elevated me one moment only that he might debase me the more the next moment and finally, sir, concluded that I was a 'bull without judgment,' and as without inspiration. I grant you sir, that the thought was negatively expressed by that peculiar trick of rhetoric which affirms a truth in the form of a denial of it, but in his graciousness and some pity, perhaps, coming into his heart, he finally gave me an alternative from those dire comparisons. I might be Napoleon flying from Leipzig, imprisoned at Elba, back to Waterloo, thence banished to St. Helena to die in solitude, or if I chose I might be compared with the proud spirit that knocked omnipotence in the eye and told him good was evil. I thank the gentleman for the alternative.

"I presume that either Napoleon or the devil would be preferable to Baalam's ass, especially when inspiration did not accompany it (laughter). But the gentleman overshot the mark if he intended to wound my feelings because, sir, he kept me in such a state of suspense to know what my final destiny would be that in my anxiety to find that place, I forgot that I was receiving a castigation. However, if the gentleman were satisfied with his elegant comparisons, and, of course, he is a gentleman of refined tastes, as we all know, a poet too of no mean ability, for if his remarks are satisfying to his soul, why then I shall not complain. But I would be pleased to know what reference all this had to the discussion that was brought upon this floor. I can see only one means of explaining it, and that is this gentleman sought to break down the force of my argument by making me appear contemptible.

"Well, sir, I am not very proud, I have no reason to be, and I am willing in this long list of comparisons to take the humblest of them all. And in doing that I presume I shall please the gentleman, and at the same time I think I shall be able even in the capacity of Baalam's ass to still instruct our poet-delegate (laughter and applause). The facts in the case in regard to Baalam's ass, if the gentleman will read the story, are decidedly instructive, especially, sir, as there are so many points of resemblance to this case. One Balack, the son of the King of Moab, discovered how merciless was the war that Israel waged upon the Amorites and sent for this prophet Baalam to curse Israel, offering him high honors and rich reward if he would do it. It seemed that the prophet, deferred for a moment by the glamor of the promise of the king, forgot his true office to God and the people and started out on this mission of cursing. It is said, sir, in the narrative, that an angel with a drawn sword stood in the way to head off the prophet, and the ass, taking alarm at threatened danger, fled into a field nearby. The prophet, if he did not use implications, at least did use blows and finally brought the ass back into the road. Presently when the road entered into a narrow lane with a wall on either side, the ass was again confronted by the danger that threatened the prophet, and in his mad effort to get by the danger, he jammed the prophet's foot against the wall. This again aroused the wrath of the misguided prophet, and with blows he brought the poor ass back into the middle of the road. The next time the danger was confronted, the prophet was in the still narrower way where there was no escape whatever from the threatened danger, and the ass lay down and refused to go any further in the direction of the danger, and the mad prophet beat him again. At last the kindly powers above, in pity of the dumb brute, spake through him, and the ass reasoned and said (to the prophet), 'Have I not been thine ass these many years. Have you ever known me before to treat you after his manner?' As if he would say, 'Know you not there is some danger in the way. You ought to know that an ass so docile, so faithful, so careful of you as I have been would not have taken the course I have unless there was some obstacle of danger threatening?' (applause). Then, sir, the eyes of the prophet were opened, and he at last saw what the ass had seen. He beheld the danger and in humiliation he said: 'I have sinned.'

"Now, sir, when this question of suffrage was first brought upon the floor of this convention, knowing, believing, I—and I was not mistaken in the words which first came to my lips, knowing that there was danger for statehood for Utah if this matter (of suffrage) was pushed to the extreme—I sounded the note of warning to this convention: your ass, running away with you into the field, as you will (applause), was beaten back into the narrow way. I again endeavored to show the danger and again was belabored and beaten. We come now into the narrow pass, and I lie down. I ask these gentlemen who have known me if I am an alarmist by nature, or am I disposed to cry there is danger when I really see none? And now in this third issue in the narrow pass, I would to God that some kind power would touch the eyes of my blind prophet friend, that he too might see the danger and find that I am not mistaken (applause) that I might not see the humiliating spectacle of an ass instructing a prophet (laughter)."

The summary of the chief points in argument was made at the conclusion of my third speech. The first speech, it will be remembered, was on the inexpedience of suffrage, the second speech entered into the merits of the question, and the third speech was made in answer to my opponents as already indicated. Closing the third speech, I made a summary of the various propositions. I claimed to have proven in my arguments all the phases of the question, and that summary stands in the verbatim minutes of the convention as follows:

"I laid down first the proposition that the franchise ought to be confined to those who are capable of acting independently. Has that proposition been controverted by argument? I have failed to hear them if it has. Still further, I stated that such was the relationship of woman in the family that she was not capable of acting thus independently without the dictation or the suspicion of dictation from her husband—has that been controverted? Gentlemen will deny that there will be such dictation, but is that an argument? Do we not know from the great facts of human nature that it will be so? Do we not know from the difference of man's nature and woman's nature that it will be so?

"Second, I laid down the proposition that the elective franchise was a privilege (conferred on the individual by the state), not a right. Has it been proved to be an inherent right? On the contrary, did I not show that this doctrine, first announced in the Declaration of Independence, that 'governments derived their just powers from the consent of the governed,' is subject to such modification as to lead our statesmen to exclude women from expressing their consent?

"Third, have they proved that the great mass of women of voting age are not already sufficiently represented in politics by husbands, fathers, sons, or brothers?

"Fourth, that in the case of unmarried property owners, have they proved that there is discrimination made against woman in the matter of taxation? And here let me refer to this great clamor of theirs about taxation without representation. The married women have representation, those who are unmarried and are property owners may have none. I went so far as to say that if gentlemen who intended to enfranchise these, I had no serious objection. It would meet the demand for no taxation without representation, and the number would be so few as not to materially interfere with the welfare of society or domestic peace. But I argue that there was no real occasion for this, for the reason that women in taxation are not discriminated against, that there was no possible means by which they could reduce taxation, and, therefore, even this much of a concession was not necessary.

"Fifth, have my opponents proved that the steady refusal of statements to grant women the elective franchise for the past two hundred years was unwise? All change is not progress. All the customs that have been bequeathed to us by antiquity ought not to be stricken down, because some customs ought to be. Some of these customs, sir, are monuments that bespeak the wisdom of our ancestors, and we ought to have a decent respect for them.

"Sixth, have my opponents pointed out how women are to work wonders and the reformation that they make will when given the ballot? Have they told us what laws women would change, or what law is desirable to change? Have they explained to us in what manner they will be able to elect all good men to office to administer the laws?

"I have heard nothing of all this. These, I take it, are the arguments that ought to have occupied the attention of my friend, and it would have been more effectual than to undertake to break their force by an attempt to debase me. Mr. Wells gave us a beautiful reference to the force of Wellington and Blucher. Why, sir, had Wellington and Blucher let the grand army of France alone, had they ceased to pursue the old guard and turned all their attention to capturing the 'Little Corporal,' it is quite possible that under Ney or some other mighty leader the broken army might have been gathered together through the night and hurled with renewed force upon the British and the Germans the next morning, and we would have had another history for Europe than we have now. The gentleman made a mistake in pursuing his 'Napoleon' and leaving the grand old guard of his argument to live and meet him here again today (applause)."

The convention was so far stirred by the opposition to incorporating suffrage in the constitution that an alternative proposition was brought upon the floor of the convention, namely, to submit the suffrage clause prepared for the constitution to a separate vote. But this effort to modify the action of the convention on the subject was voted down, and ultimately the suffrage clause was inserted in the constitution and won out in a vote upon the constitution – very largely I thought because men would rather have statehood with suffrage than to defeat statehood in order to defeat suffrage. Happily there was a president of the United States, who had to sign the admission of the State of Utah, too big to allow personal prejudices against suffrage to turn him from signing the bill for the admission of Utah.

As to the opinions entertained and expressed of the debate itself, of course, comment was divided. Suffragist members of the convention saw the weight of argument on the side of my opponents, while very many, both in the convention and out of it, and the press of the state, were equally favorable to my anti-suffragist arguments, and applause and favorable comment first held with one side and then with the other. In the comments of the *Salt Lake Tribune*, scarcely ever favorable to the notices it gives of my work, the editorial of April 20, 1895 said:

"The debate on woman suffrage in the convention yesterday was vigorous, and again Mr. Roberts won the honors. His speech on Thursday went to the expediency of the proposition at this time and in this way to confer the suffrage on women, and his conclusion was that it was not only inexpedient but might be perilous. Yesterday he spoke to the main proposition and his argument was masterly. His opponents did not disturb his points at all, but their reliance was chiefly on the promise alleged to have been made to grant woman suffrage and the declarations of both political platforms. But the very fact that both party platforms carried a woman suffrage plan deprived the opposition to this fad of any chance to be heard; men voted their party tickets without reference to this question. Further, it is true that the convention gave no expression on this subject. Further yet, the incorporation of this plank at Provo was not in any real sense a test; it was reported as a surprise to the convention without notice, and no one cared to get up a fight about it; in fact most of the delegates paid no particular attention to the matter. Then the Democrats took it up so as not to seem at a disadvantage with the ladies and not because they really wanted to make it a Democratic point of faith. It is a case of both parties getting caught in an easy trap, the consequences of the capture attracting very little attention at the time. It is idle, therefore, to seek to establish any binding realty as due to such expressions. The danger, Delegate Roberts declared, and three-fourths of the members agreed with him, and if their real sentiments actuated their votes, they would vote with him against woman suffrage."

After the final or third speech the same leading Utah newspaper printed in headlines on April 3, 1895: "ROBERTS ANNIHILATES THE WOMAN SUFFRAGISTS WITH LOGIC AND ELOQUENCE; WHITNEY, WELLS AND THURMAN DISPOSED OF; CONVENTION HALL JAMMED. A squad of police required to preserve order–Hundreds clamored vainly for admission–Mr. Roberts's speech the event of the day; Woman suffrage means Bitterness, Strife, and Unsettled Conditions; Peril of the proposed action clearly pointed out–Delegates simply playing political advantage–not even 'Bull Sense.' (Mr. Roberts said at this point,) 'I beg your pardon for using such an expression but I learned it from the 'poet delegate.' "

Then the newspaper commented editorially: "We print this morning in full, in obedience to a very general popular demand, the great speech delivered yesterday in the constitutional convention by Delegate Roberts of Davis County. All who heard it agree that it is the master effort of the convention to date; that it utterly demolishes both Richards and Whitney; that it is to them what a grand river is to a stagnant slough. By common accord, it is a great speech. It closed the debate, and closed it fitly. That it did not carry the convention with it is merely another way of saying that the majority of the delegates were not open to reason, considering themselves bound by a fictitious party action."

Mr. Orson F. Whitney was, of course, well satisfied with his own position and effort and received laudations for his excoriation of me in the debate. In his autobiography under the title *Through Memory's Halls*, Mr. Whitney refers quite extensively to his debate in which such references as these are made to it:

"My most conspicuous service was in championing the cause of equal suffrage. I was among those who advocated the placing of an article in the state constitution enabling the women of Utah to vote and hold office. The Gentile members were much opposed to this, fearing that it would strengthen 'the Mormon Power,' of which they were still apprehensive, notwithstanding the pronounced change in public sentiment. A few 'Mormon' members also disfavored it for prudential reasons, thinking it might create trouble by reviving old animosities. Upon this issue a lively battle was fought.

"In defense of the proposed article, I crossed blades with the Hon. B. H. Roberts, of Davis County . . . Opposed to woman's participation in politics, he spoke against it, and was answered by several members. . . . I had not intended to say anything upon the subject but was urged by Mr. Richards and others to take the floor and reply to the gentleman from Davis County."

Mr. Whitney complains of the leading papers in the state, the *Salt Lake Herald* and the *Salt Lake Tribune*, both under Gentile management, who according to Mr. Whitney published my speeches in full on the front page and gave him a brief synopsis. The *Deseret News*, edited by a life-long suffragist, was equally economical. But the women appreciated what had been done, and the Utah Suffrage Association printed his speeches in full and scattered them over the country.

One thing Mr. Whitney charged against me was resented as follows: "The gentleman, (Mr. Whitney), as I remember, makes two complaints against me. One is he thinks I have tried to absorb myself all the virtues of noble motives in this convention and that I brand the rest of you with cowardice. I will explain, I hope to the gentleman's satisfaction, and also to the convention's satisfaction, the meaning of my remarks in that particular line. With the gentleman from Salt Lake who has so earnestly declared that his convictions run parallel with his action on this issue and with all gentlemen that are in the same condition as he, on that subject, I take no issue, and I give them credit for all the noble sentiments and motives that belong to honorable men. But, sir, I am aware and so is this convention, from positive declarations made upon the floor of this house by gentlemen, that their actions run one way and their convictions another. Whenever I see men occupying the equivocal position, I have some misgivings in my own mind as to the result of their action under such circumstances. And when men would come to me and speak their fears to me, and tell me their convictions being against this (action on suffrage) and yet they were bound down by those ill-considered party pledges, and were going to do something for the people which they believed would work an injury to the people and to the coming state, I brand all such with cowardice, and they may make the most of it. (Applause.)"

If I should add personal expressions supporting my stand upon the question of suffrage made to me through letters, telegrams, and petitions from mass meetings signed by hundreds of people, it would require scores of pages to record it from my scrapbook of letters on that subject. One only, however, will be noted, because it relates to the bond given to secure my appearance before the commissioner's court on the charge of unlawful cohabitation. It was a letter received at the height of the suffrage debate from Federal Commissioner William McKay. It bears the date March 30, 1895, and is marked personal.

Hon. B. H. Roberts
Constitutional Convention
Salt Lake City, Utah

Dear Sir:

I appreciate most highly the manly stand you have taken in the Convention upon the question of Woman Suffrage; and though you and I differ in national politics I see in that fact all the more reason why I should say to you that in the discussion of the question thus far you are in my opinion the only man with the possible exception of Mr. (Anthony C.) Lund who has approached the subject entirely free from the speech and art of the demagogue.

In years passed the enclosed (which had reference to the bond given under the case of unlawful cohabitation) has been the subject of some comment and inquiry, it may be of interest to you now, if only as a souvenir, against which the statute of limitations have interposed its fate.

Yours truly

(Signed)   William McKay

Also there is in this collection of manuscript commendations a notification from the Alta Social Club of Salt Lake City extending to me at the request of Mr. O. G. Sharp, a member of the convention, the privileges of the Alta Club for a period of thirty days from April 4th. It is also signed by R. McIntosh, president and member of the convention, and by C. L. Robertson, secretary.

I took a general interest in nearly all the questions which reached discussion stage in the convention. This was especially true in the matter of locations for the higher educational institutions of the state, the location of the Agricultural College of Logan and the University of Utah at Salt Lake City. I also fought the effort to discontinue the state Agricultural College and amalgamate it with the university. This would have been at the sacrifice of the agricultural college plant in Utah and the discontinuance of the federal appropriations for agricultural college.

I introduced and engineered the passage of the section of the constitution prohibiting the use of the credit of the state in support of private or corporate organizations in the form of bonuses and bounties. This legislative article has an interesting incident connected with it which does not appear, of course, in the record of the convention. The committee on legislature consisted of the following gentlemen: Mr. W. G. Van Horn, chairman, myself, Mr. D. C. Eichnor, Mr. John N. Kimball, and Mr. Franklin S. Richards. The legislative committee met at the offices of Mr. Van Horn, and several drafts of the legislative article were presented and read. Mr. Richards and I were Democrats; the other three members of the committee were Republicans. The several articles submitted were commented upon; objections were made and discussed. During this time Mr. Kimball sat silent and part of the time at least apparently asleep, doubtless from a little overindulgence. After quite a long time his chair, which had been tilted back against the wall, dropped forward. Mr. Kimball, seemingly aroused, said, "I move, Mr. Chairman, that this committee accept the draft of the representative article presented by Mr. Roberts and report it to the convention." Mr. Richards immediately seconded the motion, and there was nothing for the chairman but to present the motion of Mr. Kimball. With the two Democrats, Richards and me, this gave the majority of the committee in favor of Mr. Kimball's motion. Much to the chagrin of both Mr. Van Horn and Mr. Eichnor, the democratic draft of the legislative article by me was adopted by majority vote of the committee and reported to the convention. In all committees the convention, having a majority of Republicans, always gave the majority and chairmanship of committees to the committee of the convention, and in nearly every case the reports of articles presented were formulated by Republicans. But in this case the important article on legislation was a Democratic draft and passed through the convention with very few amendments.

The prohibition question came up in the convention from the committee on schedule who prepared a majority and minority report, recommending a clause for the constitution to be separately submitted to the vote of the people and a minority report favoring simply the recommendation of a clause for insertion in the constitution. The discussion though professedly made in the main in the interests of temperance was rather decidedly intemperate, and some fanatical members made radical addresses. The main issue, however, was deliberately discussed by several prominent members among whom and perhaps the most thoughtful was made by Mr. Anthony W. Ivins, Mr. Elias Morris of Salt Lake City, and others most strongly in favor of prohibition. Largely influenced by contact with constitutional and legislative prohibition in other states, I opposed its admission into the constitution but favored the recommendation of the majority of the committee to submit the question to a separate vote of the people. There was an evident desire to make this submission without entering into a discussion of the merits of prohibition on the convention floor. When this appeared, I said:

"I cannot for the life of me understand how you can consider it separate and apart from the merits of the question. The merits of the question are inevitably involved in it and necessarily ought to be, because upon the merits of the question depend the propriety of either putting it directly into the constitution or permitting the people by their vote to put it into the constitution. And I hold, sir, that the majority report of the committee is correct, wherein it states that prohibition is but an experiment, not only in the way of legislative enactment but also by constitutional provision. I think it was only last year that the good people of the state of Iowa rooted out of their constitution the prohibitory clause on this subject. I lived for some length of time myself in the state of Iowa, when that was a prohibition state by legislative enactment. And I know not what the experience of other gentlemen may be in prohibition states, but I wish to declare that I know that in that state prohibition was nothing but a hollow mockery. The very fact that the people have but recently in their constitutions repudiated the constitutional prohibition is very strong evidence to me that this matter is but in its experimental state and that we cannot afford to undertake that experiment by constitutional provision; and as stated in the majority report, if tried at all, it should be undertaken by legislative enactment.

"Now, sir, I am of the opinion that there are things worse even than intemperance in the use of intoxicating liquors, and one of those things worse than intemperate use of intoxicants is the demoralization which comes to a community which threatens civil government itself, and that is disrespect and disregard of law. Such is the nature of this question that it is not a difficult matter to evade the law. Wherever it has been tried, men have evaded the law, and that successfully – more successfully in respect to sumptuary laws than in respect to other kinds of law. I say that it is easy to evade this class of law, and when you teach a community or when you create conditions which lead a community to disregard law, you create a greater evil even than the evil you attempt to crush by law. And for this reason I do not want to engraft into the constitution this prohibition clause. I believe it is the right of this convention to determine what to put into a constitution and what would be more proper to leave to legislature, and for that reason I think it is quite competent for this constitutional convention to say to the people, notwithstanding the petitions that are before us, it is not a proper matter to insert into the constitution. I believe, sir, that that right and power is here in this convention and that it is a proper exercise of that kind of judgment. Now, sir, prohibition being an experiment, and for the most part an experiment that has failed, I hold that there is nothing binding upon us to attempt it by constitutional provision.

"There is no gentleman upon this floor but what is aware of the evil of intemperance. It is not because I am in favor of patronizing saloons and have no regard for the evils of intemperance that I am connected with those gentlemen who made the majority on this question. But my observation teaches me that the proposed remedy for that evil is not equal to the task proposed for it. I am against it. It is for that reason that I shall vote against submitting this clause or a separate article on prohibition.

"There is another question connected with this subject, and this is recognizing the impracticability of prohibition either by constitutional provision or legislative enactment. In consequence of our being surrounded by states and territories where they may manufacture and sell these intoxicants as beverages in spite of all that we could do, they would import these beverages into our territory and they would be sold. The result would be that we would not materially lessen the evil, but we would pay out a revenue to surrounding states and territories that we absolutely need here in our own new state. And I cannot close my eyes to the fact that it would be increasing the burdens of taxation upon the people of this territory and at the same time not curing the evil at which this prohibition clause is leveled. Now these are considerations from which we cannot remove ourselves, and I think it is competent and proper for this convention to favor the adoption of the majority report of this committee on this issue. I believe that we can better control this question—this evil of intemperance—by locating it where we know where the evil is and where it can be under the guardianship of the law and strictly regulated, instead of having blind institutions (speak-easies are meant) about us producing evil and yet we know not the source of that evil. I am persuaded that it is impossible to make men temperate by legislative enactment. I do not close my eyes to the fact that there are other forces in the world than legislative enactment and congressional provisions. Why, sir, I want ministers of the gospel to have something to do, and there are better forces, meaning the moral forces of religion, to be arrayed against this evil than legislative enactment. I believe in the liberty of the individual, and if you want to know how dear to me the liberty of the individual is, I want to tell you that quite contrary from the position taken upon the floor here this morning by a gentleman from Sevier County, notwithstanding all the array of blood-curdling incidents that may be related as growing out of the acts of men under the influence of intoxicating liquors, notwithstanding all that, so dear to me is the liberty of the individual that I would pay that price for it (the evils that had been recounted), and if I could, I would not destroy the liberty and agency of man."

Mr. Miller: "May I ask the gentleman a question? How about the weaker ones—the wives and children of the unfortunate men?"

Myself: "You may add that to the list also, if you will. I recognize, sir, that Omnipotence has the power to blot this thing out of existence and yet He withholds His hand. He permits it to exist (i.e. in the elements of nature, the corn and the grains from which intoxicants are produced). You will see therefore, gentlemen, that I am prepared to vote against the amendment which adopts the minority report and in favor of the motion to adopt the majority report and shall vote against any anti-constitutional proceedings on prohibition going into the constitution."

In the main I have not changed my views above expressed on the subject of prohibition. Yet I feel that after fifty years perhaps other remarks ought to be made in order to set forth my views on the subject of this so-called moral reform. I believe in prohibition, but it is the prohibition self-administered and that is without pains and penalties attached, a prohibition that abstains from the use of intoxicating liquors mild or violent, a prohibition self-conducted and from a conviction of their mis-chievous effects and likely destructive effects. I believe and accept fully the statement of my church on the subject of such matters voiced in the Word of Wisdom given to the church. Known and very excellently phrased as the Word of Wisdom, it is not, however, given by compulsion or restraint nor are any negative or punitive consequences attached. Rather glorious promises are made as a consequence of obedience to those declarations and the observance in connection therewith of the "commandments" of God. Of course the principle set forth in this Word of Wisdom is according to the mind and will of God, and it is for a divine purpose that they shall be observed but not in or by compulsion. It is to be the free response to a counsel or word of wisdom from God.

The consitutional convention completed its work on May 8th, and the members signed the constitution on that date, the names following John Henry Smith, president, and Parley P. Christiansen, secretary. As a whole the constitution by common acclaim was a good document, the evidence of which consists in the fact that very few amendments have up to this time, 1933, nearly fifty years later, been made to it, though a number of amendments have been proposed to the people.

CHAPTER 22.

Election to Congress, Part One

During the convention and especially following the debate on woman's suffrage, I was urged by many friends to become a candidate for the U.S. Senate or for the House of Representatives, and these urgent requests finally resulted in my nomination for the House of Representatives by acclamation at the Democratic Convention held in Ogden in June 1895, the first statehood election. As such candidate I canvassed the state, largely in company with John T. Caine, candidate for governor, and Richard W. Young, later Brigadier General Young of the 65th brigade of the 40th division of the world war, and candidate for the supreme court. Other nominees of the Democratic party were Thomas S. Maloney of Ogden and Mr. Samuel R. Thurman, both candidates for the supreme court. Moses Thatcher of Logan and Joseph L. Rawlins were nominated for senators, Fisher B. Harris for secretary of state, O. W. Powers, chairman for the State Democratic Committee. The campaign that year was very intense, as partisan spirit ran high, and there was injected into the campaign what was regarded at the time as ecclesiastical interference.

Joseph F. Smith of the First Presidency of the Church of Jesus Christ of Latter-day Saints in a priesthood meeting in the Assembly Hall during the semi-annual conference of that religious organization very abruptly and severely censured two of the Democratic nominees, Moses Thatcher and me, as having accepted and entered into the campaign without consultation with the authorities of the church as to a right to become candidates for political office. As this criticism came but a short time before the election in November, it was regarded as an interference with Democratic candidates, as it was well know that Mr. Smith was an intense Republican. The charge was freely made that his criticism was made in aid of the state Republican party. The charge was held to be justified by church leaders on the ground that before engaging in work that would take church officers from their duties to the church, a consultation should be had with their fellow officers before engaging in occupations of this kind whether in politics or business, and undoubtedly there was much to say from this point of view.

The only thing in answer to the charge was that in the election for members preceding the constitutional convention, this matter of running for political office had been discussed among the authorities of the church, and while at first it was decided that it would be better for high churchmen of the dominant church organization in Utah to refrain from participation in politics, yet this was subsequently reconsidered and the decision arrived at that to require high church officials to refrain from entering politics would deny to the people some of the most patriotic and efficient service in the interest of the affairs of the people in civil government. Therefore the first decision was overthrown and the second installed as the policy, namely that prominent church leaders would be at liberty to seek public political office. It was under this supposition that both Elder Thatcher and I accepted the nomination as delegates to the constitutional convention–my nomination taking place while I was absent from the state–and also was the reason why I had accepted the nomination of the parties respectively for congressman and senator.

The question of church and state was developed out of this incident in the remainder of the campaign (1895, the first statehood election). It was very exciting and the people very much aroused. My treatment of the situation was very admirably set forth throughout a series of meetings held in Summit and Wasatch counties through three days ending October 18th. Mr. H. G. Whitney, representing the *Salt Lake Herald*, accompanied the party through these counties and wrote elaborate accounts of the enthusiastic meetings that were held. Of my speeches he reported:

"It is only necessary to say that Roberts literally electrified his audiences in every one of the eight meetings held in three days. He has no set speech, his addresses differing according to the character of his audiences. But his four great points–hard time, the tariff, silver, and the issue of bonds–are admirably worked up and fortified with unassailable authorities. Only one theme does he bring forward, with little or no deviation, at each meeting, and this is the most thrilling part of his speech. In calm earnest language he tells of the events of the priesthood meeting. No names are quoted; his words are temperate, and his allusions to his church superiors respectful. He concedes their right to criticize him and Moses Thatcher if they have done anything deserving of criticism, but he protests against the use petty politicians are making of the occurrence, and the infamy of those who whisper about that Brother Thatcher and Roberts are out of favor with the church authorities, and hence should be defeated. He makes indignant allusion to Frank Cannon and his grapevine wire warnings, says he wants no election by such means, and appeals to his friends to see that if he is not to be benefited by messages from this mysterious source, he is not damaged by them. Everywhere the most thunderous responses tell of the feeling of the people on this subject. I made it a special point to inquire at every place visited what effect the utterances of President Joseph F. Smith had had and without exception was told that the Republicans who had hitherto been depressed by the outlook had 'perked up' wonderfully in their feelings since conference, and that Democrats were correspondingly anxious. In Midway, when Roberts spoke of the underhanded way Republicans had used the occurrence against Thatcher and himself in Logan, half a dozen men jumped up in the audience and shouted: 'They're doing the same thing here.' Requests were left with the committee in every place to forward affidavits immediately if any such attempts to influence voters were detected."

The excitement of the campaign continued and various opinions were offered as the proper thing to be done to resent what seemed to be the suitable conviction that the criticism of Thatcher and me constituted an ecclesiastical interference with the affairs of the great political parties. Some talk there was of taking down the state ticket and working to defeat the adoption of the constitution and hence also defeat statehood. In this crisis Chairman Powers conducting the campaign called a state committee together, and it was resolved to re-convene the convention which had nominated the Democratic state candidates and submit that proposition to the convention. Such convention was called to meet in Salt Lake City, October 22, 1895. The delegates of Democracy accordingly met. The headlines announcing the reconvened convention as that which appeared in the *Salt Lake Tribune* of Wednesday, October 23rd, were as follows:

THE MIGHTY VOICE OF DEMOCRACY
IN THUNDER TONES IT HAS DEMANDED THE COMPLETE SEPARATION OF
CHURCH AND STATE
IN A VAST CONVENTION
NEVER HAS THE CITY WITNESSED SUCH A MOMENTOUS GATHERING
THATCHER IN LINE
A LETTER MAKING PLAIN THE ISSUE NOW BEFORE THE PEOPLE
A MASTERLY ADDRESS
IT SHOWS HOW A CHAIN OF EVENTS HAVE BROUGHT THE CRISIS
CONFIDENCE IN THE PEOPLE
THE DEMOCRATIC PARTY WILL BE CONTENT TO REST ITS CASE WITH THEM

Resolutions to take down the ticket and defeat statehood overwhelmingly defeated – Great attendance of delegates from all counties – enthusiasm intense and satisfaction – general speeches from Powers, Judd, King, Mrs. Jakeman, Roberts, Rawlins, Sloan, Mrs. Ferguson, Harris and Other Prominent Democrats – over $1,500 raised by subscription in fifteen minutes – an impromptu Torchlight Parade that amazed the onlookers – Music in profusion.

My remarks near the close of the reconvened convention are as follows:
"B. H. Roberts followed. He said he was opposed to the resolution to recall from the field the Democratic ticket and to undertake a fight against statehood. 'In the address already read,' said he, 'there is a detailed statement of the grievance endured by the Democratic party in the past. They have been wonderfully patient. I believe the party this year was

marching toward a glorious victory, when, as if an earthquake had rolled under our feet, we came to a standstill and began to wonder if again it could be true that the unwelcome influence of the church was to rob us of victory. I grant there is a temptation to resist it by such means as the resolution before the house proposes. But despite all the adverse influence used in 1894, let it be known that 19,000 good Democrats and true resisted it. I ask if this does not give good earnest that in this territory and state-to-be there is a firm and determined resolution in the hearts of enough people to divorce the church from the state? (Prolonged cheers and waving of handkerchiefs.)

" 'I want to ask the gentleman offering the resolution if he now intends to desert Utah's cause and relegate it to territorial vassalage? Have we now shown ourselves worthy of trust by the demonstration of this great body of 19,000 Democrats, mostly of the Mormon faith? How then, are we to settle this question? Are we to go back to territorial bondage? (Cries of No! No!)

" 'How must the question be settled then? Not that way assuredly. The lines of battle are now drawn up and we stand face to face with the issue. Shall it be written that the Democratic party retreated? I always thought the Democratic spirit grew higher and higher as the difficulties confronting it became greater and greater. If our friends, offering this resolution, will only stand by the 19,000 who gave their best to church and state separate.

" 'The constitution of Utah says there shall be no union of church and state nor shall any church dominate the state or usurp its functions. With 103 others I signed that document and mean to maintain that principle. The people are going to vote on it, and I hope in the name of justice and liberty they will vote aye, and then teach that they are bound to obey and honor it, for it becomes the supreme law of the land. The Democratic Party asks no odds of the church, but we propose to carry this question to the source of all political power, the people, and that appeal will not be in vain. We will take the question to the people now, and now it can be settled as well as fifteen or twenty years hence.' "

The motion to take the Democratic ticket from the field was defeated, and the campaign went on to its conclusion, but the Republican party was successful in the contest. The vote was C. E. Allen, Republican, 20,563, B. H. Roberts, Democrat, 19,666, the majority for the Republicans being 897. I ran ahead of my ticket by nearly 1000. So closed the campaign of 1895.

After the smoke of the campaign had passed, the General Authorities of the LDS church were called in consultation and an understanding had with reference to what was known as the Political Manifesto. It was disclaimed by church authorities that there was any intention on their part to control men in their political activities; it was wholly for the protection of the services due from the general officers to the church.

The manifesto finally agreed upon and known as the Political Manifesto, signed by all the General Authorities of the church, the First

Presidency, the Twelve Apostles, the First Council of the Seventy, and the Presiding Patriarch, is as follows:

"In view of all the occurrences to which reference has been made and to the diversity of views that have arisen among the people in consequence, we feel it to be our duty to clearly define our position, so there may be no cause hereafter for dispute or controversy upon the subject:

"First. We unanimously agree to and promulgate as a rule that should always be observed in the church and by every political or otherwise, which would interfere with the proper and complete discharge of his ecclesiastical duties, and before accepting a nomination or entering into engagements to perform new duties, said official should apply to the proper authorities and learn from them whether he can, consistently with the obligations already entered into with the church upon assuming his office, take upon himself the added duties and labors and responsibilities of the new position. To maintain proper discipline and order in the church, we deem this absolutely necessary; and in asserting this rule we do not consider that we are infringing in the least degree upon the individual rights of the citizen. Our position is that a man, having accepted the honors and obligations of ecclesiastical office in the church, can not properly of his own volition make these honors subordinate to, or even coordinate with, new ones of an entirely different character. We hold that unless he is willing to consult with and obtain the consent of his fellow-laborers and presiding officers in the priesthood he should be released from all obligations associated with the latter before accepting any new position.

"Second. We declare that in making these requirements of ourselves and our brethren in the ministry, we do not in the least desire to dictate to them concerning their duties as American citizens, or to interfere with the affairs of the state; neither do we consider that in the remotest degree we are seeking the union of church and state. We once more here repudiate the insinuation that there is or ever has been an attempt by our leading men to repass upon the ground occupied by the state, or that there has been or is the wish to curtail in any manner any of its functions."

Then follow the signatures.

Undoubtedly if the statement were accepted as here so emphatically declared that all this would be in the interest of service due to the church from its leading officers, then no mischief could grow out of it. At the same time it cannot wholly be disregarded that it was an instrument to be used with exceeding great care, because it could be so easy either by the giving or withholding of consent to indicate the wishes of the administration of the church to the desirability or undesirability of men in opposite parties running for office. Especially in a community where there is much anxious willingness to comply with the slightest wishes of ecclesiastical authorities. But if really honest, as I believed it was, then there could be no incompatibility between seeking this consent described above and for the purposes described and the exercise of political liberty.

That there had been good grounds for suspecting ecclesiastical intention to control the political affairs of the state can scarcely be denied, nor when all the circumstances are considered could that be a matter of wonderment. Naturally the conditions obtaining under territorial government had separated the people into Mormon and anti-Mormon parties, the latter led chiefly by the representatives of federal authorities appointed from Washington to the territory, the governor, the secretary of the territory, the federal judges, Indian agents, etc., etc. These latter were interested in the perpetuation of territorial conditions, and they had hungrily sought to substitute the legislature of the people by an appointed legislative committee. As these measures were first of all sought in the separation of the Mormon people into a church party, they were driven into an offensive organization under the title of "The People's Party" to contend for their rights. Consequently when changing political conditions in the territory made necessary the division of the people not upon religious lines but upon national party lines, there was a tendency for all the Gentile people to adhere to the Republican party, while in the main the Mormon people flocked to the Democratic party. For a time it looked as if there might be a change of name without really bringing to pass a change in political party adherence and therefore little to be gained by a division on national party lines.

Observing this, leading men of the church, who had been prominent in their political affiliations, suggested a steadying of the "political ark" by calling attention to these conditions and advising, at least, those who had no pronounced partisan views to enter the Republican party, which was supposed quite generally to be in the minority in Utah. Indeed one prominent ecclesiastic suggested that the position of the church leaders might be as a "jackman" on a teter board to throw his weight now upon one end of the board to press it down and then upon the other, pressing lighter weight on the other end of the plank to allow it to rise and thus to equalize the parties as the best interests of the state might determine. It is needless to say that such a function performed by churchmen would be absolutely incompatible with accepted views of relations of church and state in America and, however honestly conceived, could never be tolerated in an American state and under the American form of government. There would be in spite of all good intentions domination of parties under such an arrangement, and that would be inconsistent with peace and the smooth moving of political activities. That a position had been occupied by leading church authorities of political dominance under the old anti-church regime would go without saying, and it would go over into the period of statehood. From time to time there were manifestations of ecclesiastical influence being employed in state affairs, but the Political Manifesto as given above was drawn, as I believed, honestly and with the best intentions, and hence I signed it with the other General Authorities of the church. How it has worked out in subsequent years, the people will judge for themselves, but unquestionably the campaign of 1895 was more or less influenced and my defeat as well as that of the Democratic party in general was more or less influenced by the criticism of myself and Moses Thatcher.

With the close of the constitutional convention followed by defeat of the Democratic party in 1895, I was left somewhat in suspense as to what course I was to pursue as to a vocation. The reputation established for aptness in civil political matters opened to me opportunities for entering a career in the law. Mr. David Evans of Ogden, a wealthy mining man, member of the constitutional convention, a lawyer, and also active in politics, offered me an opportunity for entering with him into a law partnership. He offered me a salary from the firm as well as an opportunity to attend some two years in the Ann Arbor Michigan Law School for equipping myself for this vocation. About the same time Mr. Orlando Powers, perhaps the leading criminal lawyer, certainly in Utah, and perhaps the whole west, made a proposition for me to enter his law office, accounting me entirely prepared for entrance at once in the practice of the law. A few years later he made still another offer to me to enter into the practice of law in partnership with himself. The second offer especially created some wonder why Mr. Powers was so anxious apparently to have me join him in the practice of the law, since I had attended no law school nor had ever engaged in the practice. The answer of Mr. Powers was that in a firm such as he proposed, my general information and logical mind and ability to handle facts would more than equip me for equal standing in any law firm that could be organized, and in a short time the technicalities of the practice would come naturally to me, and therefore he desired this partnership.

These matters were referred to the General Authorities by letter, asking that permission be granted to me for entering this professional life, but the applications and the arguments used in defense of the proposition were never answered. I did not feel at liberty to wrench myself away without permission to do so from my church office as one of the First Council of Seventy, and the obligations of my office in the church were of such a nature that I did not feel at liberty to resign in order to engage in the proposed business of law.

Signing with the other General Authorities of the church the so-called Political Manifesto offended nearly all my gentile friends. They looked upon it as an improper surrender of political independence, and those who had been so ardently my supporters from that class of the population avoided contact with me. Not infrequently I could observe some leading characters even crossing the street to avoid meeting with me, and my fortunes with them were fallen to a low estate. However, I continued my own independent way, meeting my obligations to church and state according to my own conceptions of my duty, allowing friends and foes alike to fall on the one side or the other in their approval or disapproval of me.

In the spring of 1896 I was called by the church authorities to deliver a course of lectures in some of the large cities of the United States and was given as companions in this tour Melvin J. Ballard—later to become one of the Twelve Apostles—George D. Pyper, tenor soloist of the Tabernacle choir to furnish music of the lecture course, and later Edward Midgley as accompanist. The mission so organized began its work at Kansas City, Missouri, with a side visit to St. Johns, Kansas, the headquarters of the Bickertonites section that sprang out of the Rigdonite faction.

At St. Johns I met William Bickerton, the head of the section. He was a man of much force of character but without education. He at first became a disciple of Sidney Rigdon and was ordained a "Seventy" in the organization created by that deposed leader, and when the Rigdonite church "became disorganized," Bickerton continued to preach and finally, under what he claimed as a "divine direction," he affected an organization with a "First Presidency" of three, himself the chief, a "Quorum of Twelve Apostles," and some "Seventy." A number of people accepted the teachings of Bickerton both in Pennsylvania and Kansas, but the organization as such amounted to nothing.

The special mission next went to St. Louis, where on account of the excessive heat in the summer of 1896, we were compelled to suspend our activities. After two or three weeks, however, an abandoned church was rented, centrally located in St. Louis, for one month, and here we held thirty meetings which were fairly well attended. At the conclusion a small branch of the church comprising thirty members was organized. Thence the mission went to Cincinnati, thence to Pittsburgh, Philadelphia, New York, and Chicago. In all these places a number of meetings were held, suitable halls being hired, and considerable publicity obtained for the church in all these cities. The mission continued about a year and then on account of failing funds returned to Salt Lake City with a report of a successful tour.

These missionary tours in these cities kept me absent from Utah during the exciting campaign of 1896, and it was quite generally reported that the church authorities had maneuvered my absence from the state during the national campaign of 1896, when Mr. William Bryan of Nebraska conducted his first campaign for the presidency and when the free coinage of silver was the leading feature at a ratio 16 to 1 of gold. There was little evidence, however, to support this contention. During the summer shortly after the Democratic convention at Chicago that year, I personally met William Jennings Bryan at Kansas City and exchanged courtesies with him.

Mr. Bryan had been present at the Ogden convention when I was first nominated for congress, but we had not met at that time. Mr. Bryan was then in the very heyday and pride of his rather remarkable political career and at the time was the Democratic nominee for president of the United States. His physical development (he was then thirty-six years of age) was perfect, tall, slender, keen-eyed, easy to approach, frank in his communication, and fearlessly confident of himself and his future. It was magnificent to contact him under these circumstances, and our meeting registered the beginning of a friendship intensified through occasional contact. I subsequently introduced Mr. Bryan at a great public gathering in Salt Lake as Mr. Bryan passed through and spoke of his experience of membership in the Wilson cabinet as secretary of state.

Meanwhile political agitation was going on as to the forthcoming congressional election, the candidate for which would be nominated in the fall of 1898. A justice of the Utah Supreme Court and a congressman were to be elected in Utah. My friends commenced somewhat systematic urgency for my nomination, and when the convention convened Judge Baskin, a former so-called Liberal leader and an anti-Mormon, was nominated for the supreme bench in Utah and I was made the Democratic candidate for Congress. Soon afterwards the campaign turned into a most malicious and bitter contest on the question of the undesirability of a man such as I who had been involved in the plural marriage practice of the Mormon church, although there had been a settlement of that question in the constitutional convention, which seemed to have settled the status of those who had been involved in that system of marriage and made it not at all incompatible for those so involved to seek political preference. The settlement of this question in the constitutional convention briefly stated was as follows:

The Enabling Act itself required–First: "That perfect toleration of religious sentiment shall be secured, and that no inhabitant of the said state should ever be molested in personal property on account of his or her mode of religious worship: provided that polygamous or plural marriages are forever prohibited."

It is to be observed in this connection that this prohibition went to polygamous marriages alone. It was provided for in the action of the convention, which adopted the very language of the second clause in the Enabling Act, which provided that polygamous or plural marriages are forever prohibited. The United States statutes applicable to Utah in her later territorial years had made a distinction between polygamy or polygamous marriages and polygamous living. The latter was characterized only as a misdemeanor under the title of "unlawful cohabitation." In 1892 the territorial legislature, to make the territory harmonious in its characterization of this "crime" and also to seemingly give effect to President Wilford Woodruff's manifesto forbidding polygamy, entered the field and enacted a law expressly like the federal statute, forbidding polygamy or polygamous marriages and also adopting the federal act respecting unlawful cohabitation and fixing penalties in both cases like the federal law. After adopting the far range of the Enabling Act, it was supposed that the convention had sufficiently met the requirements of the Enabling Act.

But later the thought was developed in the convention that it was doubtful if the simple declaration that plural marriages are forever prohibited would be sufficient to comply with the Enabling Act, as there were no penalties affixed in case of any violation of the simple constitutional declaration. It was a question among the lawyers of the constitutional convention as to the constitutionality of the territorial legislation of 1892, making polygamous marriages a felony and unlawful cohabitation being carried over into the state jurisprudence. Hence Mr. Varian, a delegate from Salt Lake County, introduced an amendment of the constitutional declaration specifically providing that the act of the governor and legislative assembly of the territory of Utah, entitled An Act to Punish Polygamy and other Kindred Offenses, and approved February 4, 1892, "In so far as the same defines and imposes penalties for polygamy, is hereby declared to be in force in the State of Utah."

It will be observed that Mr. Varian's words called for adoption of only part of the Act of 1892, "in so far" as it "defines and imposes penalties for polygamy," which the act defined as marriage to more than one living spouse. This amendment thus cut in two the territorial act of 1892, retaining the law against polygamy or polygamous marriages and leaving the defined crime of unlawful cohabitation out. It was plain that it was not intended that the part of the act defining and punishing unlawful cohabitation was to be made an offense in the state being created. This question was submitted to Mr. Varian on the floor of the convention by Mr. David Evans, an attorney from Ogden, in the following form:

Mr. Evans: "Suppose the Act of 1892 were valid . . . Would the amendment not then repeal everything except the polygamy (i.e., polygamous marriages)"?

To which Mr. Varian answered: "If the law were valid, it might repeal by implication. Although repeals by implication are not favored" (*Proceedings of the Constitutional Convention*, 1895, vol. 11, p. 1748).

Undoubtedly, however, the intent of the convention was to make polygamous marriages irrevocably prohibited in the state, but by not including the part of the law against unlawful cohabitation, it was not intended to have this constitutional provision address that part of the polygamous offense.

Ultimately this amendment by Mr. Varian was adopted by a vote of 72 for it, 16 registered against it, 16 absent, and two paired (p. 1748).

The question was still extensively debated, chiefly among the lawyers. However, others participated in the discussion, among them Mr. Goodwin, the then brilliant editor of the *Salt Lake Tribune*. He gave his support to Mr. Varian's amendment, though his reasons for supporting it were rather unfortunate and at least gave color to the charge made against him that he was not sincere in his support of the amendment, that the action of the convention would be merely to forestall opposition by President Cleveland to sign the constitution and admit Utah into the Union.

Among other things he said: "There is no state where the laws are enforced against the public sentiment of the people. Now if public sentiment of the people of this territory is that the ordinance shall be backed by legislation, which will make penalties and enforce them, that will be done. If a change should come and the sentiment should be that it was nobody's business, we'll do what we please, that will be the rule. . . . We know that almost every church organization outside of Utah in the U.S. will scan this constitution. They will study it with a disposition to, if possible, find some fault in it. Now when they do that and there is merely a declaration (i.e., in the constitution) that there will be no more polygamy, they will simply laugh. They will say, those people have simply made a declaration and have provided no means on earth to enforce it. It is not what should be after statehood is obtained, but it is how to obtain statehood. For instance the President of the United States is, I am told, a member of the Presbyterian Church. . . . He is a lawyer. He construes things exactly as I would construe them when he has the capacity to (laughter). Now when this constitution is carried up to him . . . we will suppose in the same election by which this constitution is approved there should be Republican officers elected all over this state. He not only will have the Presbyterian Church behind him, but he will have every Democratic office holder in Washington and all through the country telling him that there is a point where he can afford to delay. It won't make a bit of difference to Utah what is in the constitution in regard to that particular matter. The idea is to have something to present to the President, which he and his friends can find no flaw in; that is, that the Enabling Act has not only been carried out in the matter, but the means have been provided to enforce its mandate. . . . If two years hence or four years hence, the legislature decided to do anything else, it can do it. If the constitution is adopted and Utah is admitted as a state, the people can revise or call a convention, and make a new constitution within a year or two. . . . But let us fix it so that the President of the United States at least cannot in his obstinate way say 'it does not suit me, you had better go back and try it over.' . . . Let us act in absolute good faith so far as our words are concerned, and have it fixed so that a penalty, if that is disobeyed, can be inflicted (i.e., provided the Varian amendment to adopt the territorial act of 1892 for punishing polygamous marriages should be adopted)."

To these remarks I replied on the afternoon of the same day they were uttered by Mr. Goodwin: "Mr. President, I am in favor of adopting the amendment offered by the gentleman from Salt Lake (Mr. Varian). I think, sir, that it should prevail. First and principally, that it may appear without any equivocation whatsoever, that in absolute good faith, the people of Utah intend to carry out the condition upon which statehood is to be granted to the territory, for Congress did require, by its Enabling Act, an express stipulation upon this subject, and I believe its intention was to have a declaration that would be effective and not merely an empty assertion, and I think a provision of this character is absolutely necessary to the document we are drafting in order to establish beyond all question the fact that we intend to carry out to the letter our agreement as expressed in the compact with the United States; but, sir, I do not think that this amendment should be adopted by this Convention in the spirit in which it was discussed by the gentleman from Salt Lake this morning (Mr. Goodwin). One of the reasons urged for having a stenographic report of these debates, as I understand it, was for the purpose of assisting those who will interpret the constitution, in understanding what the intent of the convention that framed the constitution was; and, sir, if we adopt this amendment in the spirit in which that gentleman discussed it, those who shall interpret the constitution in the light of what was said upon the various propositions would be led to conclude that this amendment was not adopted by the convention with any real intention to have it put in force, but merely for the purpose of removing from the eyes of the President of the United States, who is to pass upon this instrument, and his counselors, and to silence any opposition that might be raised against it on the part of sectarian peoples throughout the United States, and that it was not a real bona fide determination on the part of this constitutional convention to carry out that provision with good intent.

"Now, sir, I scorn all such proceedings as that. I believe that what we do here, we do with real intent of heart and without nonsense, and for that reason, and in this spirit we should adopt this amendment and then have it carried out just as it is intended to carry it out. I hope, sir, that these remarks and the remarks that other gentlemen have made and doubtless will make upon this provision of the constitution will have the effect of removing from the proceedings of this constitution this seeming insincerity, which ought not to exist in a convention of this character. Why, sir, we would give little credit to the intelligence of the man who is to pass upon this instrument, before our labors shall finally be completed, in bringing Utah into the Union, if we suppose that he could not see through this flimsy screen that it is proposed to cast over our conduct here, if we let this provision go in under the spirit of that discussion; and, sir, I hold that we ought to adopt it in a spirit of earnestness and with honest intention to make it effectual."

Mr. Varian himself also severely criticized the remarks of Mr. Goodwin, saying among other things: "I agree with my friend from Davis County. I do not put it (the amendment) upon the grounds that were stated here this morning. I do not like a sneak. I would not desire anything to be done that was not done in good faith, but I believe that this people (i.e., of Utah) intend this in good faith, and therefore I believe that they will ratify this action here today."

This was known as the constitutional settlement of the subject of polygamy as required by the Enabling Act, and it will be observed that it merely provided for the elimination of polygamy or polygamous marriages. Nothing was said in relation to polygamous living or unlawful cohabitation as it was called. And the entrance of Utah into the Union was understood to cancel all the political disagreeabilities supposed to be attached to the relationships that had been formed under the Mormon system of plural or polygamous marriages. The idea was that the fountain (polygamous marriages) if dried up, the stream from that source entered into previous to that time would run to waste and finally be obliterated with the lapse of years, and meantime no political inabilities would be held to exist against those in the plural marriage relationship which had been established.

In view of this no objections were raised against the election of a man such as I living in such polygamous relationships contracted before the Woodruff Manifesto of September 1890. No objection was urged against my election to the convention on that account, and altogether there were fifteen or twenty members of the convention in that status, including the man chosen to be the very president of the convention, Mr. John Henry Smith, also Mr. Moses Thatcher, a prominent outstanding member with the rest. At the nominating convention of 1896, no objection was urged against my nomination on the ground of my marital relations, but soon after the campaign was in progress, gradually there rose protests against me upon this ground, and the congressional campaign became very offensively redolent with such objections and especially so in the excessive use of cartooning me and my domestic relations.

This, however, did not deter Mr. R. N. Baskin running as candidate for the supreme court with me. In manifesting his support of me as congressman, he campaigned the entire state with me, although he had been a particularly violent anti-Mormon and especially committed to opposition of the polygamous practices of the Mormon church and very willingly cheered in the triumphant election of the Democratic party in that year. Judge Orlando W. Powers, national Democratic chairman of the state of Utah that year, made no opposition to my marital relations but ardently defended me against those assaults as did also Mr. Fisher Harris, who in the previous campaign of 1895 had been the Democratic nominee for secretary of state, though with me was shamefully cartooned in connection with my supposed domestic family life.

CHAPTER 23.

Election to Congress, Part Two

With the close of the campaign in Utah, in which I obtained nearly seven thousand plurality of votes cast, the opposition to me as a successful candidate in the campaign was shifted from state opposition to a nationwide opposition. Some of the leading papers of the United States took up the cudgel against me and also a sectarian opposition, among them the so-called Christian sects, was awakened and arose to national proportions. Special conferences and conventions of the churches and Sunday Schools adopted resolutions, and finally by the time Congress was to convene, petitions signed by upwards of seven million names were pasted together and rolled up like cheese and wheeled into the House of Representatives, protesting my being allowed to take my seat. The Randolph Hearst papers in New York and throughout the country thought it necessary to make special warfare upon me, and because I went east a few weeks before the assembling of Congress and resided in New York, they heralded me each day with special articles in their leading papers denouncing me as a fugitive from justice.

When Congress convened I had already been in Washington, D.C., several days looking over the ground, and by contact with incoming members I sought to forecast the coming events. Prospects were not encouraging. The members of the House were met generally by committees representing protesting situations and by the newspaper men. Some were frankly willing to concede the right of a state to pass upon the moral standing and intellectual value of their representatives, providing that they possessed the constitutional qualifications of members of the House, but these, as soon as they were engulfed in a stream of opposition and prejudice, changed their views. Among those notably was Mr. Cannon, at that time Speaker of the House but preparing for retirement. A rapid fire exchange of views with Mr. Richardson, who had been elected minority leader for the Democrats, evoked a spirited controversy concerning Mr. Cannon's change of attitude, as alleged by Mr. Richardson, between his views on first arrival and afterwards. Mr. Richardson alleged they were changed by Mrs. Cannon and representatives of the anti-Mormon Women's Organization, who by this time had been signed up to make war upon my membership in the House.

In the midst of these things, I could not but feel to be encouraged by prominent people in the United States and some prominent newspapers who stood in my favor. Among these was the foremost paper of the nation, namely the *New York Times*, which solicited and obtained a written account of my case, and especially the details of my defense.

In the course of the article I said: "It is falsely charged that the Congressman from Utah was elected to represent polygamy. That if he is seated and retains his seat it will mean that Congress endorses polygamy, and that there will be an immediate revival of the Mormon plural marriage system in Utah.

"In the name of all that is consistent, I would like to know how the Mormon people could hope to base a revival of the practice of plural marriage—even if they had the disposition to do so—on the fact of the Representative from Utah taking and retaining his seat in the House. Does the House of Representatives endorse individual views of all the men it admits to membership? If Socialists should from some congressional district elect a congressman, would his admission to the House say to the world that the American congress endorsed Socialism? Surely my enemies give the Mormon people and even Congress little credit for common sense when they trump up such a charge as this. I don't go to Washington as a representative of polygamy. I am not sent there by my constituents to ask Congress to consent to the repeal of the clause in our state constitution which defines, prohibits, and punishes polygamy—and it should be remembered that this particular clause in our state constitution cannot be repealed without the consent of the United States. I shall not go to Washington to advocate or even defend polygamy. The question has passed the point where either is necessary in the American congress. By the settlement of the matter between the people of the United States and the people of the State of Utah, the question has been taken from the field of political controversy. What views and beliefs individuals may entertain is a matter of indifference in this connection. We have not yet undertaken, I think, the task of prescribing opinion, or barring men from political preferment for mere opinions they may entertain."

Respecting danger to the "American Home," I said: "It is falsely charged that the Representative from Utah now advocates polygamy—that is, the present contracting of polygamous marriages, notwithstanding the Utah constitutional prohibition of such marriages.

"The only evidence adduced in support of the charge is a quotation from a magazine article written some two years ago by him in response to inquiries of a number of gentlemen in New York, who asked on what grounds the Mormon Church in the past had justified the doctrine of plural marriages. The question was presented in such form that it involved the consideration of whether or not the Bible sanctioned polygamy; and my answer to that question is now so misrepresented as to make it appear that I am an advocate of polygamy in the sense of advocating plural marriages now, whereas in every way I stand committed to sustain the settlement of that question as fixed by the terms of the Utah constitution forever prohibiting plural marriages; and my article merely explained the grounds on which the Mormon Church in the past based its justification of plural marriages. Would the men trying to unseat the Representative from Utah hold that one may not make an explanation of past conditions without offense? Are these sectarian ministers who are at the bottom of the agitation against this representative so sensitive over the fact that it was by the force of representative and harsh legislation often cruelly administered that led to the suppression of Mormon plural marriages rather than their 'Christian love,' the arguments of the Rev. Dr. Newman against Orson Pratt, or their own little popgun arguments on the same subject–are they so sensitive on this matter that they can bear no explanation of this past controversy without stuffing their fingers in their ears and running through the nation screaming 'the Mormons are advocating polygamy, the Mormons are threatening the American home?' It would be interesting to learn what views these gentlemen entertain on the freedom of opinion and freedom of speech. Where were they reared? In Spain or Russia or some petty despotism of the Orient? Surely they never breathed the free air of the great Western Republic. Come they down from the ninth or thirteenth century? Surely they do not belong to the close of the nineteenth century.

"I pass by the many other falsehoods that have been uttered relative to myself in this present agitation, knowing that the time is near when those who uttered them and myself will be face to face. I can then answer to the charges accusing me of being guilty of a misdemeanor in the State of Utah. I can answer to the House of Representatives–the first parliamentary body in the world–if it can consent to so far forget its dignity as to resolve itself into a police court, to ascertain if one of its members is guilty of misdemeanor alleged to have been committed in a distant state and punishable there. I could have answered then in some Justice of Peace court in Utah if the complaint had been made before such a magistrate instead of before the whole American people. But to so lay the complaint did not suit the starters of this present agitation, bent as they were upon an anti-Mormon crusade. It could not have been made to appear by proceeding so that the 'American Home,' enshrined as it is in the hearts of the eighty millions of people, protected by the force of a 'Christian Civilization,' and shielded by American law, including the Utah constitution–it could not have been made to appear that this American home was in danger if this man had been haled before a Justice of Peace and his guilt or innocence quietly ascertained. No; they must use this case for agitation purposes, to show the great Republic what danger it is really in. I pass by all this now, however, and only point out in part the misrepresentations and falsehoods on which the agitation against the Congressman from Utah and the people of that State is based, and by reason of which many worthy people are being misled and induced to join in a hue and cry over a question, the real merits of which they know little or nothing.

"The danger to the American home, in the protection of which this present agitation is invoked and which is urged as its justification, does not lurk in the sun-blessed valleys of Utah, filled with farming villages, there to greet the morn and crown the hours with its quiet joy. The good people of New York City and other cities can find it much nearer home. In this city where I am writing–the city of Helen Gould, and I mention that lady's name with the profoundest respect and admiration of her good works, her womanly charity, and, withal, her broadmindedness, and only regret that she has been misled in relation to conditions in Utah–but here in the city of her home within any thousand feet square may be found more that menaces the American home than ever existed, or I hope ever will exist, in the whole state of Utah. And knowing this it looks just a little ridiculous to see well-meaning reformers so far misled by misrepresentation of Utah affairs as to be found standing knee deep in the swamps of social evils about them, vainly trying to tiptoe themselves into a position where they can peek over the rugged summits of the Rocky Mountains to find some desperate menace to the American home. Leave Utah alone; she is able and will work out her own salvation, if, indeed, she is not already as far along that road as any other state in the Union." (*New York Times*, November 19, 1899.)

Also the *New York World* did strong editorial service. Dr. Charles W. Elliot, president at the time of Harvard University, was quoted as follows: "If Mr. Roberts was a polygamist before polygamy became illegal in the territory, I think he was absolutely right in continuing to maintain his wives and their children if there were any. . . . In my judgment, that was the only proper thing for a Mormon to do. . . . I should not consider him an unsuitable member of Congress on the ground of polygamous relations if these were the facts."

Mary A. Livermore in the same dispatch says: "It seems to me that Mr. Roberts who, as I understand it, was a polygamist before Utah became a state, ought to deal honorably with his wives and not cast them off from his support. I understand that he is now doing this, but is not living in polygamy. Aside from polygamy (i.e., polygamous marriages) there is no reason why we should expect to excoriate Mormonism that I know of. Convert Mormonism to something better, but don't persecute them."

Susan B. Anthony wrote me personally and also published her letter espousing my cause, and there were many others.

For the most part the correspondent representatives of the newspapers throughout the country, seated as they were in the gallery above the speaker's desk and generally referred to as the "third house," were quite generally favorable to my cause and had many fair and vigorous things to say in support of my right to a seat in the House of Representatives.

There was much else said in the press to the same effect enough to make several volumes, but not even a digest of them can be attempted here.

Senator Rawlins, Democrat from Utah elected to the U.S. Senate, took a loyal interest in my case and sometimes attended the hearings of the committee making the investigation and participated both by testimony and argument in the case. Early in the session of the U.S. Senate, he introduced a resolution, which he asked should be referred to the judiciary committee of the body, calling up the case of the people of Utah, who were charged with violating a "compact" with the U.S. in reference to polygamy and the election of a member to the House of Representatives charged with polygamy. He would provide for an investigation of all the charges as to whether there had been appointments of polygamists by the president in violation of the said "compact" and would make a report thereon to the Senate. Accompanying the resolution, information was supplied that it was alleged that before the election of the representative from Utah, polygamous appointment had been made of postmasters in Utah by the president, Mr. John C. Graham at Provo, and Mr. Orson F. Smith at Logan. Protests against the appointment of these men had been filed in Washington, but the protests were set aside. The administration knew by testimony of affidavits to that effect that these men were living in polygamous relations, and, that being true, the alleged "compact" had been violated by the people in my election to the House of Representatives. Thus the first offense against the alleged "compact" in the matter of polygamists holding office was first set by the administration. This action in the Senate brought up the question in the discussion in the House on the subject of my seat, and I treated it in the following manner:

"So, sir, I take it that the resolution offered by the gentleman from Tennessee (Mr. Richardson, minority leader on the floor of the House) is directly in point and that it would be better that the entire investigation of this case be referred to the committee on the judiciary. For I tell you, sir, that making a charge against a sovereign state for breaking its 'compact' with its government is a very serious matter, especially since it may involve a question in regard to the action of the executive of this nation in relation thereto. For, I assert this, that if the people of Utah were guilty of breaking a compact by electing a man charged with being a violator of these particular laws about unlawful cohabitation, the administration of the government may also be charged with breaking that contract by also appointing to federal offices against whom like protests supported by affidavits were made. Therefore it is immanently proper that they (such charges) should go to a committee that we will be assured are men of trained abilities and learned in the law" (*Congressional Record*, December 5, 1899, p. 48).

The charge that the executive of that nation had made appointments under these circumstances acted like a bomb in the House, and a number of representatives sprang to their feet, and Mr. Grosvenor, representative from

Ohio, in a most dramatic manner made a denial of such appointments. But all to no effect, for the thing established in the record of the case was that such appointments had been made and that the postmasters in question were dismissed from office, but this was too late to evade or effect the charge that such appointments had knowingly been made. During the debate upon the case on the floor of the House, I had been excluded from perfecting my membership therein by an act of exclusion, pending the investigation of my case by a special committee.

But I was accorded from first to last two brief opportunities of representing my case on the floor of the House, not from the view point and with the privileges of membership in the House but as an act of courtesy on the part of the House. I was accorded for my first speech thirty minutes by unanimous consent, and this was afterwards extended ten minutes more by the act of courtesy on the part of Mr. Taylor, chairman of the special committee having my case in hand. Near the close of the debate, I was again accorded by unanimous consent a similar amount of time. Of course these limitations hampered a full and free discussion of issues involved in his case, for a single member withdrawing his consent at any time would silence my voice and prevent the conclusions of my argument. The floor of the House was crowded by an influx of members from the Senate to hear the discussion, and such was the public interest that the gallery of the House was also crowded and they frequently applauded the utterance of the Utah man.

At the conclusion of the second speech, I made allusion to the impatient vehemence of some of the members to drive me in disgrace from the House. On this I said: "Some, in discussing the Roberts case, have said: 'Brand this man with shame and send him back to his people.' Mr. Speaker, I thank God that the power to brand me with shame is something quite beyond the power of this House, great as that power is. The power to brand with shame rests with each man and nowhere else. I have lived up to this day in all good conscience in harmony with the moral teachings of the communities in which I was reared and am sensible of no act of shame in my life. Brand me with shame! Why, if you finally determine either to exclude or expel me, I shall leave this august assembly with head erect and brow undaunted and walk God's earth as the angels walk the clouds, with no sense of shame upon me (applause on the floor and hisses from the gallery). Each in response must consider the sectarian clamor that has been invoked against the member from Utah, who violated the constitution of your country either in excluding or expelling me. All the shame that there is in this case will be left behind me and rest with this House. Mr. Speaker, I see my time has expired; I thank the House for its attention" (applause).

The resolution fashioned in this case by the majority of the special committee read as follows: "Resolved that under the facts and circumstances of this case Brigham H. Roberts, Representative-elect from the State of Utah ought not to have or hold a seat in the House of Representatives and that the seat to which he was elected is hereby declared vacant. The ayes and nays were ordered, the question was taken, and there were ayes, 268, nays 50, not voting 36, so the resolution was agreed to."

The case had furnished the sectarian "Christian" ministry an opportunity to air their anti-Mormon prejudices and in a way to proclaim their great holiness and impeccability in relation to loyalty to monogamous marriage, etc., and each sought to proclaim his own sanctity by throwing stones at the member from Utah. Writers for the press availed themselves of like opportunities both for themselves and for their own people, especially those of the sensational order. This, however, was not an entirely one-sided battle which gathered around me, the Mormon victim. As already noted very many prominent and influential persons and dignified papers of the United States held against the violation of constitutional rights for me and said noble words in the interests of constitutional morality, which may be explained as adherence to constitutional principles. The spirit of some of the writers upon the subject was extremely fair, as in the case of an article by a woman correspondent to the *Washington Star* of November 30, 1899, signed by one Pauline Pry, who sought and obtained an interview which opened as follows:

"I have given Mr. Roberts of Utah a very great shock—the opportunity to talk to a woman disposed to do him justice. There was another woman present rendering Mr. Roberts honor and devotion. The latter is a very charming young woman about twenty years old, of attractive face and figure, immeasurable force of character and most womanly dignity. She has a peculiarly pleasing manner of speech, entirely free from affectation of any sort, her style of address being characterized by a simplicity and directness, which together with reserve wins your heart and respect at once. Her voice is gentle and well modulated, bears every evidence of culture, and refinement is graceful in her bearing. She is unusually self-possessed for a woman of her years and taken altogether would appear an irresistible argument in favor of polygamy, if Mr. Roberts chose to represent her in Congress.

"However, she is not here for that purpose. 'You were very courageous to bring your daughter to Washington,' I said to Mr. Roberts.

"With a single impulse the father and daughter turned toward each other and clasped hands.

"After a moment, Mr. Roberts answered me, saying: 'There's a story of a hard battle behind her coming here, and I confess it is her triumph. I was not in favor of it at first, but her persistency won the day. She thinks she can be a sort of help to me I'll need, that no man can give me, and when it was about settled that a man who wished to be of assistance to me should join me, she wrote to me begging so hard to take his place that I was forced to yield. She said she was like Gavroche, in the case of Jean Valjean. She wanted to be in the fight, and, insignificant as her defense might be, she was bound to give it. So here she is.'

"Now you know I'm a woman, which is to say, emotional and impressionable, and I'll admit the devotion of his daughter and his appreciation of it caused the celebrated Mr. Roberts to quite lose his dreadful identity in my sight. As a father he is eminently to be trusted and much to be admired.

"In the character of the representative elect from Utah, whom the women of the United States propose unseating by 'brushing aside all technical defense' and 'taking a stand on the broad principles at stake,' Mr. Roberts impressed me as a man somewhat to be feared – rather outside all calculations that have yet been made about him. He seems to possess a certain immobility of purpose that looks at you out of his clear, steady blue eyes, that inspires you, caution appearing in the firm lines of his square-cut clean fleshed jaw, and, above all, that addresses you in the rare poise of the whole man, the impressive quiet of his voice, and telling moderation of his language. The keynote of his character is self control. He knows Mr. Roberts perfectly, believes in him implicitly, and in any event directs the destiny of Mr. Roberts without reference to contrary opinion or storms of opposition. He will fight to defend his principles and his position. I think he will give us a very interesting chapter of the coming congress."

Other phases of the case, not pertinent to these pages, were also considered in a defensive manner, and trustworthily reported by the lady correspondent of the *Star*.

CHAPTER 24.

A General Authority – Writing Church Literature

Returning to Utah I faced chaos in my affairs. No answer had been given to my expressed wish to be so far released from ecclesiastical duties as to enter into the career of the law, from which I had turned more especially to politics. Now, of course, my prospects in that line were ruined. It had been suggested in Washington, D.C., by a number of apologists who had voted for my exclusion that I would doubtless receive vindication from the people of Utah by being elected governor of the state and continue a career in state politics. But there was no appearance of evidence that such an act would be taken by the Democrats of Utah. The campaign through which I had passed and the denial of *per diem* and traveling expenses together with hotel and other necessary expenses had left me stranded in debt. Subsequently, however, and chiefly by the interest and skill of William H. King, who was elected to succeed both to my unexpired term and the term following in the House, the travelling allowance from my home to Washington and return was secured, from which I was able to relieve myself from some of the indebtedness noted above.

Apparently nothing was left to me but the inadequate compensation to meet living expenses from my church position, by now fixed upon as a small but regular income. There was nothing left but to turn to such church literature as I could work out to supplement my church compensation. About this time an interesting incident happened in that line, which at least carried something like a sense of humor in it.

Some few years before, and following the publication of my biography of John Taylor, third president of the church, I had published my *Outlines of Ecclesiastical History*. The first edition was devoted as a text book for the instruction of the Seventy, and it turned out to be a popular book not only for the Seventies but other priesthood church organizations. Mr. Abraham Cannon meantime had taken over publication of the *Contributor*, a magazine which was the organ of the Mutual Improvement Association, both of which had been founded by Mr. Junius F. Wells of blessed memory. And one day I received a note from Mr. Cannon asking what royalty I would ask allowing the *Contributor* publishers to offer the *Outlines of Ecclesiastical History* as a premium for subscriptions to the *Contributor*. To this I answered that the royalty would be 50 cents per copy. The note making the inquiry had come per hand of a messenger from Mr. Cannon's office, and on receiving the reply he immediately wrote back that "no such royalty had ever been paid on books published west of the Mississippi River." To which I on the same note I had received from Mr. Cannon wrote and returned by the hand of the messenger, "No such book as the *Ecclesiastical History* had ever been published west of the Mississippi River or anywhere else in the United States." The matter was finally agreed upon at 40 cents per copy.

By the way, authorship of the *Life of John Taylor* mentioned above deserves a further slight notice. It had been rather understood throughout the church the relations of Mr. George Q. Cannon to the Taylor family (President Taylor had married the daughter of Captain Cannon, grandfather of President Cannon, and "Uncle John Taylor" was always the title used within the families). Also his long official association with President Taylor as his counselor led to the supposition that he would be President Taylor's biographer, and the selection by the family of me to write this biography gave umbrage to Mr. Cannon, which doubtless accounted for some of the very evident prejudices which Mr. Cannon always manifested towards me.

I now placed new emphasis upon my church work. During this time I was the assistant superintendent in the M.I.A. and had held this position through the administrations of Presidents Wilford Woodruff, Lorenzo Snow, and later in the administration of Heber J. Grant. For nine years I was the chairman of the manual committee for the M.I.A. and entirely supplied the material and publication of it of three of the annuals dealing with the subject of "New Witnesses for God." These chiefly dealt with the Book of Mormon and afterwards became my prominent work in three volumes. I set forth the divine mission of Joseph Smith in one volume and assembled the evidences in the other two volumes for the truth of the Book of Mormon, as a witness for God. This was regarded by many as my greatest contribution to the literature of the church.

Also I was appointed with President Heber J. Grant to raise Utah's quota of a contribution to the erection of the monument in memorium of the sinking of the *Maine* in a Cuban Harbor. The amount reported as Utah's contribution was received from the chairman of the movement, and he congratulated Utah as having raised a certain percent of the sum.

By this time the writing of the LDS church history began to take form. For a number of years beginning back during my ministry and editing the *Latter-day Saints' Millennial Star* in England, I had begun the collection of the frequent reproduction of Joseph Smith's journal on the New Dispensation movement, under the title of "History of Joseph Smith," which was merely the publication of the daily journal he kept during his lifetime. And so for a number of years I had been purchasing copies of the *Millennial Star* as they annually appeared with this publication appearing therein, chiefly copied from the publication of the articles in the *Deseret News*. It was a difficult task to get the numbers of these volumes, and some of them were so scarce that they were held at almost prohibitive prices. However, the volumes from 14 to 26 were obtained and then just the articles on Joseph Smith's History were ripped out of the volumes and finally bound together, which made three volumes. They were placed within the covers of volumes of the *Star*, so that the student of history had the prophet's journal in a condensed compass, which made reference to the subject matter easy.

Some of the apostles, notably Francis M. Lyman, finding that such collection had been made, made the suggestion to the Quorum of the Twelve that he believed that it would be worth while to take this journal of the prophet and have it published and suggested that I be employed to make the publication. The idea appealed to the Twelve, and Elder Lyman was authorized to see on what terms I would undertake the work. When he reported back to the Twelve, it was thought that the price of doing the work was rather high, and George Q. Cannon of the presidency, who was present at the meeting, spoke up and said that he would do the work for less than that which I had stated. Of course, in any event, had he volunteered to do the work, it would have been accorded to him without reference to the price, because his wide experience, owing to his longer term of office in the church and his identification with the publishing business of the church, would have warranted the work being assigned to him.

In any event, the work was taken out of my hands, and Brother Cannon set one of his sons at work making the compilation. He superintended the printing and proofreading of the work, which was carried on without any reference to unification or annotation, just merely the reproduction of the journal as it had been brought forth through the years that it ran in the *Millennial Star*. In the course of a few months, however, President Cannon died in California. And only ninety-six pages of the work, which would amount into several volumes, had been printed. President Woodruff had also passed away, and Lorenzo Snow, by then the president of the Twelve Apostles, had been chosen and elected by the voice of the people to become president of the church in succession of President Woodruff. Among the unfinished business which came to his administration from the one which passed was the compilation of the history of the church.

I was sent for by the president and appointed to complete that work without reference to any compensation. Then came my dismay as the new editor-to-be of the work, because the mere reproduction of the matter that had been printed in the *Millennial Star* was not at all the idea that I had in the production of the work. My scheme had contemplated the publication with each volume an introduction, which would deal with and harmonize in editorial comment each volume of the work (which I estimated would be six volumes in number), and also explanatory notes in the margin, which would also help in unifying the text of the prophet. To go on with President Cannon's procedure with the work would not at all reach the dignity of it as conceived by me. I also had contemplated the publication of all the revelations received by the prophet in the chronological order in which they had been given, with marginal references to current editions of the Doctrine and Covenants in which also they appear. This plan would give the historical circumstances attending upon their being received, which would greatly help in the matter of interpretation and understanding of the revelations. A commentary, in fact, was planned upon each one as it was given.

The contemplation of giving up this plan was painful to me, and so after much hesitation, I called upon President Snow and explained what I had hoped to do in getting out this work, and yet to install it now would lead to the destruction of ninety-six pages of forms of a ten thousand edition that had been produced under the Cannon plan. But after this presentation, President Snow smilingly said: "Well then, let them be destroyed and carry out your original purpose." And this was done, and the "History of Joseph Smith," under the title of *Church History, Period 1*, volumes 1-6, was produced, averaging over 600 pages to the volume. To this in 1932 a seventh volume was added, made up in uniform style with the first six volumes and condensed from the manuscript "History of Brigham Young" and other authoritative documents.

This was done and the work was carried through on the original plans devised by me. There is no question but what the seven volumes which bring us from the commencement of Joseph Smith to the establishment of the Saints in the valley of the Rocky Mountains in Utah will remain for a long time as a standard historic work for that period. Reference to the volume will be ample vindication of the plan on which they were originally completed.

During the time that the *History of the Church, Period 1*, was edited and published, five annual *Seventy's Yearbooks on Theology* were produced. Some time previous to their commencement, namely in 1896, I had performed a mission with George Albert Smith, later of the Quorum of the Twelve Apostles, visiting the Eastern States and Southern States missions, and at the close of the tour of these two missions in connection with Elder Smith, I reported on the conditions existing, especially among the missionaries in those fields of labor. It was pointed out that the missionaries were, for the most part, very young men, the average being under twenty-one years of age. They lacked historical and doctrinal background for the work they were expected to do, and they really had no commanding knowledge to give them assurance of the things whereof they were to be witnesses. That some steps should be taken to raise the standard and age and efficiency among the missionaries was insistently evident.

This led to the recommendation that greater opportunity should be secured for the quorums of the Seventy, who according to the genius of the organization of the New Dispensation were the traveling ministry or missionary force of the church, the apostles being required by the revelations to choose the Seventies to fill the several calls for mission labor in the world "instead of any others" (D&C 107). And it was suggested in the report that being this special source for missionary material, they would be given larger opportunities as students of the gospel by being permitted to meet some time on the Sabbath day. Then the quorums regarded as theological classes could hope for larger and more constant attendance upon these missionary themes for instruction. Many of the Seventies were engaged in the auxiliary world of teaching Sunday school classes, and some objection was raised to releasing them for this activity, but it was pointed out that surely the quorums of high priests and elders could be regarded as sufficient for supplying teachers for Sunday school and the like. The Seventies released from that auxiliary work could give stricter attention to their preparation for the work of the church missionary service.

The battle for the arrangement was won from the administration of the church and then almost immediately lost, as it was held that it too much interfered with Sunday school work. However, the vigorous presentation of the claims of the Seventy to be prepared for their mission work was again won and liberty granted to have the Seventies meet in their quorum classes on Sunday morning.

This gave encouragement to the preparation of the "Seventy's Course of Theology," which ran through five year books and was prepared by me. The titles of the year books were as follows. The first was the "Outline History of the Seventy," which included a treatise on the scriptures under the general idea that a workman must know his tools, and hence this yearbook dealt with recognized scriptures of the church as books, more especially their nature as books and relative importance. The design was to create a general knowledge of the scriptures as books. The Old Testament, the New Testament, the Book of Mormon, the Doctrine and Covenants, and the Pearl of Great Price were included, the last being a collection of books brought forth by Joseph Smith, the Book of Moses, the Book of Abraham, and the brief historical narrative of Joseph Smith with some translations of the scriptures, etc. These four books were recommended to become permanent and indispensible in the library of the Seventies.

The second yearbook dealt with the "Outline History of the Dispensations of the Gospel." The third yearbook dealt with the "Doctrine of Deity." The fourth with the rather difficult doctrine of the "Atonement," and the fifth with the "Divine Immanence and the Holy Ghost." The arrangement for the Seventies to meet on Sunday morning followed through fifteen glorious months, when the seventies organization functioned as never before as classes of theological students. The attendance increased, and everywhere an intense interest in the course of study was maintained. The elder everywhere looked forward with great desire for promotion to the Seventies quorum, and Seventies' affairs touched the highwater mark in this period. Could it have continued, in a few years the church undoubtedly at home and in its foreign missions would have felt tremendous uplift in doctrinal power and the efficiency of its witnesses to the world.

However, the foreign ministry of the church was allowed to continue only for fifteen months and then jealousy for increased advantages of the auxiliary work by the Sunday schools succeeded in defeating the advantages with which for so short a time had been accorded these special quorums of the holy priesthood. Sunday morning meetings were discontinued, and with that discontinuance the interest broke and the quorums were drawn back into such hard working conditions that they could not so well succeed, and the interests of priesthood were sacrificed to the interests of an auxiliary organization, more a help in government instead of the church government itself. They have never since quite regained the status which they held during this short time, which was secured by them from the recommendation obtained through the reports of Elder Smith and me urging the need of improvement in background and efficiency of functioning in the quorums of the Seventy.

During these years of historical and doctrinal development of my writings, another large incident was coming to the fore. I observed that the *Salt Lake Tribune*, then a bitterly anti-Mormon publication and doubtless the chief newspaper in the state of Utah, was publishing a series of articles revamping into life the old exploded Solomon Spaulding story of the origin of the Book of Mormon. It was a series of papers, the origin of which was not disclosed and how long the series would be was not announced. But judging from the trend of them, I was satisfied that they could be effectively answered and accordingly wrote to Colonel Nelson, then the editor of the *Salt Lake Tribune*, and asked if he would be willing to publish a refutation of the theory on which the series was based if it was prepared by a member of the LDS church. In his reply Mr. Nelson disclosed the fact that the articles were reproduced by the *Tribune* from a magazine published in New York known as the *New York Historical Magazine* and that they were written by a Mr. Theodore Schroeder. Some years before he was a practicing attorney in Utah, who had been disbarred by action of the supreme court for unprofessional conduct. By one of those whims of fortune which sometimes seem to bless the disreputable, he fell heir to a property which rendered him independent of the practice of law, and he had returned to the East and had there so ingratiated himself into the favors of the publisher of the *Historical Magazine* that he got them to publish his attack upon the Book of Mormon.

This, as characterized above, may be known as the "re-galvanizing" into life of the exploded theory of the Solomon Spaulding stories as to the origin of the Book of Mormon. The Spaulding manuscript, which had for so long been relied upon by opponents to the Book of Mormon, had really been discovered in the Sandwich Islands in the possession of a Mr. Rice of

Dansville, Ohio, who had formerly been a printer in Ohio. Mr. Fairchild of the Oberlin College of Ohio, visiting this one-time publisher in the Sandwich Islands, induced him to rummage among his papers which he had taken with him to Hawaii in search of important anti-slavery documents, and he found the original of the Solomon Spaulding story brought to him by an apostate Mormon of the name of Hurlbut. This was published, and the utter impossibility of its being the origin of the Book of Mormon was demonstrated by its publication. Hence the importance of it had vanished and had been practically forgotten until Mr. Schroeder assumed the existence of a second Spaulding Manuscript and gave it galvanic life and was now publishing it in this historical magazine.

Regarding this assault upon the Book of Mormon as invincible, Mr. Nelson of the *Tribune* expressed a willingness to publish any answer a Mormon might make to the secondly assumed Spaulding manuscript, providing that the *Deseret News*, known as the LDS church organ, would publish the Schroeder articles. But he suggested also that perhaps the publisher of the Schroeder articles might be glad to publish the LDS church's answer to it, if he were solicited to do so. Regarding the suggestions for publication in the *Tribune* as too complex, I conferred directly with the publisher of the *Historical Magazine* in New York, a Mr. Nelke. Not a very enthusiastic answer was given to the effect that if I would prepare an answer to Mr. Schroeder's article, if it was acceptable as reaching the standard of literature of the *Historical Magazine* publication, then it might be published if approved.

I accepted the chance fulfillment of this proposition and prepared a series of four articles, which corresponded to the four articles written for the magazine by Mr. Schroeder, and gave such an analysis of this second Spaulding manuscript that the publishers of the *Historical Magazine* accepted them and published them. Afterwards both Mr. Schroeder's articles and my reply thereto were published in the volume of miscellaneous discourses published by me under the title *Defense of the Faith and Saints* (2:1-229).

At the conclusion of these Book of Mormon articles, Mr. Nelke, the publisher of the *Historical Magazine*, wrote saying that the publishers were willing to publish a "detailed history of the church" if I would write it. This coming after the guarded acceptance of the articles on the Book of Mormon was somewhat astonishing and was proof that the literature of the Book of Mormon articles had reached the high level of the *Historical Magazine* literature. But this time it was I who gave the guarded answer, saying to the publishers that in their proposition to publish the history of the church in detail in their magazine that the publisher could scarcely understand the largeness of such an order. The magazine was bi-monthly, and it would require a continuous article through six or eight years to reproduce the history of the Mormon church in detail. The reply of the publishers was that they would enlarge the magazine to admit this article and would make it monthly rather than a bi-monthly publication, as they desired to make it an illustrated article. Their proposition to publish the history held good if the church would meet the expense of making the plates for illustrations.

This proposition was presented to President Joseph F. Smith, and he promptly encouraged me to avail myself of this opportunity of a hearing for the church through the New York magazine, and the church would meet the expense of the illustrations. Needless to say no compensation was contemplated either from the church or from the magazine publishers for me. The advantage to the church was to be the publication of its message through these historical documents. It was, however, finally arranged that while Mr. Nelke and the publishers of the eastern magazine would hold the copyright to the first edition of the completed history, if it should be republished in separate book form, the secondary copyright was to inhere in all subsequent editions after the first to me.

Under these arrangements the articles were begun. The *Historical Magazine* was changed to a monthly periodical and enlarged to admit this article on the "History of Mormonism," as it was entitled. The article ran through six years of the rather majestic magazine publication at an average of forty-two pages per month. As soon as the first number of the article was completed, it was sent to the publishers. This began in the July number of the *Americana*, the new name for the old *Historical Magazine*, with the frontpiece engraving of Joseph Smith and throughout all the six years was richly illustrated with choice steel engravings.

It was expected of course that the articles would at least be collected and published in a series of volumes unconnected with the miscellaneous articles published in the magazine. Mr. Nelke expected really to obtain some compensation for the expense of publishing this article by reproducing it in a book form. But this was not accomplished in his life time, and I also was disappointed in this non-reproduction of my long and laborious work. The statement I made that the publication of it in book form would amount to more than $50,000 was more than the Trustee-in-Trust of the church could afford to have expended for such purpose. Bitter years of disappointment followed, but finally when the centennial anniversary of the organization of the church was approaching, it was recommended to the church authorities by a committee of which I was a member to provide for publishing this monumental work. This really gave a new value to the time selected for the publication and an added value to it, which went far to wipe out the years of disappointment through which I had suffered over it.

The authorities accepted the committee's suggestion, and preparation was made to complete this publication in six volumes at an average of between six and seven hundred pages per volume, and the tremendous labor of reproducing such a series of volumes was accomplished in less than two years' time. The title adopted was the *Comprehensive History of the*

Church of Jesus Christ of Latter-day Saints, Century 1. This title was a change
from the one used in the *Americana* article, namely, "History of the Mormon
Church." There was no serious objection to this title "Mormon Church,"
since what was intended as a derisive appellation has long since lost its
odium, and for familiar and popular use there is little objection to the word
"Mormon." Hence in the *Americana* articles "History of the Mormon
Church" was used. But now that the history appeared in a more permanent
form, it was thought to be sufficiently pretentious to bear the official title of
the church given here by revelation from God – The Church of Jesus Christ
of Latter-day Saints: "for thus shall my church be called in the last days,
saith the Lord" (D&C 115:3-5).

The prefix "comprehensive" came because of an incidental reference to
the work in the annual "Christmas Greetings of the First Presidency to the
members of the Church in all the World, for the Year 1915." When referring
to the things achieved by the church that year, the presidency said of the
work then recently completed in the *Americana*: "The Comprehensive
History of the Mormon Church by Elder B. H. Roberts and published in the
Americana and completed to recent date and will form six large volumes
when bound in book form, containing data and details collated in forcible
style, most comprehensive and valuable for reference." Hence the word
"comprehensive" in the formal title of the work.

My object as the author of this history was to make it both the advocate
and the defense of this New Dispensation based upon God's revelations to
the great prophet of that dispensation, Joseph Smith – and this through
setting forth the truth step by step as it was developed in those revelations
and by the administration of those into whose hands God had placed the
responsibility of this development. This work tells the truth of that
historical development, not only its incidents that contribute to the propi-
tious prophecies, things connected with the church, but also those things
which seem to have a contrary effect upon those developments. For as
stated in the views of the late president, Theodore Roosevelt: History to be
of any worth must not only tell of your successes but also of your failures or
semi-failures in your work. And this I endeavored to do, meeting adverse
problems with the same frankness, being mindful also of the fact that while
the servants of God, chosen as presidents, apostles, and other leaders of the
great New Dispensation movement, carried heavenly treasures in their
hands and high truths, yet they bore these in earthen vessels, liable at times
to be broken and the heavenly treasures marred.

It must be said of those entrusted with this great mission of God that
they were not always 100 percent perfect and right in their administrations.
Neither were those who fought them always and every time 100 percent
wrong. Even in the divine things human frailty touches them or enters into
their development and are liable to take on human limitations and
uncertainties. Where truth has to be met in such manner, the historian's

line of delineation between things must follow justly, firmly, and without hesitation, or he will fail in his absolute duty to the truth of things. This I religiously held in mind and followed to such an extent that it may be said to constitute the *Comprehensive History*'s chief characteristic.

The nature of this fair treatment of both friends and foes in context was brought forth by an incidental remark by one who greatly admired my work—namely, the late Elder David McKenzie, who for years was clerk in the office of successive presidencies of the church and a man of very fine literary ability himself. When the bundles of the *Americana* would appear, he was generally the first to open it and read the current article. One day meeting me in the office he said in his broad rich Scot dialect, "Well, I have read your story in this month's *Americana,* and aye, mon, the frankness of it. The frankness o' it. How dare you do it, mon?"

This frankness, another name for fairness, was sometimes subject to criticism by others, who would have been glad to express some of the manifestations of weakness on the pro-Mormon side of things. But I was of the conviction that to have this history both advocate and defend this New Dispensation, it must be kept honest and fearless and full as well when the tide of events were not favorable for the church and also when the tides seemed to run against it—hence the claim of fullness and fairness in the writing of this marvelous story of the New Dispensation. And all the while the reputation of it grows as it finds its way among individual readers, and library possessions of it increases. Especially is this true of reading clubs, some twenty of them in Salt Lake City alone, which have been organized for not only the reading but the study of it.

After this claim of fairness is made for the work, the next valuable feature of it is the extensive use of official documents both of the church and of the government—and then the more than 4,000 notes and references to be found in the margin and the independent quoted notes following the chapter which assemble the widely scattered documents as the basic authorities for the historical narrative. These are so voluminous and impartially selected both pro and con that it is possible for the reader to examine from original sources every question of fact, conclusion, and doctrine set forth in the text, and but for this collection of authorities, the facts on which Mormon authority are founded would be left scattered over immensely wide ranges. This may seem like much vaunting of praise for the work, but undoubtedly it is the masterpiece of historical writings in the first century of the church's history.

CHAPTER 25.

President of the Eastern States Mission

Connecting up the final form in which the centennial history of the church was completed in book form has carried us past some important matters in my life's work, which must be picked up and inserted here, apparently a little out of their order.

For example, there was the call to preside over the Eastern States Mission beginning the Spring (May 29) of 1922. Several alternatives to activity had been presented to me in connection with this call to the Eastern States. The brethren of the First Presidency told me I might select a mission within the United States as a field of labor, and there was some talk made also in relation to my taking editorial charge of the *Deseret News*, a newspaper recognized as a church organ. The choice I finally expressed was to become president of the Eastern States Mission. This was the most populous mission in the United States and comprised at that time eleven states within its boundary, including the industrial section of the American Union and its population exceeding thirty-three millions of people – truly a noble field. Also it had the attraction of including within it the territory of the early activities of the church, the birthplace of the prophet (Vermont), the early scenes of the prophet's life, the first vision, and the coming forth of the Book of Mormon (the Hill Cumorah), the cradle of the church organization (Fayette, New York). Also the Harmony, Colesville, and Susquehanna valleys, where the priesthood was restored, both the Aaronic and the Melchizedek priesthood. These many adventures of the prophet naturally would endear this section of the country to my mind and heart.

I succeeded in this presidency Elder George W. McCune, who had been in charge of the mission for three or four years and was accounted an efficient presiding officer but in need of being released largely on account of the uncertainty in the continuance of his health. The mission when turned over to me numbered about 140 missionaries, chiefly young men and ladies who had been called by the general authorities of the church into this immense region of country with its large population. The first summer of my labors in this mission was occupied in visiting the eight or ten conference districts into which the mission was divided. This took me to the conference headquarters in Maine, Vermont, Massachusetts; to five conferences in New York State, including Brooklyn, Manhattan, Rochester, Buffalo, Albany; also conferences in Pittsburgh, Philadelphia, Delaware,

Baltimore, Washington, D.C., Charleston, and Fairmont, West Virginia, and Huntington in the valley of the Ohio at the confluence of the Big Sandy River bordering Kentucky and West Virginia.

The following summer the plan was projected for a widespread missionary tour throughout the country districts of the mission, preaching and baptizing by the way without purse and scrip for the elders. A converging of all these elders traveling through the mission territory was arranged for at the Hill Cumorah and Sacred Grove and the old Smith Farm Home, near the town of Palmyra, the place of publication of the Book of Mormon and largely identified with the early movements of the church. This conference was to convene on the 21st of September 1923 in commemoration of the centennial anniversary of the revealed existence of the Book of Mormon. The 21st was the anniversary of Moroni's first visit to the prophet at the first home of his father on the Smith farm, just south of the line between Manchester and Wayne township. The missionaries converging at the meeting place of this conference had prepared a pennant blue in color and across it in white letters Cumorah, in the upper left hand corner in green and gold a picture of the Hill Cumorah, and underneath it in white letters "1823, September 21-22-23, 1923." This was worn across the shoulders of the incoming missionaries and was meant as a challenge to all observers to inquire concerning the destination and purpose of the traveling elders who wore it, and it brought about many a conversation about the coming forth of the Book of Mormon. In all about 150 missionaries assembled on the Hill Cumorah on the 21st day of September.

In the celebration, provision had been made for sleeping quarters in tents obtained from the military authorities in Rochester, New York, and placed about the Smith home. Also there was a large tent that would comfortably seat the congregation and could be used in the emergencies of rains. On several occasions, rains occurring, the large tent was crowded with missionaries and the large throngs that attended the meetings.

Of course, the invitations had been extended to the General Authorities of the church in Utah, but not until the last moment was action taken by any of them to attend the conference. However, President Grant and Sister Grant, together with their son-in-law John Taylor and his wife, then residing in the Northern States Mission, and also Rudger Clawson, Dr. James E. Talmage, and Joseph Fielding Smith, all of the Council of the Twelve, attended. These brethren were very welcome and undoubtedly added importance to the occasion.

Careful preparation had been made with caterers in Palmyra to bring food to the Smith farm three times a day. It was served in the open at improvised tables through the three days. A flag pole had been cut from the Sacred Grove forty feet in length and raised just south of the Smith farmhouse with the United States flag raised upon it. Another flag pole was raised upon the Hill Cumorah and the United States flag flown from its apex, while just below was a flag representing the Jaredite and Nephite nations. The Jaredite portion of the flag representing the oldest empire was of purple with their name for the scared hill in white letters RAMAH, while on the blue division of the flag was CUMORAH in white letters – the Nephite name for the hill – over which this united flag of purple and blue and white waved.

Meetings were held in the open both on the summit of the Hill Cumorah, whence came the Book of Mormon, and also in the Sacred Grove, where the holy sacrament was administered to the missionaries and to the members of the church who had gathered there in large numbers. Carefully written statements of each prominent event celebrated on this occasion were read, and appointed missionaries read written remarks from missionaries in the various conferences and fields of labor in the mission. Of course, valuable instructions and discourses and reminiscences were given by the General Authorities of the church who were present, and altogether a profitable and inspiring time was had throughout in which sociability and fellowship furnished important features.

I had given widespread notice of this anniversary event, and several of the most important papers in New York State had designed sending special correspondents and photographers to Cumorah to chronicle in story and by pictures these events. It so happened that just within the week when this conference was staged, there was a general newspaper strike called in New York, and these prominent papers were unable to feature the conference as they had intended to do. However, the local papers in Palmyra, Rochester, Syracuse, and other points gave liberal space to the description of the conference proceeding, and usually their representations were without bias and very fair. The editor of the *Rochester (N.Y.) Herald* under date of September 22, 1923, said:

"Unfolding like some graphic panorama of the past epic in implications and dramatic in content, the story of an ancient civilization that peopled the plains and hills in this vicinity was the chief topic of discussion before the centennial conference of the Church of Jesus Christ of Latter-day Saints today. Reaching so far back into the dim yesterdays of history, back to days more than 2,500 years ago, this story came with a strange emphasis in the very place where its climaxes and denouements are supposed to have been reached. The narrative is the very basis of Mormon theology and belief and leads directly up to the revelation given through Joseph Smith of the foundations of the Mormon Church."

Then under sub-heading it said: "A NORSE SAGA. The speaker at the conference told the story with the simplicity and directness of a Norse Saga. As point after point of the drama of the lost tribes, of their rise to a great civilization and of their final downfall in the bitterness of war was related, those not conversant with the tale were gripped and fascinated by the strangeness of the recital, and when a speaker dramatically pointed to the earth and mentioned that upon the very spot where he stood some to the epic events might have taken place there was a decided thrill to being there."

It was at this conference that my hitherto sturdy health collapsed. The excessive work of providing for this centennial conference had required such ceaseless exertions both mental and physical that I suffered a series of nervous chills, and the physician discovered what was entirely new to me, namely that I was a victim of the dread incurable disease of diabetes. I was only able to remain on my seat and attend about half of the meetings of this conference. It was estimated that more than five thousand people attended, notwithstanding the untoward circumstances of it being rainy part of the time.

At the close of the great gathering, as I walked weakly to the automobile which was to take me to Buffalo and thence continue the journey westward to attend the general semi-annual conference of the church early in October in Salt Lake City, one of the Twelve present remarked, though not within my hearing–it was afterwards related to me–"There goes the last of Elder Roberts, he will never recover."

It had been my intention to make the journey alone, but at the solicitation of President Grant and others, one of the returning elders was detailed to be my companion. The journey was safely made without incident, and Dr. C. F. Wilcox, a physician of long and high standing, met me at the depot on the arrival of the train and immediately took charge of me. Within an hour he had administered a dose of insulin, which had recently come into use in such cases, and I was glad of the relaxation and sense of security which the care of the doctor and the loving care and rest of my family and my friends afforded me. Gradually I began to be restored to normal conditions, with the exception that I was very emaciated and weak. In the course of a few weeks, however, I mustered the strength and courage to return to my field of labor as if there had been no break in my general health.

A review of the status of missionaries in the Eastern States from the standpoint of efficiency revealed to my mind the necessity of in some way planning for a systematic course of study among the missionaries, and I hit upon the idea of establishing a mission school for imparting such instructions and creating a background of general knowledge and specific instructions which would lead to a general improvement in efficiency and morale of missionaries, and this without discontinuing the active mission work in the respective conferences. I therefore decided upon taking one-third of the missionaries in the field (about fifty to eighty) at a time, leaving the remaining two-thirds in their respective fields of labor. The time for the school could not be longer than four weeks of intensive instruction and drill.

A circular letter was sent to the respective conference or district presidents to make the selection from their respective fields, and the letter of instruction with the call for these appointments set forth the character of the work to be carried on in the school. The following paragraph is quoted from my letter of instruction:

"I wish to impress upon all those who come to the school that they are coming here for a period of INTENSIVE WORK as thorough-going students. It will be a time of great economy for them, as I want expenses kept down at an *absolute minimum*. They must not think of coming to New York as coming upon a pleasure trip; it will be a time of sacrifice as to shows, outings, socials, and the like. Every day will be fully occupied in class work and drill. The evenings will all be occupied and remaining hours to be devoted to rest and needful sleep preparatory to early rising. All folly and lightmindedness must be eliminated and there must be a perfect *willingness* to participate earnestly in all the activities of the school, and drink in the spirit of it. If there are any brethren or sisters who will come from your conference that cannot fully and willingly subscribe to every one of these requirements, including willingness to be criticized sharply, and corrected as their exercises, general work, appearance, and conduct, and stand reproof, if necessary, I do not want them to come to this school at all; for we shall have no time for continually explaining why we correct or reprove, and we will have no apologies to make for such correction and reproof. I ask you to emphasize this to all those you will send from your conference, and if there is any hesitancy or unwillingness to submit to the whole program as to conduct here set forth, please tell them they are excused."

The first school for this four-week course was assembled, and they were a body of very earnest, anxious students, desirous of availing themselves of the lessons and drill proposed, including hearty compliance with the above-quoted paragraph from the letter announcing the school. A day apart from the four weeks was devoted to registration and preliminary organization and instruction, so as to not intrude upon the full four weeks of instruction planned. A simple daily program was followed, a sample of which is hereunto attached:

FOURTH WEEK

9 A.M.
(a) Inspection: 5 minutes
(b) Devotion exercises: 15 minutes
(c) Scripture Reading Drill (selections from the Old Testament and the Pearl of Great Price): 40 minutes
Instructor: Pearl Snow

10 A.M.
The Needed Personal Qualities of Missionaries
Introspection
Instructor: President B. H. Roberts

11 A.M.
(a) Hymnology and Singing Practice – 20 minutes.
Instructor: Elsie Cook
(b) Mission Economics: Organization and Methods – Elders Only
Instructor: Fred L. Markham
(c) Self-Knowledge, Physical, Moral, and Spiritual – Lady
Missionaries Only
Instructor: Dr. M. C. Roberts

12 Noon. INTERMISSION AND LUNCHEON

1 P.M.
Outline History: (Succession of Dispensations): The Dispensation of the
Fullness of Times
The New Dispensation of the One and Only Gospel
Instructor: President B. H. Roberts

2 P.M.
Tracting: Theory of, Objective Lessons in; Experiences Renewed
Instructor: Elizabeth Skolfield

3 P.M.
Preaching: Theory of, Objective Lessons in: Street Meetings,
Cottage Meetings, Hall Meetings
Instructor: President B. H. Roberts

4 P.M.
Directed Study Period
Instructor: Dixie Brimhall

4:30 P.M.
Physical Culture and Setting-up Exercises
Instructor: Willard Bean

5 to 8 P.M.
Home-Going and Relaxation – Dinner

8 to 10 P.M.
Home Study Period: (Report on Call).

As stated above this is merely a sample of the lessons that ran through
the entire course of four weeks in the five sessions of the Mission School,
varying of course with the progressive building up of the several subjects
and exercises. The earnestness and the enthusiasm of each of these schools
was very commendable, and it was quite generally conceded by those who
attended them and those who were witnesses of the effects of these courses
of intensive study that the four full weeks were equal in value to six months
of the ordinary mission work in the field without the school, so that it was
really a great economizing of the time of the missionaries.

The arrangement of lodgings for the missionaries was by securing them before their arrival within walking distance of the Brooklyn chapel, and sufficient places were found for the young missionaries. In fact before the close of the schools, more lodging places were offered than were found necessary, and the expense of the school was so managed that the cost of attendance upon the school did not materially increase the expense of the missionaries.

Another good effect of lodging the missionaries in suitable homes around the Brooklyn chapel district was the fact of the association of these young missionaries in the homes, for the deportment of the missionaries won the respect of these neighborhoods to the Mormon people and their faith. It often happened that the neighbors to the chapel would come to the services and at times materially increased the attendance at special meetings, and throughout the deportment of these mission students won golden opinion for the church they represented.

Five schools in all were held, the last closing on February 6, 1927. Some of the visiting authorities of the church to the mission were inclined to criticize this increasing the efficiency of the missionaries, holding that it scarcely justified the withdrawal for so many missionaries from the respective fields of labor. But this was because they either did not sufficiently realize how much needed the instructions were which were imparted through the school or else were invincible to the value of the background created for those who attended the school. But the missionaries who had the advantage of them were fully persuaded of the high value of these schools and quite generally rated them as the most profitable and interesting period of their mission experience. The atmosphere of the mission home, "that of a spiritual and cultural center," and the school have frequently been referred to as the most enjoyable and ideal periods of spiritual living which had ever touched their lives. How could it be otherwise given all the objectives and elements that entered into those attendant upon the Eastern States Mission School.

CHAPTER 26.

The First Council of the Seventy

I was released from the presidency of the Eastern States Mission in the spring of 1927 and was succeeded in that presidency by Judge Henry H. Rolap of Ogden, Utah, very prominent in Sunday school activities of the church and for a number of years upon the supreme bench of the state court.

On returning to Salt Lake, I renewed my activities in connection with the First Council of the Seventy and attended upon stake conferences and other public meetings with which the First Council, as General Authorities of the church, were officially connected. In this capacity, I visited stakes of the church in Wyoming, Idaho, Utah, Arizona, and California. The First Council had been somewhat disrupted by the calls upon those members to preside over missions. In addition to my own presidency for more than five years in the Eastern States Mission, Elder Joseph W. McMurrin was presiding in the California Mission, Charles H. Hart in the Canadian Mission, Rey L. Pratt in the Mexican Mission, and Levi Edgar Young over the Temple Square Mission.

This left in practicality only two of the council to function in the regular administration of the affairs of the council, Elder J. Golden Kimball and Elder Rulon S. Wells. Meantime much of the work of the council with their quorums had been taken over by members of the Quorum of the Twelve. They undoubtedly, of course, had the right to assist in keeping up and administering in the affairs of these quorums as witnesses for the Lord Jesus Christ. Seventies were established in the church to be the assistants to the Twelve in the responsibilities of preaching the gospel in all the world. Indeed the Twelve are directed by the revelations of God to call upon the Seventy instead of any others to fill the several calls for preaching the gospel in the foreign missions outside of the stakes of Zion. The place of these quorums is as witnesses for the Christ—witnesses that he is the very son of God, that he is the revelation of God to mankind, that he is the redeemer of the world by bringing to pass the universal resurrection of the dead, that he is the individual savior of man from sin and its effects through repentance and baptism in the likeness of his death and burial and resurrection, and also that through him comes the baptism of the spirit which links up the life of man to the life of God through the Holy Ghost.

These quorums, as before has been pointed out, are not quorums in the wards or in the stakes but general special quorums of the church, as indicated by their ordinal numbers from one to more than two hundred. At one time an effort was made to abolish these general ordinal numbers and resolve these general quorums of the church into stake quorums, from one to three or four as the case might be in the respective stakes, even as the quorums of the standing ministry, the elders, are numbered in the respective stakes. Happily, through the resistance offered by me, this movement was checked and foiled, it is to be hoped permanently. In pursuance of maintaining the integrity of the Seventies organization, I on several occasions asked for a meeting with the First Presidency and the Twelve Apostles, both in speech and in writing. This was done by an elaborate letter written from the Eastern States Mission following an opportunity sought by me to present the case of the Seventies verbally before the Twelve and the Presidency. Not being satisfied with the temporary verbal presentation, I wrote to President Grant the following letter on the organization of the Seventy:

October 25, 1926

To the Presidency of the Church and
the Quorum of the Twelve Apostles
47 East South Temple St.
Salt Lake City, Utah

Dear Brethren:

I have the pleasure of announcing that I arrived at the headquarters of the Eastern States Mission Sunday morning, October 17th. The return journey was much more pleasant than I anticipated.

Placing in order my papers which had accumulated through correspondence and otherwise during my absence, I read again the letter, copy of which I obtained at the meeting of the First Council with the Presidency and Twelve at their late meeting in the Salt Lake Temple, October 7th, to consider matters pertaining to the organization and government of the Seventy's quorums. This letter bears the date March 25, 1926, is addressed to President Heber J. Grant and counselors, and is signed by Rudger Clawson as President of the Council of Twelve. This was the letter that came up in the aforesaid meeting, as containing the very latest recommendations of the Twelve concerning Seventy affairs, and while I know I had an opportunity of quite freely expressing my views at aforesaid meeting, it was only in a rather general way, and not specifically addressed to the several items of this letter. As I have just now read the letter, I feel that it is my duty as one of the Council of Seventy, and especially its senior member, to put in writing my very definite objections to the several recommendations which are therein contained, that you may have my views in hand in considering the conclusions that you no doubt will formulate when you again consider these recommendations from the Twelve.

In setting forth my views, permit me to say that I shall confine such statement to the parts of the letter as fundamentally affect the presidency and management of the Seventy's quorums.

You will remember that I made as the basis of my remarks at the above mentioned meeting with the presidency and the Twelve the following passage from Section 107 of the Doctrine and Covenants:

> And it is according to the vision showing the order of the Seventy, that they should have seven presidents to preside over them, chosen out of the number of the Seventy; And the seventh president of these presidents is to preside over the six; and these seven presidents are to CHOOSE other seventy beside the first seventy to whom they belong AND ARE TO PRESIDE OVER THEM; and also *other seventy*, until seven times seventy, if the labor in the vineyard of necessity requires it. And these seventy are to be traveling ministers, unto the Gentile first and also unto the Jews. Whereas other officers of the church, who belong not unto the Twelve, neither to the Seventy, are not under the responsibility to travel among all nations, but are to travel as their circumstances shall allow, notwithstanding they may hold as high and responsible offices in the church.

This, you will remember in my remarks at the temple meeting, I insisted very definitely fixed the *choosing* and *presiding over the quorums of the Seventy* by the First Council of Seventy. It rests with the First Council of the Seventy both to do the *choosing* and the *presiding* and there is nowhere mentioned, nor contemplated, the bringing in of presidents of stakes nor of committees from high councils to do this work of choosing and presiding. Of course, I recognized that in the choosing or selection of Seventies for ordination, it is necessary to be sure of the standing of men in the ward and stake as to their being worthy of such choosing and ordination: and, therefore, an endorsement of bishops and presidents of stakes as to the standing of these candidates for ordination, such assurance is both desirable and necessary; and it has always been the practice of the First Council to secure such recommendations.

But, now, in the face of the above very definite statement in the revelation of God about the *choosing and presiding over the Seventy*, what is it that the Twelve recommended?

They ask that a letter be formulated to the presidents of stakes, advising them that the First Presidency and Council of the Twelve have had under consideration for a long time the quorums of Seventies and their work, and after conference with the First Council of Seventy have reached the following conclusions:

"A" That the presidencies of stakes have the same general supervision over quorums of Seventies within their stakes that they now exercise over other quorums of the Melchizedek priesthood and that the presidencies of stakes collaborate with the First Council of Seventies in choosing and setting apart presidents of the several quorums.

One only has to read this paragraph "A" to see that the proposition is to change entirely the whole genius of the Seventies organization. By the revelation of God, *choosing* and *presiding over the Seventies*, even should the number of quorums be increased to seven times seventy, and more, should the ministry require it, is lodged with the First Council of Seventy. And now, this paragraph proposes:

It proposes, (1) to give the presidents of stakes the same general supervision of quorums of Seventies within their stakes that they now exercise over other quorums in the Melchizedek priesthood; a thing not at all provided for, nor contemplated in the revelation of God.

Let me urge upon your attention that these quorums of Seventy are *not stake quorums* and therefore, as quorums, are not and cannot be legally under the jurisdiction of the stake president. They are specifically general quorums of the church, have always been held so through the seventy years of their existence, and have been numbered accordingly from one to now more than two hundred. They constitute a traveling ministry (D&C 107:97) and exist in contra-distinction to quorums of elders, which are stake quorums and are standing ministers (D&C 124:137-40).

The paragraph of the apostles' letter here considered says that the presidents of stakes are to have the same supervision over quorums of Seventies within their stakes that they now exercise over other quorums of Melchizedek priesthood in their stakes. This cannot be done, unless you strike out of existence the First Council of Seventy, or strip them of all the main functions of their office–which, of course, would in effect destroy them.

The principle function of the First Council is to "choose" the Seventies, preside over them, and prepare them for their ministry.

In the supervision of the quorums of the high priests and the several quorums of elders in the respective stakes of Zion, the jurisdiction of the presidents of stakes over such quorums is direct, undivided, and complete. *They are stake quorums*, and fell under the general presidency of these stake officers. But when it is proposed to place the quorums of Seventies–general church quorums–under the same local jurisdiction, there is at once divided authority and a double jurisdiction created, inevitably producing confusion and irritation as at the present time, where this divided authority and double supervision is to be attempted. And that is the present cause of irritation where it exists. The presidents of stakes cannot have the same jurisdiction or "general supervision" over the quorums of Seventy within their respective stakes that they now exercise over other quorums of the Melchizedek priesthood, as long as the First Council exists and holds its appointed place by the revelation of God to "choose" and "preside" over the quorums of Seventy now in the church, or hereafter to be organized. For even in this proposed plan by the Twelve to divide the authority between stake presidents and the quorums of elders in the stakes, the First Council would have at least a meddling hand at supervision of the quorums of Seventy, unknown in the case of the other quorums of the high priesthood in the stakes of Zion. Every way, the proposition of the Twelve is turned, it violates the order that God provides for the management of these Seventy's quorums and fails to attain the end proposed, viz., to reduce them to the status of the stake quorums. From the very nature of their structure, these quorums refuse to become what they are not–stake quorums.

Again in this said paragraph "A."

It is directed that the presidencies of stakes collaborate with the First Council of Seventies in *choosing* and setting apart presidents of the several quorums.

Why? And where in the revelation of God is the authorization for this intrusion of local officers into the affairs of these general church quorums. More on this a little later.

I next take up the paragraph "B," and for convenience divide it into three parts:

1. "That in such supervision (viz., that "general supervision" provided for in paragraph "A") the same supervision that presidents of stakes have over elder's quorums the stake presidents are authorized, *with the co-operation of bishops, to advance brethren in the priesthood to the office of Seventy*."

Yes, but what then becomes of the word of God which says: "And these seven presidents (The First Council) are to CHOOSE *other seventy* beside the first seventy to which they belong (all Seventies, that means) and are to preside over them"!

The Twelve to propose to change this direction given of God, and the "stake presidencies" are "to be authorized, with the co-operation of the bishops, to *advance brethren in the priesthood to the office of Seventy*." In other words, these local officers, stake presidents and bishops, are to "choose" the Seventies, instead of the "Seven Presidents" that are appointed of God "to CHOOSE" them and "other Seventy besides the first Seventy to whom they belong; . . . and also other Seventy, until seven times seventy if the labor in the vineyard requires it."–The First Council is to CHOOSE all Seventies in fact.

I respectfully ask when was it that the Lord changed his mind on this subject, and where is the revelation proclaiming such change? For, surely, it would require a revelation to justify such a radical change.

The next part of paragraph "B":

11. "And also" presidents of stakes with the co-operation of bishops are to be authorized "to make nominations and recommendations to the First Council of Seventies for the presidents of quorums."

That sounds all very well; but in too many cases where presidents of stakes have already undertaken that method of procedure, it has been done in the spirit of expecting the First Council to accept out of hand those recommendations, and when we have doubted the wisdom and desirability of some of these recommendations for our work (as surely we have the right to doubt when there is reason for it), it has been the cause of irritation and sometimes ill feeling. The First Council are expected–in such cases, to use a figure of speech–"to sign on the dotted line," and so in large part would be the expectation if this proposed procedure by the Twelve were specifically authorized. Indeed, so little would be left for the First Council to do in connection with the work of the Seventies that the First Council might as well, for all practical purposes, be absolutely abolished and all their functions relegated to the presidents of stakes and ward bishops, who would doubtless perform their offices much better, since, as it might be urged, that they are on the ground and in immediate contact with the men to be made presidents and Seventies. And since the effect of all this procedure would be to reduce the Seventies quorums, on the same level with the elders quorums–why have Seventies quorums at all? Why not abolish them?

Returning, however, to the serious part of this section of paragraph "B," and on the specific point of the presidents of stakes "choosing" and nominating to the First Council of Seventy men to be "presidents of quorums"–why are the respective quorums of Seventies to be presided over ignored? And what of the quorum council with whom the new members will serve? What has become of the principle that governments derive their just power from the consent of the governed, and this operates as well in ecclesiastical as in Civil government? Will it be enough to say that the consent of the governed can come later–when nominations have been made by the presidents of stakes to the First Council and that council has accepted them, then the names may be submitted to the quorums and councils thereof to be voted upon, and through the consent of the governed obtained? The procedure may be so, and the quorums and the councils of them thus ignored may silently submit, and matters go on in a dull, gray and a sullen manner; but you will have no *corps d'esprit* in the quorums; and young men of active minds will grow restive, and either become indifferent to the organization and ignore it or leave it.

A quorum of Seventy as God has given it to the church is the most wonderful organization of all our quorums and is best capable of self government and the best calculated to resist disintegration and can be converted into a veritable flying column to carry God's message to the world, but it would require more space to set it forth than I am here allowing myself. But since each quorum of Seventy has its own local council as the presidency of it and usually they have been chosen with some care and are usually men of established character nearly in every instance and ranging in age from twenty-five years to sixty, why not regard them as having some judgment and *right to a voice in a choice in nominating* those with whom they are to work, and who are to work with them–going beyond the matter of merely giving a formal vote of acceptance after others have done all the considering and choosing and nominating? Why are the councils of these quorums and the quorums themselves ignored by the plan of procedure proposed by the Twelve? The choice for presidents of the quorums must be limited under Section 107 of the Doctrine and Covenants to the Seventies. It is purely a matter that pertains to the Seventy and to the respective quorums thereof. *Why not permit the Seventies to do the business pertaining to the Seventies*, under the direction of the First Council? This suggestion, of course, does not preclude the submission of names of Seventies chosen for presidents to both bishops of wards and presidents of stakes for endorsement as to their good standing as members in the wards where they hold their fellowship. And also, in the matter of securing members–i.e., candidates for ordination to the office of Seventy–the Seventies must and do recognize the fact that these candidates coming from quorums of elders over which presidents of stakes have direct jurisdiction, being stake quorums; and that bishops have immediate watch care over their membership in their wards. Therefore it is becoming and necessary and desirable that there should be complete agreement and understanding had between the councils of quorums, the First Council and presidents of stakes, and bishops with reference to the worthiness and desirability of making these ordinations and promotions. And it has always been the custom and the law of the First Council so to proceed, but all this does not require that the choosing and promotion of men to be Seventies should be taken out of the hands of the officers where God has placed it.

In outline the procedure under the First Council in filling vacancies in quorum councils has been:

On receiving notice of a vacancy or vacancies in a council, the First Council has advised that the quorum council consider the quorum members and from their number recommend the names of the most desirable men to fill the vacancies, preferring that several names for each vacancy be given that the First Council might have some margin of choice from among those who would be acceptable to the quorum. Always these names, thus submitted to the First Council, are to be previously submitted to the bishop and president of the stake for their endorsement *as being in good standing in the ward and stake and worthy of the appointment proposed.*

And this procedure has worked reasonably well and with as little

THE AUTOBIOGRAPHY OF B. H. ROBERTS

friction as may be hoped for in working so large a number of quorums and harmonizing so many interests in the respective organizations. I see no good reason nor justification for departing from this procedure so long our custom.

The third part of paragraph "B" says: "Seventies should be ordained in quorum meetings by the presidents of the quorums and received into the quorum by a vote of the members."

Why change from having the Seventies ordained by the First Council or immediately under their direction at a meeting called for the purpose and at which they are present? Why change this to their being "ordained" in a local quorum meeting by the presidents of the local quorums? What requires it or justifies it? since "These Seven Presidents (i.e. the First Council) are to choose other seventy beside the first Seventy to which they belong . . . and also other Seventy until seven times seventy, if the labor in the vineyard of necessity requires it."

Does it not seem reasonable that this universal choosing of all the Seventies by the First Council implies their ordaining them also? Or at least being ordained under their immediate supervision and not by the local presidents alone? The choosing is so closely allied to the ordination of them that have done the "choosing," they could as well do the ordaining or directly supervise it, and as the two things could about as easily be done as the one. And in any event why change the usage grown into a custom, and a satisfactory one by those immediately concerned? The only reason that occurs to me for the change would be to make the Seventies quorums like the elders quorums in this respect of being ordained. It helped strike down the distinction between the elder and Seventies, which seems to be the whole tendency of this plan urged by the Twelve. If that be the intent then why not go further and strike down the distinction in the presidency of these quorums? Dismiss the seven presidents of each quorum and have the one president and two counselors as in the case of the elders quorums? This would make for uniformity indeed! And why should Seventies have seven presidents instead of one president and two counselors? *Strike out the seven and make them conform to the type of quorums generally. What is the use of these distinctions?*

Moreover, why should they have a seemingly, special presidency – the First Council of Seventy – outside of ward and stake organizations and located at a distance from these quorums? The elders and high priests have no such presidency! Why not abolish this distant presidency, this anomaly in priesthood organization? The presidents of stakes or even bishops of wards could do the presiding just as well, or even better. Besides, it would simplify things, make things uniform and save a lot of trouble! And when we get the Seventies quorums conformed to the same likeness as the elders quorums, it may occur to some genius in ecclesiastical government to suggest that since Seventies quorums are like elders quorums, why have the

Seventies quorums at all? And indeed, why? No reason at all; except that *God* has placed them in the church, as definitely as he has the apostles and prescribed the way in which they are to be "chosen" and "presided over," which order of procedure for choosing and presiding over, the Twelve propose to change.

Respecting paragraph "C," it is enough to say that making quorums proficient, passing worthy Seventies to high priests quorums, and reducing the numbers of quorums in some stakes are all matters of mere detail and are largely now in progress of operation. But why the last line of the paragraph: "*Each stake should have at least one quorum of Seventies.*"

Why? Seventies quorums are not stake quorums. They do not function as stake quorums. There is nothing for them to do as a quorum in a stake. They are not essential in any way to a stake organization. The Seventies quorums exist and have existed throughout their duration in the church independent of stake lines. We have had single quorums existing in several stakes, in as high as three stakes. Being general church quorums they are not necessarily affected by stake lines, and having a local presidency in the council of the quorum and a general presidency in the First Council, they were and are in such cases completely officered and can function fully in their office under these circumstances. And the stakes may be fully organized without having a quorum of Seventies at all.

At this point may be considered no. 2 of the preliminary set of propositions in this letter by the Twelve, dealing with the designation of Seventies quorums by numbers. They say:

> 2. "That quorums of Seventies in the stakes of the church be designated by specifying the number of the quorum and also the numerical order of the stake where it is maintained, as, for instance, the 145th being the 1st quorum of Seventies in the Cache Stake of Zion."

Why this double numberage of the quorums of Seventy? What is feigned by it but confusion and lumbering of things up? The Twelve have previously suggested that the ordinal number of the quorums of Seventy throughout the church—"Except as to the first" (sic!) be dropped and the Seventies quorums be numbered in each stake as elders' quorums are numbered. This proposition, however, met with stout opposition from the First Council, and so now we have the proposition split, or is it doubled? Anyway, the quorums are to receive double numbers, one ordinal to show their number as church quorums and one to show their number as stake quorums—which they are not and which no designation by numbers can make them, number them as you may.

The fact is, these quorums of Seventy are general church quorums, not stake quorums, and for seventy years they have been numbered as such, and there has been no mistake made in so numbering as such, and there has been no mistake made in so numbering them throughout the presidencies of all previous presidential administrations of the church. The 115th quorum of Seventies is not the 115th of any stake, nor the 3rd, nor the 4th of any stake of Zion but is the *115th quorum of the Church of Jesus Christ of Latter-day Saints* and should remain so unconfused with any stake numberings.

What is to be gained by this proposed innovation by the Twelve's plan of numbering the Seventies quorums? It will help nothing in the stake; it is nothing but lumber not fitted to the structure. It does, however, add comfort to those who are evidently determined that these general church quorums shall gravitate to the status of stake quorums, and to this end it is doubtless proposed.

Conclusion.

The sum of the matter is this: God has placed in his church prophets, apostles, evangelists and pastors; also he has placed Seventies and Seventies quorums in his church and given them their special and peculiar quorum organization and directed how and by whom they shall be "chosen" and "presided over" and what shall be their specific duty and calling in the church. They are to be God's special witnesses in all the world. The special calling resembles the calling of the twelve apostles at that particular point: That is to say, they are (1) special witnesses of the name of Christ; and (2) their calling and mission is to all the world – their mission is a universal one. This universality, this unlimited sphere of their activities, coupled with the fact of their being special witnesses, is what gives their calling its apostolic flavor; for they are apostles. God's first great prophet of this new dispensation so designated them. Lest some of the Twelve have overlooked the passage of history containing that designation, I quote it.

During the dedicatory service in the Kirtland Temple, March 27, 1838, when the various officers of the church were sustained, the Seventies were sustained as "Apostles and special witnesses to the nations to assist the Twelve," etc. I quote the passage in full, the Prophet Joseph Smith speaking.

I then called upon the quorums and congregation of Saints to acknowledge the Twelve Apostles who were present, as prophets, seers, revelators, and special witnesses to all the nations of the earth, holding the keys of the kingdom, to unlock it, or cause it to be done, among them, and uphold them by their prayers, which they assented to by rising. I next called upon the quorums and congregation of Saints to acknowledge the presidents of Seventies who act as their representatives, as apostles, and special witnesses to the nations, to assist the Twelve in opening the gospel kingdoms among all the people and to uphold them by their prayers, which they did by rising. (*History of the Church*, vol. 11, 417-18.)

While this action was taken with reference to the First Council of Seventy, yet in a general way the like apostolic feature adheres to the priesthood of the Seventy generally.

Being, then, of this dignity in their calling and office and having received this appointment in the church of God, it seems to me that tampering with their organization as God has given it requires some caution; and those changes proposed by the Twelve here discussed ought not to be made.

After careful thought and reflection on these matters, I say deliberately that these proposed changes made by the Twelve do not meet with my approval. Of course I speak for myself alone, not for the First Council or any member of it.

All this is respectfully submitted.

Signed: B. H. Roberts.

P.S. I would here call attention to the revelation given of the Lord to President John Taylor in April 1883 and read by me and commented upon at the late temple meeting. While not specifically naming any of the points raised by the letter of the Twelve here discussed, yet in its whole letter and spirit it contemplates throughout having the business of Seventies attended to by the Seventies. I would make that revelation part of this communication. It will be found in the *Seventies Course in Theology—First Year*, pp. 9-10.

It was remarked by one of the apostles that my theory as to the organization and government of the Seventy might be right, but he doubted its being practical. Believing that what was referred to as my theory of the management of the Seventies organization is what God has ordained, I cannot believe that God has given us an impractical plan for such choosing and presiding over Seventies. The plan as God has given it is entirely practical if allowed to function as planned. But if changed and distorted I am sure it will not be practical. The multiplication table in mathematics works all right if allowed to stand as it is, but if you go to changing it, making it say that three times nine is twenty-one or that three times eight is sixteen and so throughout, then you will have trouble. The application of the illustration is obvious.

B. H. R.

In connection with this letter is the following letter written by J. Golden Kimball to me:

November 4, 1926

President B. H. Roberts
273 Gates Ave.
Brooklyn, N.Y.

Dear Brother Roberts:

Your letter addressed to the First Presidency and the Council of the Twelve, a copy of which you mailed to me, was presented to the First

Council of the Seventy at our Thursday meeting held today. There were present at this meeting Brothers Wells, Hart, and Kimball. We instructed our general secretary to strike off a copy for each member of the First Council which would include Brothers McMurrin and Pratt.

Brothers Wells and Hart have not yet had ample time to fully consider your letter, but the information they now have as to the contents of your letter gives them assurances that you have performed a wonderful work in placing in writing before the Brethren of the Authorities a concise and complete answer to each and every question they have presented to us as a change in the status of the Seventy organization.

As far as I am individually concerned, I do not hesitate in saying that I appreciate and concur as well as approve of the clean-cut, honest, frank manner in which you have presented your views before the Brethren of the Authorities. I am very pleased that you made your statement in writing, as the General Authorities, in my judgment, are warped and twisted regarding the Seventies organization, and if they will give your letter proper consideration, it would seem to me impossible for them to carry out the conclusions of the Council of the Twelve. It is just as well for the First Council of the Seventy to take the matter at heart and continue to plead with the Lord to inspire His servants to follow out to the letter the revelations regarding the Seventies. Unless they can give to us a revelation "Thus saith the Lord," it will always leave me in doubt and uncertainty if they conclude to follow their suggestions as presented by the Council of Twelve. Personally I have been so disturbed in my feelings, especially when appointed to meet with the Seventy quorums and set them in order, that it has been the most trying period of my labors as one of the First Council of Seventy, as it practically destroys every conception I have had concerning the Seventies during the thirty-five years of my labors in the First Council. God knows I have given to the Seventies the best that was in me, and I have been unsparing in my efforts to awaken the presidents and Seventies to their high and holy calling as special witnesses of the Lord to the nations of the earth. At no time have I enjoyed more of the spirit of my office and calling than in meeting in some dark corner with a few representatives of a quorum of Seventy. I need not express myself further because I know that you know that I have the spirit of my office and calling as one of the First Council of the Seventy, notwithstanding all my weaknesses and imperfections. I know you have the same spirit and have always had it, as I have traveled with you a great deal in years past and would have great joy in again associating myself with you in looking after the interests of the Seventies in the church.

In conclusion, I may say that the members of the First Council of the Seventy here at home have not heard a whisper, but all has been silence since the First Council met with the presidency of the church and the Council of the Twelve, although we have accompanied the apostles in visiting stake conferences.

We are very glad that the election has passed as there never was a time in the history of the state where there was more abuse and mud slinging from both parties. I think if the Democrats nominated a great leader and a man whom the people had confidence in, the election would have been very different, although it is neither here nor there with me as I am practically non-partisan and try to vote for a good man, although I have to admit that I hardly knew half a dozen men listed with the two parties. They were entire strangers to me, but it is very evident to all that the leading men of Utah, at least very few of them, are chosen to lead the people politically. The outlook is very discouraging for it must be that we have in the state of Utah worthy men to take care of our financial and political affairs.

At present the First Council are enjoying their usual health, although I can see that Brother Wells is not as well as usual. I have been very much better during the year but have a breaking out occasionally of some new trouble that perplexes and annoys me. You can feel sure that the First Council of the Seventy uphold and sustain you as Senior President of the First Council of the Seventy, and we are proud to have a senior president who is ever ready and willing to labor for the interests of the Seventies and defend their cause, even unto death.

> Praying for your success and improvement of health, I am,
> Very truly your friend and brother,
> Signed.   J. Golden Kimball

Subsequently the question of the place of the Seventy in the church came up during the production of volume 7 of the *History of the Church, Period I*, which I was preparing, in which President Brigham Young's views from the decision of his in the Nauvoo Temple came up, namely, that Seventies outranked high priests, since they were apostles and authorized to set in order the church in all the world. Therefore they could ordain high priests, could bring into existence high councils, and attend to any of the general business of the church they were appointed to transact. This decision of President Young's was based upon complaints coming from the high priests that some of the presidents of the Seventy had washed and anointed in the temple the high priests, against which the high priests had protested. But President Young declared their right to do this washing and anointing and gave the above ideas of ordaining high priests and regulating the affairs of the church.

When the feasibility of suppressing President Young's decision taken from his own manuscript history was presented to the First Presidency and the Twelve, I again asked the privilege of setting forth my views on the subject, and this was granted, and in a lengthy speech I upheld the views of President Brigham Young. But I was the only one in the meeting who expressed my views. After my remarks, the First Council of Seventy were excused from the temple, and the Twelve went to their luncheon in the temple. Afterwards the matter was considered by the First Presidency and the Twelve alone, and ultimately without deciding the question upon its merits, they concluded that to follow the line of decision in the matter by President Young, it would disturb the minds of many members of the church.

Therefore President Heber J. Grant wrote me to that effect and advised the elimination of President Young's decision and doctrine, so it was not included in the printed history but remains in the manuscript. Of course I had to comply with this decision, but in doing so and answering the letter to President Grant, I protested the mutilation of the history of the church I was compiling in the seventh volume of Period I and stated to him that while he had the physical power to insist upon such a marring of the history by refusing to admit the very important decision of President Young, I felt that he had no moral right to mar the record in that way. For myself I accepted the doctrine by President Young in his decision at the Nauvoo Temple and felt that it was true, in harmony with the revealed word of God, a position that I had maintained in my speech when the matter was before the First Presidency and the Twelve and the First Council. I added that he should retain and maintain the attitude of President Young, the second prophet of the church, who in the ordaining of Seventies followed the very pointed instruction he had received from Joseph Smith, the first prophet of the New Dispensation.

In order that my full position may be known my letter to President Grant follows:

April 27, 1931

President Heber J. Grant
Church Office Building

My dear President Grant:

Recalling the delightful conversations I had with you at my room on Monday last, I think, in relation to the Seventies, etc., etc., and dwelling upon its substance, impels me to write you further in regard to some of these things that were then briefly mentioned.

Among these was the attention you gave to the apparent incongruity of the First Council of the Seventy being unable to participate with members of the Twelve when out in conferences, when ordaining high priests and bishop's counselors when occasion should arise. The answer to all this has been that the presidency of the Seventies, not being high priests, were barred from these functions; also in regard to performing marriage ceremonies, etc. Perhaps you will remember that I said I thought the decisions that had led to this policy of excluding the seven presidents from such functions was too tightly drawn and that if it were considered that these brethren have an APOSTOLIC CALLING, that calling would warrant them to do along these lines whatsoever might be necessary in the course of their ministry (as stated in Doctrine and Covenants): . . . "in building up the Church and regulating all the affairs of the same in all nations, first to the gentiles and then to the Jews" (107:34).

To review this matter a little further I call your attention to the fact that the Doc. & Cov. Sec. 107, given primarily on the subject of priesthood and establishing the relationship of councils, etc., etc., says: "The Seventy are also called to preach the gospel, and to be especial witnesses unto the gentiles and in all the world. Thus differing from other officers in the Church in the duties of their calling; and they form a quorum *equal in authority to that of the Twelve special witnesses or apostles just named.*"

You will observe that the language making these Seventies especial witnesses of the Lord Jesus Christ is practically the same as that which so designates the Twelve. Now if this quorum is "equal in authority to that of the Twelve special witnesses or Apostles just named," then it must follow that what the Apostles can do the Seventy can do when appointed to do those things, "in building up and regulating the affairs of the Church."

I trust you will not grow impatient just yet at this point, which may have become more or less trite in the consideration of this subject, for I have something further I want to add which may be of great interest to you. But, if my deductions are right so far as I have gone, then in order to get the full measure of service from the Seventy, especially from the First Council and its direct quorum (the First Quorum) "in building up the Kingdom," then there would be no need of wishing that the presiding council over the Seventy held the office of high priests.

Further on in the revelation it is said: "it is according to the vision showing the order of the Seventy that they should have seven presidents to preside over them, chosen out of the number of the Seventy. And the seventh president (of course from the last ordained) of these presidents is to preside over the six. And these seven presidents are to choose other seventy besides the first Seventy *to whom they belong*, and are to preside over them; and also other Seventy until seven times seventy, if the labor in the vineyard of necessity required it. (Section 107:93-96.) This gives to them a general presidency over all the quorums and NOT quorums of the wards or stakes.

President Joseph Smith, the Prophet, when some were being sent to ordain Seventy, said: "Brethren you are going to ordain Seventies. Do not forget to confer the High Priesthood upon them. Ordain each of them to the High Priesthood, and to be one of the Seventy Apostles." (i.e., observe ORDAIN THEM TO THE HIGH PRIESTHOOD and TO THE APOSTLESHIP.) Discourse by B. Young, May 25, 1877. *Deseret Weekly*, June 6, 1877, p. 274.

In the prophet Joseph's History, under date of December 28, 1835, he says: "This day the Council of the Seventy met to render an account of their travels and ministry, since they were ordained to that Apostleship. The meeting was interesting indeed, and my heart was made glad while listening to the relation of those who have been laboring in the vineyard of the Lord, with such marvelous success." etc. (Hist. of Ch., 2:346)

There are other passages to the same effect, but being at the hospital I cannot now lay my hands on them. But here it is clear that the Seventy were ordained to the apostleship, and, of course, with all that that phrase means.

During the dedicatory services in the Kirtland, Temple, March 27, 1836, wherein the various officers of the church, were sustained, the Seventy were sustained as "Apostles and special witnesses to the nations to assist the Twelve," etc. I quote: "I (Joseph Smith) then called upon the quorums and congregation of Saints to acknowledge the Twelve Apostles, who were present, as Prophet, Seers, Revelators and special witnesses to all the nations of the earth, holding the keys of the kingdom, to unlock it, or cause it to be done among them, and uphold them by their prayers, which they assented to by rising.

I next called upon the quorums and congregation of Saints to acknowledge the presidents of Seventies who act as their representatives as apostles and special witnesses to the nations, to assist the Twelve in opening the gospel kingdom among all people, and to uphold them by their prayers, which they did by rising." History of Church, 2:417-18.

And of course, from all the descriptions in the Doc. & Cov., their calling is an Apostolic one.

In my recent research and study of the Manuscript History of Brigham Young, I incidentally came upon what I am now going to quote you, under date of Dec. 14, 1845. Pres. Young and others of the Twelve with their wives spent that Sunday in the Nauvoo Temple, meeting in the attic story of the temple. And now quoting Pres. B. Young: "I stated that the Seventy were ordained Apostles (i.e., according to the instructions that had been given to the Prophet Joseph respecting their ordination above) and when they went forth into the ministry they went with power to build up the kingdom in all the world, and consequently they have power to ordain High Priests and also to ordain a High Council. Some of the High Priests have been ready to quarrel on the subject supposing they had power and authority above the Seventy and some in their zeal for power have abused and trampled on the feelings of some of the Seventy."

If Pres. Young is to be regarded as an expounder of the priesthood it would seem to me that this circumstance in the temple and bearing directly upon the point of the authority of the presidents of Seventies, should go a far way towards establishing the suggestion that I made to you, that it would not be necessary to ordain presidents of Seventies, high priests in order to function in all things that would become necessary "in building up the kingdom in all the world, first among the Gentiles and then among the Jews."

I trust you will not think me over persistent in the matter, but I did think that since this information had come into my hands and also is in strict harmony with the interpretation I gave with the Seventies holding an APOSTOLIC CALLING, it would authorize the First Council to do whatever the Apostles do when necessary, and when appointed to do it, should be made known to you and your counselors and to the present quorum of the Twelve; and in this spirit I submit it to your consideration.

Very truly yours,

B. H. Roberts

Under these decisions the operation of the work among the Seventies has continued until the present time, 1933, and while not altogether satisfactory, yet in the main the genius of the organization has been maintained, and it is my hope that it will yet more pronouncedly be formulated and preserved.

EDITOR'S AFTERWORD

While B. H. Roberts chronicled in his autobiography a few incidents in his life after the mid-1920s, such as his concern over the status and role of the Seventy, he failed to mention other significant personal events, including the deaths of two of his wives and his arguments with church officials. It is difficult to account satisfactorily for these omissions. Perhaps he did not believe they were important or relevant enough to note. Perhaps he avoided discussion of them because they involved family members and ecclesiastical colleagues. More likely they were too painful for the aging and increasingly melancholy Roberts to recall in detail.

Roberts's first wife, Sarah Louisa Smith, twenty-three years old when they married on 31 January 1878, gave birth to seven children before passing away on 21 May 1923. She was followed less than three years later by Roberts's third wife, Margaret Curtis (Shipp). Seven years Roberts's senior, she married Roberts in April 1890 and died at the age of sixty-nine on 13 March 1926. Celia Dibble, Roberts's second wife, was twenty years old at the time of her marriage on 2 October 1884. She bore eight children and outlived her husband by two-and-one-half years, passing away on 21 March 1936. In his autobiography, B. H. Roberts notes in passing only his marriages to Sarah Louisa and Celia, and his children by Celia.

In late 1921, two years after returning home from France where he served as a chaplain during World War I, Roberts was asked to respond to a series of questions regarding the historicity of the Book of Mormon. In response, he produced two manuscripts, "Book of Mormon Difficulties" and "A Book of Mormon Study," detailing problems which could be used to question the validity of the LDS church's founding scripture as an ancient document.

The first manuscript was presented to the Council of Twelve Apostles for their consideration in late January the next year. Roberts had noted linguistic problems in the Book of Mormon, wondering, for example, how so many languages could have evolved from one language in only one thousand years. Also, Roberts was concerned about the lack of archeological evidence for Book of Mormon mention of domestic animals, iron, steel, wheat, barley, and wheeled vehicles. The second manuscript, which Roberts apparently completed in 1923 and did not present to church authorities, discussed possible Book of Mormon parallels with an early 1820s book on native Americans and ancient Israelites, entitled *View of the Hebrews*, and internal inconsistencies in the Book of Mormon.

In a cover letter to church president Heber J. Grant, which accompanied the first manuscript, Roberts explained his motives for undertaking such a project. "I am thoroughly convinced," he wrote, "of the necessity of all the brethren herein addressed becoming familiar with these Book of Mormon problems, and finding the answer for them, as it is a matter that will concern the faith of the youth of the Church now as also in the future, as well as such casual inquiries that may come to us from the outside world." Believing that "our faith is not only unshaken but unshakable," Roberts felt it was desirable to face these challenges directly. "Maintenance of the truth of the Book of Mormon is absolutely essential to the integrity of the whole Mormon movement," he wrote in another letter to Grant, "for it is inconceivable that the Book of Mormon should be untrue in its origin and character and the Church of Jesus Christ of Latter-day Saints to be a true church."

Roberts's controversial studies were interrupted when he was called in early 1922 to serve as president of the church's eastern states mission, headquartered in New York City. Although never printed during his life, Roberts's two manuscripts were first made available in 1980 by Modern Microfilm Company of Salt Lake City and then published by the University of Illinois Press in 1985 as *Studies of the Book of Mormon*, edited and introduced by Brigham D. Madsen, with a biographical essay by Sterling M. McMurrin.

After five years in New York City, Roberts was released in 1927 and began work on a new theological project he hoped would be his "masterwork." Late the next year, he submitted to the Quorum of Twelve Apostles a bulky, 747-page manuscript entitled, "The Truth, The Way, The Life: An Elementary Treatise on Theology." Designed as a lesson manual for Melchizedek priesthood quorums throughout the church, Roberts's ambitious work contained, he explained, "a full harvest of all that I have thought, and felt and written through the nearly fifty years of my ministry, that is on the theme of the title." Within three weeks, the twelve apostles appointed a reading committee, composed of Elders George Albert Smith, David O. McKay, Joseph Fielding Smith, Stephen L Richards, and Melvin J. Ballard, "to examine the manuscript of Brother Roberts' work, and make a recommendation as to its suitability for the study of the High Priesthood."

One year later, committee chair George Albert Smith reported his group's findings to the rest of the Twelve. The committee found that by and large the work was a "very worthy" treatment of church beliefs. They were, however, uncomfortable with "some objectionable doctrines advanced which are of a speculative nature and appear to be out of harmony with the revelations of the Lord and the fundamental teachings of the Church."

The committee voiced special concern with the following points: the existence of races of humans before Adam; the suggestion that Adam was a translated being subject to death who did not bring death to his posterity as a result of the Fall; Adam's placement on the earth before other life belonging to our present dispensation; the complete destruction of all life prior to Adam's advent; and God's continuing acquisition of knowledge. Other problems existed, and of the fifty-four chapters, twenty were found to contain questionable teachings.

The Twelve formally reported to President Grant in mid-May 1930, one month after Roberts lost part of his right foot to diabetes, that "[we] do not regard said work in its present form as a suitable study for the Priesthood quorums of the Church." Throughout the next months, Roberts was told that his treatise would be published if he modified or changed altogether his more controversial concepts in keeping with the committee's suggestions. Roberts refused, adamant that his work appear in its present form or not at all. Consequently, though abbreviated excerpts have since appeared in articles and books, Roberts's magnum opus, "The Truth, The Way, The Life," remains unpublished.

Joseph Fielding Smith, who had served on the committee of apostles to review Roberts's manuscript, subsequently criticized Roberts's views in public. Always ready to defend his position, the feisty Roberts immediately registered an official complaint with the First Presidency. "If Elder Smith is merely putting forth his own opinions I call in question his competency to utter such dogmatism either as a scholar or as an Apostle," he wrote to President Grant. But Grant recorded in his diary, "I think no good can be accomplished by dealing in mysteries, and that is what I feel in my heart of hearts these brethren are both doing." Roberts hoped that a formal airing of both sides would help pave the way for the publication of his own beliefs.

Hearings before the Twelve at which Roberts and Smith presented arguments in support of their views—especially on the existence of pre-Adamic races—resulted in a stalemate, and the controversy was referred back to the First Presidency for resolution. Lacking an authoritative statement on the subject, President Grant and his counselors ruled that the topic was not to be raised again by church officials, though one church authority, James E. Talmage, did eventually receive permission to counter Smith's denunciations in an 1931 address in the Salt Lake Tabernacle. Talmage argued for the existence of death before the fall of Adam and for a geologically old earth. Talmage's speech was later published and widely distributed.

The final three years of Roberts's life were marked by the publication of his six-volume *Comprehensive History of the Church* in commemoration of the centennial of the church's founding, completion of routine church assignments and administrative matters, public sermons (Roberts was a favorite speaker at funerals), attendance at the World Fellowship of Faiths in Chicago, and the preparation and dictation of his autobiography. Despite bouts of severe depression, including migraine headaches and spells of dizziness, Roberts also contemplated several new projects, including the establishment of a theological school, but poor health prevented him from accomplishing these goals.

Shortly before noon on Tuesday, 27 September 1933, Roberts passed away in Salt Lake City. He was buried four days later on 1 October. His last words, reportedly spoken to an attending nurse, were: "You had better give me my coat. I am not going to stay here in bed. I have stayed long enough."

INDEX

A

Abraham, 125, 126
Adams, Mr., 117, 118
Agricultural College of Utah, 194
Alabama, 137, 141, 161
Alexander, Elder, 156
Allen, C. E., 202
Alsup, Mr. (also Parson), 123, 124, 125, 126, 132, 133
Alta Social Club, 194
Amazon, 4, 5
American Party, 183
Americana, 227, 228
Anderson, Mr., 117
Anthony, Susan B., 215
anti-Mormon Women's Organization, 212

B

Baird, Ben, 120
Baird, James, 52, 53, 54, 59, 73, 158
Baird Mills (Tennessee), 118, 156
Ballard, Father (also President), 166, 167
Ballard, Melvin J., 167, 206, 255
Ballard rifle, 63
Baptist, 83
Barnes, John G. M., 186
Barrett, Mr. (also Captain), 170, 171
Baskin, R. N., 207, 211
Bates, Governor, 142, 154
Battle Creek, 31
Beebe's Hotel, 95
Berry, William S., 140, 154
Bible, 121, 139
Bickerton, William, 206
Bickertonites, 206
"Big Ben." See Maynard, Ben.
Bingham Canyon, 53
Black Rock, 48, 49
"Blackeye," 19
Book of Abraham, 224
Book of Mormon, 46, 79, 80, 118, 121, 123, 124, 125, 172, 221, 224, 225, 230, 231, 232
"Book of Mormon Difficulties," 254-55
"Book of Mormon Study," 254-55
Book of Moses, 224
Book of the Prophecies, 97
Books of Moses, 97
Bountiful (Utah), 25, 42, 44-47, 52, 58, 136
Bountiful Coop, 46
Bountiful Tabernacle, 46

boy scouts, 36
British Mission, 165
Broadway, 40
Bruggt family, 131
Bryan, William Jennings, 206, 207
"Buffalo Chips," 37
Bur River, 92
Burton, Charles R., 163, 164
Butcher family, 53

C

Caine, John T., 138, 182, 199
California, 39, 59
Call, Anson, 45
[Call,] "Anson V.," 45
Call, Senator, 137
Camp, Richard C., 135
Camp Florence, 22
Campbell, Alexander, 126
Campbellites, 120, 123, 134
Canada, 3, 22
Cannon, Abraham, 220, 221
Cannon, Frank J., 182, 200
Cannon, George Q., 80, 221, 222, 223
Cannon, Mr., 212
Cannon, Mrs., 212
Carpenter (Tennesse), 150, 151
Carrol, Mr., 143
Carthage (Illinois), 15, 16
Carver, Elder, 115, 117, 118
Castle Gardens, 3, 6, 21, 24
Catholic church (priest), 87, 88, 122, 134
Cedar River, 85
Centerville (Utah), 52, 53, 55, 58, 59, 68, 72, 73, 74, 81, 94, 115, 136, 156, 164, 175
Centerville Dairy, 59
"Centerville Debating Society," 58
Charleston (first lieutenant to Captain William Henry Chipman), 31, 34
Chase, George, 58
Chattanooga (Tennessee), 136, 137, 138, 141, 142, 152, 153, 154, 156, 159, 160
Chicago (Illinois), 22, 111, 112
Chidester, J. F., 184
Chimney Rock, 35
Chipman, Captain William Henry, 25, 26, 27, 28, 33, 34, 37, 38, 39, 40, 41
Christiansen, Parley P., 198
Church, Emmos, 129, 144
Church, Laura, 135, 145